THE AMERICAN CRISIS
IN
PHYSICAL ACTIVITY EDUCATION:
Confusing Winning at Sport with Total Fitness for All

Earle F. Zeigler
Ph.D., LL.D., D.Sc., FAAKPE
The University of Western Ontario
Canada

2010

Order this book online at www.trafford.com
or email orders@trafford.com

Most Trafford titles are also available at major online book retailers.

Printed in Victoria, BC, Canada.

ISBN: 978-1-4269-2546-7 (sc)

Library of Congress Control Number: 2010900174

*Our mission is to efficiently provide the world's finest, most comprehensive book publishing
service, enabling every author to experience success. To find out how to publish your book, your
way, and have it available worldwide, visit us online at www.trafford.com*

Trafford rev. 1/15/2010

 www.trafford.com

North America & international
toll-free: 1 888 232 4444 (USA & Canada)
phone: 250 383 6864 ♦ fax: 812 355 4082

Dedication

To the memory of:

Harry Abbott, Bridgeport, CT, YMCA

R. J. H. (Bob) Kiphuth, Yale University,
New Haven, CT

Paul A. Hunsicker, The University of Michigan

King J. McCristal, University of Illinois

"All fine physical activity educators who understood the type of overall program needed to develop a healthy, fit population.

Each man appreciated fully the role that "the right kind" of sport should play in this undertaking.

I am grateful to them, in addition, for giving me the opportunity to work with them in this life-enhancing field of endeavor" EFZ

Credo

Fundamentally, I believe that the *large* majority of children, youth, and young adults is not getting the quality physical and related health education program (including appropriate intramural sport competition) that we should be providing for them.

On the other hand, a *tiny* percentage of this population is being provided with acceptable to excellent varsity (extramural) sport programs.

This underlying philosophy in regard to the availability of selective school program offerings is not followed with any other aspect of public education. It is undemocratic!

In addition, there is now solid evidence in the United States that, as these athletically superior students "progress" in their sports through the years, their qualities of sportsmanship, fairness, honesty, etc. decline.

My conclusion is that extramural (varsity) competitive sport programs should receive absolutely no direct or indirect funding until such time as ALL students in a school district or specific school, college, or university receive a fine physical activity and health education program (including intramural sport competition).

Earle F. Zeigler

Prologue:

Solving the Problem of Inadequate Physical Activity Education

This book is titled "The American Crisis in Physical Activity Education: Confusing Winning at Sport With Total Fitness for All." You, the reader, may not think that this is indeed a problem, much less a crisis. However, if you will bear with me, I think that as you get into this book, you may eventually agree that the latter–a crisis–is actually the case.

Assuming that we are indeed confronted by a problem that has such serious ramifications for our future, what can be done? If these conditions are true, it means that we should assess the evolving situation carefully and then proceed to institute the appropriate remedies to the extent possible.

To provide us with an approach that should help to communicate with policy makers at all levels about this ever-increasing problem, I decided to use the five–question approach to the building of effective communication skills recommended by Mark Bowden, a communications specialist (*National Post*, Canada, 2008 11 24, FP3)

Question 1: Where are we now? The response to this question can be found in the credo stated at the front of this book. The *large* majority of children, youth, and young adults is not getting the quality physical and related health education program (including appropriate intramural sport competition) that we should be providing.

On the other hand, a *tiny* percentage of this population is being provided with acceptable to excellent varsity (extramural) sport programs within the educational structure. This underlying philosophy in regard to the availability of selective school program offerings is not followed with any other aspect of public education. ***It is undemocratic***!

In addition, there is now evidence in the United States that, as these athletically superior students "progress" in sport competition through the years, their qualities of sportsmanship, fair play, honesty, etc. decline.

Question 2. Why are we here? The answer to this question is that we are here because society has mistakenly not been convinced that regular physical activity education for all children, youth, and young adults was important enough to require them to be involved regularly throughout the required number of years spent in the educational system. This is not the case with–say–English. mathematics, and science.

Question 3. Where should we want to be? We should want to create a situation where the following "common denominators" of physical activity education are made available in all educational institutions at all levels:

1. That regular physical activity education be required for all children and young people (who are presumably still in school) up to and including 16 years of age.

2. That human movement fundamentals through various expressive activities are basic in the elementary, middle, and high school curricula.

3. That physical vigor and endurance are important for people of all ages. Progressive standards should be developed from prevailing norms.

4. That boys and girls (and young men and women) should have an experience in competitive sport at some stage of their development. The important goal here is the development of an athlete of character, one who is honest, fair, responsible, respectful, and compassionate (Stoll, S. K. & Beller, J. M. *Sport as education: On the edge*. NY: Columbia University Teachers College, 1998.

5. That remediable defects should be corrected through exercise therapy at all school levels. Where needed, adapted sport and physical recreation experiences should be stressed.

6. That a young person should develop certain positive attitudes toward his or her own health in particular and toward community hygiene in general. Basic health knowledge should be an integral part of the school curriculum.

(<u>N.B.</u>: Note that this "common denominator" should be a specific objective of the field of physical activity education *only as it relates to developmental physical activity.)*

7. That exercise, sport, and expressive movement can make a most important contribution throughout life toward the worthy use of leisure.

8. That character and/or personality development is vitally important to the development of the young person. Therefore it is especially important that men and women

with high professional standards and ethics guide all human movement experience in sport, exercise, and expressive movement at the various educational levels.

(See Zeigler, E. F. (2003) *Socio-Cultural Foundations of Physical Education and Educational Sport*. Aachen, Germany: Meyer and Meyer Sports.

Question 4. How do we get there? We "get there" by convincing the public, including the "powers that be," that we simply cannot as a society permit the continuance of the prevailing haphazard approach to an aspect of human life that is so basic (1) to profitable and enjoyable involvement in all aspects of life, and that (2) will enable us to have the benefits of such a life over a longer period of time. Society must demand that such a comprehensive program be made available at all educational levels

Question 5. What exactly should we do? Without attempting to enumerate specifically where any stumbling blocks might loom in our path, the field of physical activity education should keep in mind the four major processes proposed by March and Simon (*The Future of Human Resource Management*, 1958, pp. 129-131). They could be employed chronologically, as the field seeks to realize its desired immediate objectives and long-range goal. These four major processes to be followed in the achievement of the desired objectives and goals for the field are as follows:

> 1. **Problem-solving**: Basically, what is being proposed here is a problem for the profession of sport and physical activity education to solve or resolve. It must move as soon as possible to convince others that this proposal is truly worthwhile. Part of the approach includes assurance that the objectives are indeed operational (i.e., that their presence or absence can be tested empirically as the field progresses). In this way, even if sufficient funding were not available--and it well might not be--the various parties who are vital or necessary to the success of the venture would at least have agreed-upon objectives. However, with a professional task of this magnitude, it is quite possible, even probable that such consensus will not be achieved initially. *But it can be instituted--one step at a time!*

> 2. **Persuasion**: For the sake of argument, then, let us assume that the objectives on the way toward the achievement of long-range aims are not shared by the others whom the profession needs to convince, people who are either directly or indirectly related to our own field or are in allied fields or related disciplines. On the assumption

7

that the stance of the others is not absolutely fixed or intractable, then this second step of persuasion can (should) be employed on the assumption that at some level our objectives will be shared, and that disagreement over sub-goals can be mediated by reference to larger common goals. (Here the field should keep in mind that influencing specific leaders in each of the various "other" associations and societies with which it is seeking to cooperate can be a most effective technique for bringing about attitude change within the larger membership of our profession everywhere.)

> Note: If persuasion works, then the parties concerned can obviously return to the problem-solving level (#1).

3. **Bargaining**: We will now move along to the third stage of a theoretical plan on the assumption that the second step (persuasion) didn't fully work. This means obviously that there is still disagreement over the operational goals proposed at the problem-solving level (the first stage). Now the field has a difficult decision to make: does it attempt to strike a bargain, or do it decide that we simply must "go it alone?"

The problem with the first alternative is that bargaining implies compromise, and compromise means that each group involved will have to surrender a portion of its claim, request, or argument. The second alternative may seem more desirable, but following it may also mean eventual failure in achieving the final, most important objective.

> Note: We can appreciate, of course, that the necessity of proceeding to this stage, and then selecting either of the two alternatives, is obviously much less desirable than settling the matter at either the first or second stages.

4. **Politicking**: The implementation of the fourth stage (or plan of attack) is based on the fact that the proposed action of the first three stages has failed. The participants in the discussion cannot agree in any way about the main issue. It is at this point that the recognized profession has to somehow expand the number of parties or groups involved in consideration of the proposed project. The goal, of course, is to attempt to include potential allies so as to

improve the chance of achieving the desired final objective.
Employing so-called "power politics" is
usually tricky, however, and it may indeed backfire upon the group
bringing such a maneuver into play. However, this is the way the
world (or society) works, and the goal may be well worth the risk or
danger involved.

> Note: Obviously, the hope that it will not be
> necessary to operate at this fourth stage
> continually in connection with the development
> of the field. It would be most divisive in many
> instances and time consuming as well.
> Therefore, the field would be faced with the
> decision as to whether this type of operation
> would do more harm than good (in the
> immediate future at least).

Conceptual Index

Part Three: Looking to the Future
in Physical Activity Education
and Educational Sport

Preface

This book was written because I found myself–along with my concern about the future–terribly upset about what is happening to physical activity education and so-called educational sport within the education system. I live in North America as a dual citizen, and I feel sad that we here appear to be a large part of the world's problem! I had thought the world would be a better place for all people by the year 2000. Because now it definitely doesn't seem to be heading in that direction, I am forced to conclude:

(1) that in many ways we are confused about what our values are at the present,

(2) that we need to reconsider them and then *re-state* exactly what we believe they are in light of the changing times, and

(3) finally that we will then need to assess more carefully– *on a regular basis*--whether we are living up to those values we have chosen and so often glibly espouse.

Having reached the age of 90, it is obvious that I will not be around forever. I am especially disturbed about what is happening in the U.S.A. I believe that the world's only superpower is (and has been!) playing a very negative role with its international efforts over the years--as well-intentioned as it claims those intentions are. I grant that America's intentions have indeed been well intentioned in particular instances. At the same time, however, I also believe that the States has been disintegrating *within* from the standpoint of human values. I just happen to have been born as a citizen of the country that was once supposed to be "the last best hope on earth." Now the "last best hope" is that the rest of the world through the power and influence of a *greatly improved* United Nations will somehow be able to persuade the United States to fulfill its avowed purposes *and stay in its proper place.*

Born in 1919 at the end of World War I in Queens, a borough of New York City, I grew up there in what was subsequently viewed as the "roaring twenties." This presumed uproar and bedlam did not affect me, however. Through the devoted efforts of my grandparents and working mother, I eventually learned a bit more than on which side to butter toast. My mother had divorced my father when I was two years old (a significant "fracture" in those times). She subsequently married again, to a Baptist minister, and we three moved to South Norwalk, CT. Hence, at 12 years of age I had acquired a stepfather and, in a minor way, I suppose you could say that was the beginning of my "time of troubles."

I grant that I must have been a "handful" for a fresh-out-of-seminary Baptist minister, and that he did his best to cope with me. However, from day #1 we never were on quite the same "wave length". I admit that this fact actually helped me decide where I stood on many aspects of life. So I should be thankful, because such a relationship while an adolescent--as *the* minister's son--coupled with the developing social and political scene of the 1930s and 1940s, did much to shape my future orientation to the world around me.

I live in Canada now, and eventually became a citizen here too after moving here for the second time. Thus, I pay taxes in both countries. Frankly, as a sort of "refugee," I live here because I like the climate better (i.e., the *social* climate). That statement undoubtedly sounds a bit odd because Canada is said to be "the land of ice, snow, Indians, and people who speak French," However, I live in the lower mainland of British Columbia where that white stuff is a distinct rarity. It does rain more than occasionally, I must admit.

More seriously, when I said above that I liked the climate in Canada better, that was indeed a play on words too. What I really meant was that presently I find Canada a country in which my present beliefs and social philosophy fit much better than they did in the U.S.A. as presently constituted. I have done very well in my field of physical activity education and educational sport over a period of some 70 years divided between both countries. Therefore, I can say that moving back and forth between the two countries was actually not a question of my liking periodically to be "a bigger fish in a smaller pond." (Canada's population of 30 million+ only equates with that of the State of California.) To come to the point, there are now so many aspects about the U.S. that turn me off that I hardly know where to begin in explaining my position.

For example, I am very upset about the fact that the United States became the first country in the 21st century to defy the United Nations by waging war against Iraq ostensibly to oust an evil dictator. I know that he was a tyrant who oversaw many terrible acts by his sons and other henchmen. But that's not the point. The U.S. has continued to set a terrible precedent in a highly troubled world by its action. (I must point out that Canada did not approve this almost unilateral action.) And what or who is next? And now the United States is over there converting Afghanistan to democracy. I do believe democracy is the best form of government devised to date, of course. However, I'm forced to say: "Egad! Who's next?" in the parade of countries the U.S. is determined to democratize (or whatever!) while exporting capitalism, technology, and Christianity as well?

For a second example of the prevailing climate that disturbs me in the United States, let me move to an area where I worked professionally for another example. Having taught, administered, and periodically coached sport at Yale, Michigan, and Illinois, I can speak more authoritatively about sport in general and more specifically about intercollegiate athletics in the States. Sport in the Ivy League and similar institutions (Division 3, NCAA) is typically fine. It's doing well what it's intended to do. However, athletics in those universities where gate receipts is a vital factor has gradually and steadily throughout the 20th century gotten completely out of hand. It is semi-professional! This fact has occasioned all of the attendant vices that somehow have crept into such programs when sponsored by educational institutions.

This most unfortunate development throughout the 20th century in sport is only symptomatic of the entire society, however. My position in this realm is basically this: "Sport was created by humans to serve humans beneficially in all aspects of their lives." As it seems to be now, many professional and semi-professional athletes--not to mention the situation in overly emphasized high school sport competition--are there to serve what has become a most undesirable "sport goliath." It is accompanied and insidiously goaded by a mindless public watching with vicarious, yet often rapturous, involvement. All of this is akin to the seduction of the populace that occurred in ancient Rome. Sadly, while this is taking place, the overwhelming majority of children and young people is getting a poor (or no!) introduction to what ought to be a a fine program of health instruction, physical activity education, and physical recreation in the public schools and related institutions. Not only are "the rich getting richer, and the poor poorer," the elite athletes are getting the attention, and the normal and challenged youngsters are getting fatter!

What this boils down to is that--almost everywhere one turns--there is a crisis in human values as we move into the 21st century. This has created what I call an ethical decision-making dilemma. In recent books, *Who Knows What's Right Anymore?* and *Whatever Happened to "the Good Life?"*, both published by Trafford in 2002 <www.trafford.com>, I strove to get to the heart of this massive problem in different ways. In "Who Knows What's Right Anymore? I argued that, for several reasons, the child and adolescent in society today are missing out almost completely on a sound "experiential" introduction to ethics. This is true whether we are referring to what takes place in the home, the school system, or the church--actually an experience that occurs inadequately--*if at all!* In fact, the truth is that typically no systematic instruction in this most important subject is offered at any time. Bluntly speaking, I refuse to accept the often-heard "osmosis stance"--that such knowledge is "better caught than taught." Granted that it helps to have people around you who are setting good examples. However, in the final analysis it's the individual who makes judgments and decisions based on experiences undergone.

My objective in Part One is to assess the North American situation in what has been called the postmodern age. I believe that Americans, and many Canadians as well, do not fully comprehend their unique position in the history of the world's development. In all probability this status will change radically as the 21st century progresses. For that matter, I believe that the years ahead are going to be really difficult and trying for the large majority of the world's citizens. Basically, however, the United States, as the one major nuclear power, has deliberately assumed the ongoing, overriding task of maintaining large-scale peace. This will be increasingly difficult because a variety of countries, both large and small, may already have, or may soon have, nuclear-arms capability. That is one stark fact that makes the future so worrisome.

Physical activity education, including what is here called *educational* sport, is a field that in the 21st century is facing one more crossroad in its torturous historical development. As it happened, after approximately 200 years, during which time people were involved in subsistence physical activity and indigenous physical recreation and games, some 19th century European leaders in organized physical activity brought their varying ideas about physical training and gymnastics to the "New World." Those directing the effort after the American Civil War adopted the name "physical education" for a new national association in the 1880s. What then gradually developed on this soil has been termed a unique "American system" of physical education. Over the decades of the 20th century, this "American program" has included to greater or lesser extent, at the several levels of education, elements of health education, physical education, physical recreation, sport, and dance.

As it developed since the founding of the Association for the Advancement of Physical Education in 1985, the field of physical activity education (including sport) has had many obstacles to overcome. This book has been written to alert anyone who might be interested in the field's two confounding "predicaments" as it proceeds in the 21st century. *Sadly, yet interestingly, despite the enormous importance of what the field has to offer humankind, these two predicaments facing society are not recognized by the large majority of the population. People just don't seem to fully comprehend the seriousness of either predicament!*

The first "predicament" is the fact that the field of physical activity education (and related school health education) is not receiving the support and attention it needs (and warrants!) to serve children, youth, and young adults adequately–and certainly not fully. It appears that the public doesn't recognize this situation or, to the extent that it does, does not believe it is worth the attention and expense of doing anything significant to rectify the problem.

The second predicament relates to the evolving role of sport in society. Sport has become a social institution that is accepted in its many forms without being required to prove itself as worthwhile. Somehow it is relentlessly developing in ways that should cause the discerning onlooker to question whether it is producing more "good than bad" in the culture. It has become an ever-present factor in the daily lives of the developed world. However it is functioning with no underlying theory that is being even semi-scientifically affirmed as it evolves. People seem to think, generally speaking that sport involvement is good for children, youth, and young adults and, the more of it there is, the better off people and society will be. This rosy picture is becoming dimmer with each passing day…

Both of these predicaments should be resolved as soon as it is humanly possible. However, the "powers that be" must be convinced about the necessity for such action before we can expect change to occur. The situation is complex and seemingly difficult to explain despite the prediction that the oncoming generation will dies at an earlier age than their parents. A fine physical and related health education program is needed annually throughout the educational system. In addition to a class-oriented program, a supplementary, intramural competitive–sport program is needed for both "normal" and "special-needs" children and youth.

Keeping in mind, therefore, these glaring omissions in our educational system, why do we then turn around and devote an enormous amount of time, effort, and money to promote "varsity sport for the few"? I can see no justifiable reason to continue with the present approach unless the urgent needs of the mass of students are first met. If we are honest and fair, this situation must change at the first possible moment. The only conclusion I can come to is the following: ***As I say, or repeatedly imply throughout this book, "sport does not equate with [a fine program of] physical activity [and related] health education. A varsity team program for accelerated children and youth should be made available only after the physical activity education needs of the large majority of youth have been met!***

As you catch your breath, while contemplating the uproar that the instigation of such a proposal would produce, I can appreciate that this may seem to be a ridiculous assertion on a continent where competitive sport has become such a powerful social institution. Nevertheless, I simply ask this question: "In what other aspect of the entire educational program do we take care of the needs and wishes of a tiny minority of the school population to the detriment of the large majority of the students?

As it developed historically, this unique situation occurs only in North America! Nowhere else in the world do we find that a competitive athletics program has become an institution for the "physically gifted" within the schools at the middle-school, secondary, and tertiary educational levels. Competitive sport, although popular around the world, has never been accepted as part of the educational program such as academic subjects are.

Of course, you may reply: "Competitive sport hasn't been accepted as part of the official *educational* program here either!" This is true, but somehow it has assumed a place of importance despite the fact that its importance of its contribution cannot be verified. It is a social institution without an accompanying theory that is supported by evidence. In addition, as a matter of fact, there is now solid evident that such desirable traits a honesty, fair play, truth, and sportsmanship decline the longer that athlete continues with sport competition! (This to me was a "clincher"…)

We might also postulate another situation within education where it was a question of the provision of a fine program of English or mathematics instruction for all students. I ask: "What would the reaction of parents and the public be if programs were available only to those students who appeared to be gifted in language or numeracy?

Keeping the above in mind, I decided to divide this book on the subject into more or less four parts as follows:

Part One: An Emerging Postmodern Age
Part Two: The Status of Physical (Activity)
            Education and Educational Sport
Part Three: Looking to the Future of Physical
            Activity Education and Educational Sport

In conclusion, I wish all my colleagues well for the uncertain future that lies ahead. I know that I speak for them when I urge all who may read these words to "take up the torch" and move it much further along that we of my generation were able to do.

Earle F. Zeigler
British Columbia, Canada
2010

Part One: An Emerging Postmodern Age

Selection #1
A North American Crisis!

"A disastrous mistake"? "Crisis, what crisis?" you may ask. My response is: "It's getting closer, and it's really going to bite you, if you don't look out!" Face it! Anyway one wants to look at it, the handwriting is on the wall! North American children and youth are simply not getting regular, quality physical activity education programs throughout their entire educational experience. The result is going to be that they will "pay for it" sooner *and* later. And we, members of the general public, are really going to pay for it later in horrendous health costs and in several other vital ways.

And sadly, we will have no one else to blame but ourselves because we are being warned, and we had been forewarned down through the years. In September, 2004, The Centers for Disease Control and Prevention of the United States released a report titled "Participation in High School Physical Education–United States, 1991-2003 (MMWR Weekly, Sept, 17, 2004 / 53(36), 844-847). In essence it states the evolving situation is not good, and that "If the national health objectives are to be achieved, coordinated efforts involving schools, communities, and policy makers are needed to provide daily, quality PE for all youth" (p. 1).

Next, on May 10, 2006, a significant article written by Eleanor Randolph was published in *The New York Times* titled "The Big, Fat American Kid Crisis . . .And 10 Things We Can Do About It". In this highly significant article Ms. Randolph points out clearly and starkly that "Over the last 30 years. *obesity rates* have doubled among pre-schoolers and tripled for those age 6 to 11." After stating "Childhood obesity has become a medical crisis," she explains further that "The *National Institutes of Health* estimates that *Americans will take five years off our average lifespan* in a few years if we don't curb obesity, especially among the young." Still further, "The Centers for Disease Control and Prevention has estimated that this obesity epidemic is already costing our health care system about $79 billion a year."

Further, the June, 2009 issue of the *Research Digest* of the President's Council on Physical Fitness and Sports (Series 10, No. 2) included a report titled " School Physical Education as a Viable Change Agent to Increase School Physical Activity. The summary statement in the article, written by Professors V. Gregory Payne, San Jose State University, CA and James R. Morrow, Jr. University of North Texas, Denton, stressed that:

> School physical education has been promoted by numerous
> expert sources as one of the most promising interventions in
> our nation's battle against physical inactivity, obesity, and

morbidities. However, much room remains for
improvement. Changes to the curriculum with the adoption
of standards and enforcement of state policies can make
school physical education one of the most powerful change
agents for the serious health concerns facing our country.

Finally, on July 2, 2009, the Trust for America's Health (TFAH) and the
Robert Wood Johnson Foundation (RWJF) followed up with "F as in Fat 2009
(How Obesity Policies are Failing in America"). Their findings are even more
stark and foreboding: "Adult obesity rates increased in 23 states and did not
decrease in a single state in the past year." Calling for a National Strategy to
Combat Obesity that urges the defining of "roles and responsibilities for federal,
state, and local governments" as well as "promoting collaboration among
businesses, communities, schools, and families," A number of basic policies are
recommended. Number #3 in this list states: "Increase the frequency, intensity,
and duration of physical activity at schools."

It is obvious that the die has been cast. We in the field of physical activity
education must step up to the plate more than we have ever done so in the past.
We can no longer permit colleagues in other fields and disciplines to downgrade
the value of our potential contribution to the lives of children, youth, and young
adults. The solution for us is to relate to all those groups mentioned above to help
us make our case in both the public sector and in academe. In doing so, we should
state loudly and clearly: "We undertake physical activity regularly ourselves; we
teach it to others; we teach other how to teach it; we research all aspects physical
activity; and we administer programs of physical activity at all educational levels."
(At the university level, if we don't think physical activity education sounds
sufficiently "academic," we can say that our concern is with "developmental
physical activity in exercise, sport, and related expressive activity".) Finally, it
should be obvious that a full understanding of such involvement in human
movement depends on knowledge emanating from the physical sciences, the social
sciences, and the humanities.

A Terrible Predicament

How did America–the whole North American continent probably–get
itself into such a predicament? Historically, as the American Association for the
Advancement of Physical Education (1885) "subdivided" and eventually became
AAHPERD (and even spawned ICHPER-SD internationally), most of those "subdivided" folks (e.g., health education, recreation) blithely went their own way as
PE despite the valiant efforts of many "stumbled along" as the afterthought in the
educational system. In Canada the CAHPERD tagged right along after them *until*
it recently became Physical & Health Education Canada (a good move, I say).

This "name business" (i.e. deciding on the right name and sticking with it!)
has been "driving me crazy and our field crazy" since I first became involved in
the early 1940s. More recently I have been recommending the name *"physical*

activity education and educational sport" for the "profession" and *"developmental physical activity"* as a name for any university unit.

Thinking historically and more broadly, however, physical education as a name for the field has indeed turned out to be a "bloody misnomer"! It was so, because–soon after the term "physical education" was adopted–psychological research in the early 20th century demonstrated that we are indeed *unified* organisms, the field of general education was thereby told that *henceforth* there couldn't be three separate types of education (i.e., physical, mental, and spiritual)!

In addition, because of the historical mind-body dichotomy dating back to the ancient Greek, Plato, and the "power of the church" subsequently, our field of physical education was "assigned" lower status automatically with this tri-partite educational philosophy (e.g., witness the place of "the body" in the well-known YMCA triangle!).

Further, in North America, Britain's "sporting tradition" began to develop in the mid-1800s. It had to compete with the foreign systems of gymnastics and exercise brought over from Europe. This might have worked out just fine, *if such activity had been introduced wholeheartedly within the educational curriculum on a regular basis.* However, it was deemed "extra-curricular" by educational essentialists–and resultantly has suffered from "second-class status" ever since.

There Is No *Profession* of Physical Education!

Shifting back to what *did* happen to what was called *physical* education within education, I recommend that now–after proclaiming it loudly for 100 years–the field should stop talking about the *profession* of physical education. We must do this because we are *not* a profession! We *are* professional *educators* responsible for physical activity education within the curriculum. Also, specifically related health education is involved, although we are *not* typically school health educators unless qualified to do that too. School health education is far too important to be allotted as a second-hand responsibility of the physical activity educator. We are further typically not *professional* coaches, although based on background and training in selected sports, we carry out this function at the various educational levels. *Certainly we are not considered a separate profession by the public!*

Further, our frequent placement within departments, schools, or faculties of education at the university level (i.e., not as separate units in either the USA or Canada, for example) has somehow come to mean that our status is "automatically the 'lowest of the low' in the 'academic firmament'." I won't go into the history of this declaration at this point right now. That is just "the way it is out there"!

(Note: Many of physical education's professional programs in the United States are under the aegis of schools of education except where they managed to "escape" at some point historically. Even then, aspiring physical educators must have certain course experiences within the education unit on a campus to qualify for teacher status at the state level. The arrangement differs In Canada from province to province. In Ontario, for example, a separate degree is awarded (B.Ed.) after the baccalaureate degree in the field of physical education or kinesiology.

To broaden the outlook: Any idea of being a profession in society at large, in addition to being a professional educator responsible for physical activity education, "got away" from the field of physical education years ago and probably can never be retrieved. There are so many different professions or occupations "out there" whose practitioners promote this or that type of physical activity that to organize them "under one roof and one title" seem inconceivable. It might be worth a try, but it is "so late in the game." Thus, here we are today, as Jimmy Durante (the late comedian) was wont to say–*because the right kind of physical activity has proven to be such a good thing*– "Everybody wants to get in on the act!" And that's exactly what has been happening…

Just imagine it. Even many medics in the mid-20th century were almost "our enemies"; now they are proclaiming the benefits of physical activity daily as the beneficial results of this or that research project are reported. Of course, they should be doing just that! Why? Because we now know that "womb to tomb", developmental physical activity will not only help a person live life more fully, it will also help him or her to live longer! And yet, *somehow* (!) here we as physical activity educators are–at the beginning of the 21st century–with *inadequate* programs of physical and health education at all educational levels!

In addition, at the same time, *somehow* (!) commercialized, overemphasized, competitive sport is running rampant both within many high schools, colleges, and universities. This is actually hurting our field of physical activity education and related health education because of the misplaced expenditure of energy and the accompanying "misdirected" use of available funding in communities across the North American continent. The situation has developed (retrogressed?) to the point where the "wrong" types of sporting experiences are promoted and actually "glorified"! A case can be made to the effect that because of such misplaced emphasis that competitive sport is probably doing more harm than good in world culture.

How Did This Come About Historically?

I found myself hard pressed to explain fully and correctly how this "tale of woe" came to be historically. Then I recalled VanderZwaag's analysis about what occurred during the period from 1880-1920 in the United States (1975). He had explained that "the nineteenth century was characterized by sectional interests and struggles among systems in physical education. This would not seem to be true today. What was the turning point?" VanderZwaag found the answer in "the steadily increasing interest in sports among the American people. The popularity of athletic contests was evident long before 1880. However, the earliest interest was developed through athletic clubs and intercollegiate athletics. The mass of the people did not receive the educational benefits to be derived from such activity."

As it turned out, the English sporting pattern won out over the several foreign systems of physical education. As VanderZwaag explained further that by 1920, it was evident that the United States had evolved a program of physical education that was characterized by informality and emphasis upon national sports. Such a program was thought to be entirely natural in view of our changing educational and political philosophies. Educationally, there was a growing recognition that a sound program of education should be based upon the needs of the child. This was also being recognized in the field of physical education that rapidly came to a system of physical education for the public schools that was based upon the play activities of childhood.

Why did this acceptance of "play and sport" as "physical education" materialize, you may ask? Seeking to answer this question more fully, I remembered that many years ago, when I was thesis adviser to the late Phyllis J. Hill at the University of Illinois, UIUC, Dr. Hill had provided an explanation in her investigation completed in 1965 (*A Cultural History of Sport in Illinois, 1673-1820*). In her concluding statement, she wrote: "I am forced to the position that American cultural practices, including sport, have been forged by environmental forces, rather than by Anglo-Saxon tradition". This conclusion has merit still today because as she explained further, "work ethics and sport ethics are so close as to be virtually indistinguishable."

I sought to comprehend what this means for us today in the field of physical (activity) education and (educational) sport. Hill had concluded: "if all human behavior is, indeed, a total and patterned response, *the understanding of sport can be furthered only when it is studied in reference to other human variables within the culture*" [the emphasis is by EFZ]. What can I conclude? I can only affirm that our goal was sound. However, other societal influences were brought to bear on the ideal thereby perverting it. Our task in physical activity education and educational/recreational sport is to help **all** people of all ages and conditions understand how important it is for them to be involved in a type of developmental physical activity that will enable them to *live life more fully* based on their choice of "life values." If they choose correctly, and we in the field help them to acquire the needed knowledge and skills to live life more fully, the evidence we have from research now points to *a longer life for them* as well for those who choose wisely…

Selection #2
Perspective on "Quality of Life":
Genes, Memes, and Physical Activity

Two historical questions have important implications for the field of physical activity education and educational sport:

    1. Did humans in earlier times, equipped with their coalescing genes and evolving memes, enjoy to any significant degree what discerning people today might define as "quality living?" (Memes are sets of "cultural instructions" passed on from one generation to the next; see below, also.)

    2. Did earlier humans have an opportunity for freely chosen, beneficial physical activity in sport, exercise, play, and dance of sufficient quality and quantity to contribute to the quality of life (as viewed by us today)? Of course, the phrasing of these questions–whether humans in earlier societies enjoyed quality living, including fine types of developmental physical activity–is no doubt presumptuous. It reminds one of the comedian whose stock question in response to his foil who challenged the truth of the zany experiences his friend typically reported: "Vas you dare, Sharlie?"

What makes a question about the quality of life in earlier times doubly difficult, of course, is whether present-day humans can be both judge and jury in such a debate. On what basis can we decide whether any <u>social</u> progress has indeed been made such that would permit resolution of such a concept as "quality living." There has been progression, of course, but on what basis can we assume that change is indeed progress? It may be acceptable as a <u>human</u> criterion of progress to say that we are coming closer to approximating the good and solid accomplishments that we think humans should have achieved both individually and socially.

However, Simpson (1949) believes it is shortsighted to assume automatically that such is "the only criterion of progress and that it has a general validity in evolution." He concludes, therefore, that human progress is actually relative and not general, and "does not warrant a choice of the line of humans' ancestry as <u>the</u> central line of evolution as a whole." Nevertheless, he does concede "that man is, on the whole but not in every single respect, the pinnacle so far of evolutionary progress" <u>on this Earth</u> (pp. 240-262). .

A Conception of History (Nevins)

Of course, we should also understand initially that a number of different "approaches" to the historical analysis of human history have been taken by scholars (e.g., "x number" of great civilizations, "great man" theory). The one that I adopted after reflection early on in my writing is what I identify as a pragmatic approach. Allan Nevins' broad conception of history (1962) seemed to offer that possibility in the best possible way when he stated:

Although when we use the word "history" we instinctively think of the past, this is an error, for history is actually a bridge connecting the past with the present, and pointing the road to the future. This conception of history as a lantern carried by the side of man, moving forward with every step taken, is of course far ampler than the concept of a mere interesting tale to be told, a vivid scene to be described, or a group of picturesque characters to be delineated (p. 14).

The "Tragic Sense" of Life (Muller)

Proceeding from this conception with the topic at hand, I realized immediately that any assessment of the quality of life in prerecorded history must be a dubious evaluation at best. However, I was intrigued by the work of Herbert Muller who has written so insightfully about the struggle for freedom in human history. I was impressed, also, by his belief that recorded history has displayed a "tragic sense" of life. Whereas the philosopher Hobbes (1588-1679) stated in his *De Homine* that very early humans existed in an anarchically individualistic state of nature in which life was "solitary, poor, nasty, brutish, and short," Muller (1961) argued in rebuttal that it "might have been poor and short enough, but that it was never solitary or simply brutish" (p. 6). Accordingly, Muller's approach to history (1952) is "in the spirit of the great tragic poets, a spirit of reverence and or irony, and is based on the assumption that the tragic sense of life is not only the profoundest but the most pertinent for an understanding of both past and present" (p. vii).

Muller's rationalization for his "tragic" view is simply that the drama of human history has been characterized by high tragedy in the Aristotelian sense. As he states, "All the mighty civilizations of the past have fallen, because of tragic flaws; as we are enthralled by any Golden Age we must always add that it did not last, it did not do" (p. vii). This brings to mind the possibility that the 20th century of the modern era could turn out to be the Golden Age of the United States. This may be true because so many misgivings are developing about our blind optimism concerning history's malleability and compatibility in keeping with American ideals. As Heilbroner (1960) explained in his "future as history" concept, America's still-prevalent belief in a personal "deity of history" may be short lived in the 21st century. Arguing that technological, political, and economic forces are "bringing about a closing of our historic future," he emphasized the need to search for a greatly improved "common denominator of values" (p. 178). However, all of this could be an oversimplification, because even the concept of civilization is literally a relative newcomer on the world scene.

Arnold Toynbee (1947) came to a quite simple conclusion about it all is his monumental A study of history—that humankind must return to the one true God from whom it has gradually but steadily fallen away. There is a faint possibility that Toynbee may turn out to be right, but we on this Earth should not put all of our eggs in that one basket. We had best try to use our heads as intelligently and wisely as possible as we get on with striving to make the world as effective and efficient—and as replete with good, as opposed to evil, as we possibly can.

Here we can well be guided by the pact that Goethe's Faust made with the Devil. As a German student and instructor originally, I recall the essence of the pact struck by Faust with the then-presumed purveyor of the world's evil. It was as follows: If ever the time were to come when Faust was tempted to feel completely fulfilled and not bored by the power, wealth, and honor that the horned one had bestowed upon him, then the Devil would have won, and accordingly would take him away to a "much warmer climate." Eventually, by conforming to the terms of the agreement, Faust is saved by the ministrations of the author (Johann Wolfgang von Goethe). However, we today can never forget for a moment that previous civilizations were not somehow saved miraculously—not one made it! "Man errs, but strive he must," said Goethe, and we as world citizens today dare not forget that dictum.

The "Adventure" of Civilization

In retrospect, the adventure of civilization began to make some headway because of now-identifiable forms of early striving which embodied elements of great creativity (e.g., the invention of the wheel, the harnessing of fire). The subsequent development in technology, very slowly but steadily, offered humans some surplus of material goods over and above that needed for daily living. For example, the early harnessing of nature created the irrigation systems of Sumeria and Egypt, and these accomplishments led to the establishment of the first cities. Here material surpluses were collected, managed, and sometimes squandered. Nevertheless, necessary early accounting methods were created that were subsequently expanded in a way that introduced writing to the human scene. As we now know, the development of this form of communication in time helped humans expand their self-consciousness and to evolve gradually and steadily in all aspects of culture. For better or worse, however, the result of this social and material progress has created a mixed agenda characterized by good and evil down to the present.

As Muller (1952) concluded, "the adventure of civilization is necessarily inclusive" (p. 53). By that he meant that evil will probably always be with humankind to some degree, but it is civilization that sets the standards and accordingly works to eradicate at least the worst forms of such evil. Racial prejudice, for example, must be overcome. For better or worse, there are now more than six billion people on earth, and that number appears to be growing faster than the national debt of the USA! These earth creatures are black-, yellow- or brown-, and white-skinned, but we now know from genetic research that basically there is an "overwhelming oneness" in all humankind that we dare not forget (Huxley, 1967).

As various world evils are overcome, or at least held in check, scientific and accompanying technological development will be called upon increasingly to meet the demands of the exploding population. Gainful work and a reasonable amount of leisure will be required for further development. Unfortunately, the necessary leisure required for the many aspects of a broad, societal culture to develop fully, as well as for an individual to grow and develop similarly within it, has come slowly. The average person in the world is far from a full realization of such benefits. Why "the good life" for all has been so slow in arriving is not an easy question to answer. Of course, we might argue that times do change slowly, and that the possibility of increased leisure has really come quite rapidly once humans began to achieve a degree of control of their environment.

Of course, there have been so many wars throughout history, and there has been very little if any let-up in this regard down to the present. Sadly, nothing is so devastating to a country's economy. In retrospect, also, in the Middle Ages of the Western world the power of the Church had to be weakened to permit the separation of church and state. This development, coupled with the rising humanism of the Renaissance in the latter stages of that era, was basic to the rise of a middle class. Finally, the beginnings of the natural sciences had to be consolidated into real gains before advancing technology could lead the West into the Industrial Revolution (i.e., Toffler's "Second Wave").

Recommended Approaches for Improving Life's Quality

Csikszentmihalyi (1993), seeking to help humans "free themselves of the dead hand of the past," has proposed selected "approaches to life that will improve its quality and lead to joyful involvement." However, he stresses that humans are now confronted with a "memes versus genes" dilemma. "Meme" is the term introduced in the 1970s by the British biologist, Richard Dawkins, who coined the noun from the Greek term mimesis to describe a set of "cultural instructions" passed on by example from one generation to another. A gene is, of course, the basic physical unit of heredity about which we are hearing increasingly.

Csikszentmihalyi is fearful that humans' previous "adaptive successes"–the very ones that have helped people survive down to the present–need to be re-assessed in the light of present conditions lest they destroy our future. He refers to (1) the organization of the brain, (2) the emergence of a primitive self, (3) the genetic instructions that helped us survive through past millennia, and (4) the competition with other people that is the result of the selective forces on which evolution is based. In addition, he envisions a further danger—"the threat of the artifacts we have created to make our lives more comfortable" (p. 119). Here these "permanent patterns of matter or information are produced by an act of human intentionality" (p. 120) and, although new on the humans' evolutionary stage, can over time "assume lives of their own." For example, the results of a few "mimetic parasites," such as the mind-altering drugs, alcohol and tobacco, have been literally devastating to a number of societies or segments thereof.

Arguing that our unique heritage "brings with it an awesome responsibility" because we are at the "cutting edge" of evolution, he affirms that now we "can either direct our life energy toward achieving growth and harmony or waste the potentials we have inherited, adding to the sway of chaos and destruction" (pp. 3-4). Csikszentmihalyi is basically searching for ways that could "integrate the growth and liberation of the self with that of society as a whole" (p. 5). Essentially, he is recommending that we strive for "flow experiences" which are characterized by,

(1)   clear goals with instant feedback;
(2)   opportunities for acting decisively in situations where personal skills are suited to given challenges;
(3)   actions taken merging with awareness to facilitate concentration
(4)   resulting concentration on the task at hand such that there is complete psycho-physical involvement;
(5)   a sense of potential control prevailing;
(6)   a loss of self-consciousness involving transcendence of ego boundaries occurring as the person experiences a sense of growth and of being part of some greater entity;
(7)   a sense of time altered so as to seem to pass faster; and
(8)   an experience that becomes autotelic, and thus creating the feeling that it is worth doing for its own sake (pp. 178-179).

He theorizes further that, even though intense flow experiences are relatively rare in everyday life, such experiences should indeed be increasingly possible in the play, work, study, or religious ritual of humans, **IF AND ONLY IF** the conditions outlined above are present.

Zeldin (1994), in his highly interesting *An intimate history of humanity*, both complements and supplements the work of Csikszentmihalyi by offering what he calls a "new vision of the past." He urges humankind to revisit the various individual feelings and personal relationships evidenced throughout history. In the process he recommends that individuals "form a fresh view both of their own personal history and of humanity's whole record of cruelty, misunderstanding, and joy" (p. vii). This revised vision of the past can be gradually achieved as the 21st century develops, Zeldin affirms, also–agreeing with our conference theme-setter (Csikszentmihalyi)–by deliberate efforts to reverse, through considered re-examination now and in the future, the unpleasant and unrewarding experiences of distant generations in the past. Because of this urgent need to remove the past's "dead hand," Zeldin is telling us starkly and simply that "those who don't learn from past experiences are doomed to repeat them!"

Zeldin stresses, also, the urgent need for society to:

(1)   Help people revive their hopes as they
        search for their roots,
(2)   Acquire immunity to loneliness,
(3)   Invent new forms of love,
(4)   Hive respect instead of seeking power,
(5)   Learn how to serve as intermediaries between
        people,
(6)   Free themselves from fears,
(7)   Develop rewarding friendships,
(8)   Survive today's nuclear family crisis, and
(9)   Choose a purposeful way of life.

He sees these as some of the ways in which we can turn future achievement of now often hidden aspirations into "flow experiences."

Interestingly, Lenk (1994), from a social-philosophical perspective, also envisioned the need for "value changes" in what he calls the "achieving society." He asks the question, "Is life more about work or more about pleasure?" He answers by suggesting that societal conditions may increasingly be such that people will require additional opportunities for "creative achievement and active involvement." Proceeding from an "achievement theme" he developed previously,

Lenk affirms also that "we are in need of a new positive 'culture' of achievement and a humanized creative achievement principle" (pp. 92-93).

The Fundamental Importance of Individual Freedom

The delineation by Csikszentmihalyi of the contribution that "flow experiences" can make in people's' lives, as well as Zeldin's call for a new "vision of the past" as we move into the future would require substantive individual freedom within a positively permissive society. As we look back to earlier eras, therefore, the vital missing link in most people's lives as they sought to fulfill their purposes was the absence of the necessary individual freedom. The definition of freedom I will use here is the relatively neutral, objective one accepted by Muller (1961, p. xiii) in his *Freedom in the ancient world*: "The condition of being able to choose and to carry out purposes." This means that the individual is neither hampered by external constraints nor coerced to do other than he or she wills. It assumes the ability, coupled with a positive desire, to make a conscious choice between known alternatives.

Human Evolution

Admittedly, permitting a conscious choice between alternatives will permit the presence of "population pockets" where there is a demand to give creationism co-equal status with the teaching of a Darwinian long-range approach to human evolution in the schools. As humans we, who tend to think we are "the greatest," may be excused from wondering occasionally why the Creator took such a long and laborious route with so many odd variations of flora and fauna to get to this point of "present greatness." For literally hundreds of thousands of years, the forebears of present-day humans struggled on chipping flints and making their tools. As they used their brains and their hands, both that proved to be an enormous biological advantage, it now seems apparent that in their primitive self-consciousness they were not living only for the moment like their contemporaries, the apes.

The power that these advantages provided humans, an aid combined with technological advancement, somehow nevertheless only offered minimal levels of freedom. As mentioned above, the early development of language as a means of communication was vitally important. This distanced sub humans even more from the apes as cultural evolution became much faster than biological evolution. In a sense, culture brought with it "good news" and "bad news." The bad news was that humans were to a large degree trapped in a world that they themselves created. Fixed habits and beliefs are strong inhibitors of change, growth, and of what might be called progress. The good news is that change did occur, albeit very slowly, and growth did take place.

To most people such change and growth did represent true progress. For example, prehistoric humans interbred, and in this way broadened their genetic base. This lends credence to the present-day argument introduced above: humans today—brown or yellow, black, and white—are indeed one race. This fact helps us to appreciate the development of worldwide cultural evolution. Unfortunately, however, progress has never been a straight-line affair. In the final analysis, this must be the answer for those of us who idealistically thought that the world would be in quite good shape by the year 2000! It may also provide solace to those of who wonder (1) why education finds it so difficult to get sufficient funding; (2) why professors in so many countries must often assume a "Rodney Dangerfield complex"; and (3) why physical education/kinesiology, despite evidence mounting daily as to the value of developmental physical activity, so often finds itself in dire straits within the domain of education and in the eyes of the public.

Physical Culture Down Through the Ages

Lest we in the profession presently blame ourselves too much for our profession's perennial plight, we should keep in mind the words of Thomas Woody (1949) who produced perhaps the most scholarly work extant about physical education in the ancient world. "Turn where one will," Woody explains, "it is impossible to find physical culture adequately presented in books dealing with the general history of education" (p. vii). (To this I hastily add the opinion: or anywhere else for that matter!)

We might ask, "Why is this so?" I believe the answer is that, throughout recorded history down, supposedly learned people have simply not understood either planned or playful physical activity's potential for improving the quality of life, for providing flow experiences, if you will. We might therefore argue that the highest aim of the profession of physical (activity) education and (educational) sport could well be the ordered assembly of the scientific and scholarly principles and generalizations that underlie such developmental physical activity.

It is a safe assumption that the values and norms of a culture have a profound influence on the way people carry out their daily functions. Accordingly, we are now in a position to inquire as to how value determinations have influenced developmental physical activity historically in those activities that we now call exercise, sport, dance, and play. History has told us clearly that physical activity has been a basic part of the fundamental pattern of living of every creature of any type that has ever lived on Earth. Yet Woody (1949) tells us further that "lip-service has been paid increasingly to the dictum 'a sound mind in a sound body,' ever since western Europe began to revive the educational concepts of the Graeco-Roman world." As he avers, "there is still a lack of balance between physical and mental culture" (p. vii).

Most interestingly, the answer to our plight may well rest in Woody's words that relate to the early "wisdom" of a Greek named Plato who left the world with a mixed message on the topic of the human body. The mind-body dualism that he has evidently created led indirectly to the Roman "sound mind in a sound body" dictum of Seneca. Further, this denial of the "wholeness" of the human organism has carried through down to the 20th century. And as the world moves on in the 21st century, I believe that the field of physical education/kinesiology [or whatever silly name appeared this week!] must strongly build on the "unified organism" concept provided for us by the related discipline of psychology, along with the continuing research of its applied psychologists.

Writing in the early 21st century, I seek to leave behind a challenge to the next generation of scholars and professional practitioners that those of us in this generation were not able to meet. The challenge is for them to devise the necessary ways and means of informing the American public about the principles of developmental physical activity–of physical education and kinesiology, if you will–upon which the field's professional practice can now be based logically.

Physical Education's 14 Principal Principles

On December 28, 1951, speaking at the general session of the former College Physical Education Association in Chicago, Illinois, the eminent Arthur H. Steinhaus of George Williams College, Chicago, with "many misgivings," offered what he called the four "principal principles" of physical education to the profession (1952). He explained that the term "principal principles can and does mean the most important or chief fundamental theories, ideas, or generalizations" (p. 5).

Steinhaus' effort in 1951 preceded the analytic summary carried out in "The Contributions of Physical Activity to Human Well-Being," a supplement to the *Research Quarterly* in May, 1960. There, as explained by Ray Weiss, a joint effort was made by scholars in the allied professions to present evidence that physical activity can indeed contribute to wellbeing of humans. These scholarly professionals were stating to the best of their knowledge what we felt that *really* knew, and what we felt that we were very close to knowing at that time.

As we in physical education/kinesiology move along in the 21st century, we can affirm that our steadily growing body of knowledge has provided our profession with a much more substantive knowledge base than that which existed at the middle of the present century. With similar misgivings to those mentioned by Professor Steinhaus, we can now affirm with reasonable assurance that our "principal principles" have increased in number to thirteen! It is perhaps pointless to attempt to determine precisely to what extent this increase can be attributed more to the efforts of the profession's natural science scholars than to those of the more recently added social science and humanities scholars, not to forget the important contributions emanating from our allied professions and related disciplines. That there is some overlap in these principles will be obvious as they are read, but this increase in the number of principal principles suggested points to the wisdom of continually searching for evidence wherever it is to be found.

The following, then, are the principles or generalizations that under gird our professional practice t the beginning of the 21st century. Steinhaus' four principles have now been merged with nine others to make a total of thirteen. Many of you in this room have made a greater or lesser contribution to what has now become the "knowledge heritage" being "passed on"—as our AAKPE seal states–to recent Academy inductees and their colleagues for further investigation and development:

Principle I: The "REVERSIBILITY Principle"

The first principle affirms that circulo-respiratory (often called cardio-vascular) conditioning is inherently reversible in the human body.

> (A male, for example, typically reaches his peak at age 19 and goes downhill gradually thereafter until eventual death. This means that a person must achieve and maintain at least an "irreducible level" of such conditioning to live normally.)

Principle II: The "OVERLOAD Principle"

The principle here is that a muscle or muscle group must be taxed beyond that to which it is accustomed, or it won't develop; in fact, it will probably retrogress.

> (Thus, the individual must maintain reasonable muscular strength in his/her body to carry out life's normal duties and responsibilities and to protect the body from deterioration.)

Principle III: The "FLEXIBILITY Principle"

This principle states that the human must regularly put his or her various joints through the range of motion for which they are intended.

> (Inactive joints become increasingly inflexible until immobility sets in. If inflexibility is a sign of old age, the evidence shows that most people are becoming old about age 27! A person must not neglect maintenance of bodily flexibility.)

Principle IV: The "BONE DENSITY Principle"

The evidence explains that developmental physical activity throughout life preserves the density of a human's bones.

(The density of the human's bones after maturity is not fixed or permanent, and the decline after age 35 may be more rapid than is the case with fat and muscle. After prolonged inactivity, adequate calcium in an individual's diet and weight-bearing physical activity is essential for the preservation of bones. Prevention of bone loss is much more effective than later efforts to repair any bone damage incurred.)

Principle V: The "GRAVITY Principle"

This principle explains that maintaining muscle-group strength throughout one's life, while standing or sitting, helps a person fight against the force of gravity that is working continually to break down a body's structure.

(Maintaining muscle group strength and tonus, along with the best possible structural alignment of one's bones through the development of a proper "body consciousness," will help the individual to fight off gravity's potentially devastating effects as long as possible.)

Principle VI: The "RELAXATION Principle"

Principle VI states that the skill of relaxation is one that people should acquire in today's increasingly complex world.

(Oddly enough, people often need to be taught how to relax in today's typically stressful environment. Part of any "total fitness" package should, therefore, be the development of an understanding as to how an individual can avoid chronic or abnormal fatigue in a social and physical environment that is often overly taxing.)

Principle VII: The "AESTHETIC Principle"

This principle explains that a person has either an innate or a culturally determined need to "look good" to himself/herself and to others.

(Socrates may have decried "growing old without appreciating the beauty of which the body is capable." This is a "need": to make a good appearance to one's family, friends, and those who one meets daily at work or during leisure. Billions of dollars are spent annually by people striving to "make themselves look like something they are not" naturally. Why do people do this? Quite probably, they go through these "body rituals" both to please themselves and because of various social pressures. Thus, if a person is physically active, while following the above six principles, one's bodily appearance can be preserved normally, naturally, and inexpensively.)

Principle VIII: The "INTEGRATION Principle"

Principle VIII asserts that developmental physical activity provides an opportunity for the individual to get "fully involved" as a vital living organism.

(So many of life's activities challenge a person only fractionally in that only part of his or her sensory equipment and even less of the individual's motor mechanism are involved. By their very nature, physical activities in exercise, sport, play, and expressive movement demand full attention from the organism—often in the face of opposition—and therefore involve complete psycho-physical integration.)

Principle IX: The "INTEGRITY Principle"

The integrity principle states that a completely integrated psycho-physical activity should correspond ETHICALLY with the avowed ideals and standards of society.

(The integrity principle goes hand in hand with desirable integration of the human's various aspects (so-called unity of body and mind in the organism explained in Principle VIII immediately above). Fair play, honesty, and concern for others should be uppermost in an individual's pattern of developmental physical activity.)

Principle X: The "PRIORITY OF THE PERSON Principle"

Principle X affirms that any physical activity in sport, play, and exercise that is sponsored through public or private agencies should be conducted in such a way that the welfare of the individual comes first.

(Situations arise daily in all aspects of social living where this principle, one that stresses the sanctity of the individual, is often forgotten. In a democratic society, a man or woman, or boy or girl, should never be forced or encouraged to take part in some type of developmental physical activity where this principle is negated because of the desire of others to win. The individual's personal growth and development is more important than the reputation of any sport organization in which he or she may take part. Sport should serve as a "social servant.")

Principle XI: The "LIVE LIFE TO ITS FULLEST Principle"

This principle asserts that, unless a person moves his or her body with reasonable vigor according to principles I-VI above, it will not serve that individual best throughout life.

(Human movement is what distinguishes the individual from the rock on the ground. Regular, reasonably strenuous physical activity helps a person to meet the normal daily tasks and the unexpected sudden demands that may be required live life fully and to protect oneself from harm.)

Principle XII: The "FUN AND PLEASURE Principle"

Principle XII states that the human is normally a "seeker of fun and pleasure," and that a great deal of the opportunity for such enjoyment is achieved by full, active bodily movement.

> (The opportunity for such fun and pleasure will be missing from a person's life if he or she does not maintain at least an "irreducible minimum" level of physical fitness.)

Principle XIII: The "LONGEVITY Principle"

This penultimate principle affirms that regular developmental physical activity throughout life can help a person live longer.

> (The statistical evidence is mounting that demonstrates the wisdom of maintaining an active lifestyle throughout life. Succinctly put, all things being equal, a physically active person who is physically active will live longer!)

Principle XIV: The "Physical Fitness & Learning– Correlation Principle"

This final principle states that students who maintain physical fitness are performing better academically than those students who are not fit.

> (Evidence is now accumulating that shows a positive relationship between physical fitness and what is termed as academic achievement.)

Flow Experiences and "The Good Life"

These 13 "principal principles" represent what we believe we know about wisdom of keeping these generalizations about planned physical activity in mind throughout life. The key task for the field of physical activity education and kinesiology is to help people of all ages, whether they are "accelerated, normal, or 'special population'," to actually implement this knowledge daily into their lives. If it is possible at present for some people to deliberately plan for and then include such flow experiences in their life patterns, and thereby to improve their quality of life, it is accordingly reasonable to assume (to hope?) that many more people will have the opportunity (i.e., the freedom) to do so in the future). However, before this will happen, those presently unconvinced must be convinced of the possibility and desirability of adding such experiences to their lives. This leads inevitably to the perennial question in education as to the knowledge, competencies, character, and personality traits for which we should educate in the years ahead.

Such choices will inevitably depend on on the values and norms of the culture in which people live. As we appreciate, values are the major social forces that help to determine the direction a culture will take at any given moment. Such values as social values, educational values, scientific values, and artistic values make up the highest level of the social system in a culture. It can, therefore, be argued that these values represent the "ideal general character" (e.g., rule of law, social-structured facilitation of individual achievement, equality of opportunity). As we understand further, overall culture in itself serves a pattern-maintenance function as a society relates to the functional problems it faces. In this connection pattern-maintenance and integration are internal problems, whereas adaptation and goal-attainment are external (Johnson, 1994, 1969).

In addition, the values that people hold for themselves in a society at a given time have a direct relationship to how we conceive the nature of the human being. There have been a number of attempts to define such nature on a rough historical time scale. For example, Morris (1956) offered a fivefold chronological series of definitions as to how to conceive the human being, including analyses in the following order:

(1) rational animal,

(2) spiritual being,

(3) receptacle of knowledge,

(4) mind that can be trained by exercise, and

(5) problem-solving organism.

In the mid-1960s, Berelson and Steiner (1964) traced six images for humankind throughout recorded history, but more from the standpoint of behavioral science. They identified them as follows:

(1) philosophical image,

(2) Christian image,

(3) political image,

(4) economic image,

(5) psychoanalytic image, and

(6) behavioral-science image.

Whatever one conceives to be his or her basic nature (e.g., problem-solving organism with a behavioral science image), as this person matures we can reasonably expect that considerable thought will be given as to what constitutes "the good life." As we know people from all levels of society have been offering advice on this topic since time immemorial. Csikszentmihalyi has recommended that we search for approaches to living–that is, flow experiences–that "improve its quality and lead to joyful involvement." In so doing, "the growth and liberation of the self" will be combined "with that of society as a whole" (p. 5).

Kateb's Delineation of "The Good Life"

To help us answer the question about ways to improve the quality of life, as well as how this might be accomplished joyfully, I return to the possibilities for "Utopia and the Good Life" outlined by George Kateb (1965, pp. 454-473). He recommended a progression of possibilities or definitions of the good life as:

(1) laissez faire,

(2) the greatest amount of pleasure,

(3) play,

(4) craft,

(5) political action, and

(6) the life of the mind.

His conclusion was that the life of the mind offers the greatest potential in the world as we know it now or as we may know it in the future.

As we put these possibilities in historical perspective, it is immediately obvious that only a very small percentage of people throughout recorded history have had sufficient freedom and wherewithal to choose and carry out those purposes they might have chosen initially. For example, laissez faire (No. 1 above), the greatest amount of pleasure (2), and play (3) could only be chosen (i.e., were available) as life patterns by a minute percentage of earlier humans in any search for flow experiences.

If by craft (4) is meant pursuit of an art or manual skill, then the number of those people for whom such was possible and who were probably involved in the development and use of craft in the past for survival and/or recreation rises significantly. Undoubtedly, depending on their freedom to pursue such endeavor, flow experiences could well have been one outcome of this involvement. Number 5, political action as a possible pursuit in the search for a good life, presents a significantly lesser opportunity, numerically speaking, for flow experiences because of the station in life inherited, not to mention the freedom, temperament, and constitutional vigor required for such involvement.

Kateb's final possibility as an approach to a search for the good life was titled "the life of the mind." He felt that "the man (sic) possessed of the higher faculties in their perfection is the model for utopia and already exists outside it . . ." (p. 472). This is an interesting conclusion that might be foreseen, of course, from a university scholar. Also, it can be argued that pursuit of the so-named "life of the mind" should increasingly be part and parcel of the life of each person in enlightened societies of the future.

Flow Experiences Via a Transcending Multiple Approach

In conclusion, I believe that men and women, now and in the future, can increase their exposure to flow experiences by combining all of Kateb's approaches into one viable, multiple, all-encompassing approach. At least five of these six approaches to the good life are directly or indirectly related to the role that developmental physical activity in sport, exercise, and dance can play in a society generally, as well as in the lives of people specifically (Zeigler, 1979, p. 12).

Fine educational experience has been related historically to the mastery of various subject matters. Accordingly—and I believe mistakenly—we do not typically understand so-called formal education to fully encompass *all* of the changes that take place in individuals based on their total life experience. Because of this truncated outlook, somehow the movement experience, the quality human motor performance experience aspect of education, of recreation, of all life—these *flow* experiences of a unified organism, if you will—has been slighted historically down to the present. Huxley (1964, p. 31) called it the disregard for the "education of the non-verbal humanities," of the "psycho-physical instrument of an evolving amphibian." This is the historical reality faced by the profession in 2008 of the Common Era.

Notes

1. Sincere appreciation is expressed to the many scientists and scholars, both within our field and in related disciplines and allied professions, whose efforts have made the statement of these principles possible at the close of the 20th century.

2. Steinhaus' original principles are included in the 13 principal principles formulated above. Note, however, that his "principle of integration and integrity" has been divided in two so as to create two separate principles.

References

Berelson, B. & Steiner, G.A. (1964). *Human behavior: An inventory of scientific findings*. NY: HarcourtBrace.
Contributions of physical activity to human well-being. (May 1960) *Research Quarterly*, 31, 2 (Part II): 261-375.
Csikszentmihalyi, M. (1993). *The evolving self*. NY: HarperCollins.
Heilbroner, R.L. (1960). *The future as history*. NY: Harper & Row.
Hobbes, T. *De Homine*.

Huxley, A. (1964). *Tomorrow and tomorrow and tomorrow.* NY:
New American Library.

Huxley, J. (January 1967). The crisis in man's destiny. *Playboy,*
93-94, 212-217.

Johnson, H.M. (1969). The relevance of the theory of action to
historians. *Social Science Quarterly,* 21<2>:46-58)

Johnson, H.M. (1994). Modern organizations in the Parsonsian theory of action.
In A. Farazmand, *Modern organizations:Administrative theory in contemporary society* (pp.
57 et ff.). Westport, CT: Praeger.

Kateb, G. (Spring 1965) Utopia and the good life. *Daedalus,*
94: 454-473.

Lenk, H. (1994). Value changes and the achieving society: A
social-philosophical perspective. In *Organisation for Economic Co-operation and
Development, OECD societies in ransition* (pp. 81-94).

Morris, V.C. (1956). Physical education and the philosophy of education.
JOPHER, 27,3: 21-22, 30-31.

Muller, H.J. (1954). *The uses of the past.* NY: Mentor Books.

Muller, H.J. (1961*). Freedom in the ancient world.* NY: Harper & Bros.

Nevins, A. (1963). *The gateway to history.* Garden City, NY:
Doubleday & Co.)

Simpson, G. (1949). *The meaning of evolution.* New Haven & London: Yale
University Press.

Steinhaus, A.H. (1952). Principal principles of physical education.
In *Proceedings of the College Physical Education Association.*
Washington, DC: AAHPER, pp. 5-11.

Woody, T. (1949). Life and education in early societies. NY:
Macmillan.

Zeigler, E.F. (1979) Sport and physical activity's role in the behavioral science
image of man and women. In E. F. Zeigler, *Issues in North American sport and
physical education.* Washington, DC: AAHPER.

Zeigler, E.F. (1989). *An introduction to sport and physical
education philosophy.* Carmel, IN: Benchmark.

Zeigler, E.F. (1994). Physical education's 13 "principal
principles," *JOPERD,* 65, 7: 4-5.

Zeldin, T. (1994). *An intimate history of humanity.* NY: HarperCollins.

Selection #3
Counteracting America's Value Orientation

The term *"modernism"* is used to describe cultural movements in today's world that were caused by onrushing science, technology, and economic globalization. It is said to have started in the late nineteenth and early twentieth century. Conversely, *postmodernism*, as variously defined, can be described loosely as an effort by some intelligent and possibly wise people to react against what is happening to this *modern* world as it "races headlong" toward an indeterminate future.

It can be argued reasonably that America's thrust is modernistic to the nth degree. To the extent that this is true, I am arguing here conversely that any country should work to counteract America's value orientation as the world moves along in the 21st century. For example, I believe that Canada can--and should do this--by adopting a position that might be called "moderate" postmodernism.

Granted that it will be most difficult for countries such as Canada to consistently exhibit a different "thrust" than its neighbor to the south. Nevertheless I believe that now is the time to deliberately create a society characterized by the better elements of what has been termed postmodernism. In fact, I feel that all countries will be *forced* to grapple with the basic thrust of modernism in the 21st century if they hope to avoid the "twilight" that is descending on "American culture" (Berman, 2000). You, the reader, may well question this stark statement about our immediate neighbor. However, bear with me, and let us begin.

What is postmodernism? While most philosophers have been "elsewhere engaged" for the past 50 plus years, what has been called postmodernism, and what I believe is poorly defined for the edification of most, has gradually become a substantive factor in broader intellectual circles. I freely admit to have been grumbling about the term "postmodern" for decades. I say this because somehow it too has been used badly as have other philosophic terms such as existentialism, pragmatism, idealism, realism, etc. as they emerged to become common parlance.

In this ongoing process, postmodernism was often used by a minority to challenge prevailing knowledge, and considerably less by the few truly seeking to analyze what was the intent of those who coined the term originally. For example, I am personally not suggesting, as some have, that scientific evidence and empirical reasoning are to be taken with a grain of salt based on someone's subjective reality. Further, if anything is worth saying, I believe it should be said as carefully and understandably as possible. Accordingly, the terms used must be defined, at least tentatively. Otherwise one can't help but think that the speaker (or writer) is either deceitful, a confused person, or has an axe to grind.

If nothing in the world is absolute, and one value is as good as another in a world increasingly threatened with collapse and impending doom, as some say postmodernists claim, then one idea is possibly as good as another in any search to cope with the planet's myriad problems. This caricature of a postmodern world, as one in which we can avoid dealing with the harsh realities facing humankind, is hardly what any rational person might suggest. How can humankind choose to avoid (1) looming environmental disaster, (2) ongoing war because of daily terrorist threats, and (3) hordes of displaced, starving people, many of whom are now victims of conflicts within troubled cultures? Further, as we still occasionally hear said, *what rational being would argue that one idea is really as good as another?*

What then is humankind to do in the face of the present confusion and often conflicted assertions about postmodernism from several quarters that have been bandied about? First, I think we need to analyze the world situation as carefully as we possibly can. Perhaps this will provide us with a snapshot of the milieu where we can at least see the need for a changing (or changed) perspective that would cause humankind to abandon the eventual, destructive elements of modernism that threaten us. An initial look at some of the developments of the second half of the twentieth century may provide a perspective from which to judge the situation.

Historical Perspective on the "World Situation"

In this search for historical perspective on world society today, we need to keep in mind the significant developments of the decades immediately preceding the turn of the 21st century. For example, Naisbitt (1982) outlined the "ten new directions that are transforming our lives." Then his wife and he suggested the "megatrends" they saw insofar as women's evolving role in the societal structure (Aburdene & Naisbitt, 1992). Here I refer to:

1) the concepts of the information society and Internet,
2) "high tech/high touch,"
3) the shift to world economy,
4) the need to shift to long-term thinking in regard to ecology,
5) the move toward organizational decentralization,
6) the trend toward self-help,
7) the ongoing discussion of the wisdom of participatory democracy as opposed to representative democracy,
8) a shift toward networking,
9) a reconsideration of the "north-south" orientation, and
10) the viewing of decisions as "multiple option" instead of "either/or."

Add to this the ever-increasing, lifelong involvement of women in the workplace, politics, sports, organized religion, and social activism. Now, we can begin to understand that a new world order has descended upon us as we begin the 21st century.

Moving ahead in time slightly past the presentation of Naisbitt's first set of *Megatrends*, a second list of 10 issues facing political leaders was highlighted in the *Utne Reader*. It was titled "Ten events that shook the world between 1984 and 1994" (1994, pp. 58-74). Consider the following:

1) the fall of communism and the continuing rise of nationalism,
2) the environmental crisis and the Green movement,
3) the AIDS epidemic and the "gay response,"
4) continuing wars (29 in 1993) and the peace movement,
5) the gender war,
6) religion and racial tension,
7) the concept of "West meets East" and resultant implications,
8) the "Baby Boomers" came of age and "Generation X" has started to worry and complain because of declining expectation levels,
9) the whole idea of globalism and international markets, and
10) the computer revolution and the specter of the Internet.

It is true that the world's "economic manageability"–or adaptability to cope with such change–may have been helped by its division into three major trading blocs: (1) the Pacific Rim long dominated by Japan [and now by China as well]; (2) the European Community very heavily influenced by Germany; and (3) North America dominated by the United States of America. While this appears to be true to some observers, interestingly perhaps something even more fundamental has occurred. Succinctly put, world politics seems to be "entering a new phase in which the fundamental source of conflict will be neither ideological nor economic." In the place of these, Samuel P. Huntington, of Harvard's Institute for Strategic Studies, has asserted that now the major conflicts in the world would be clashes between different groups of civilizations espousing fundamentally different cultures.

These clashes represent a distinct shift away from viewing the world as being composed of "first, second, and third worlds" as was the case during the Cold War. Thus, Huntington is arguing that in the 21st century the world will return to a pattern of development evident several hundred years ago in which civilizations will actually rise and fall. (Interestingly, this is exactly what the late Arnold Toynbee in his now famous theory of history development stated. However, to confuse the situation even more, most recently we have been warned by scholars about the increasing number of clashes within civilizations!)

Internationally, after the dissolution of the Union of Soviet Socialist Republics (the USSR), Russia and the remaining communist regimes have been severely challenged as they sought to convert to more of a capitalistic economic system. Additionally, a number of other multinational countries are regularly showing signs of potential breakups. Further, the evidence points to the strong possibility that the developing nations are becoming ever poorer and more destitute with burgeoning populations resulting in widespread starvation caused by both social and ecological factors.

Further, Western Europe is facing a demographic time bomb even more than the United States because of the influx of refugees from African and Islamic countries, not to mention refugees from countries of the former Soviet Union. It is evident, also, that the European Community is inclined to appease Islam's demands. However, the multinational nature of the European Community will tend to bring on economic protectionism to insulate its economy against the rising costs of prevailing socialist legislation.

Still further, there is evidence that Radical Islam, possibly along with Communist China, is becoming increasingly aggressive toward the Western culture of Europe and North America. At present, Islam gives evidence of replacing Marxism as the world's main ideology of confrontation. For example, Islam is dedicated to regaining control of Jerusalem and to force Israel to give up control of land occupied earlier to provide a buffer zone against Arab aggressors. Also, China has been arming certain Arab nations. Yet, how can the West be critical in this regard when we recall that the U.S.A. has also armed selected countries in the past [and present?] when such support was deemed in its interest?)

As Hong Kong, despite its ongoing protestations, is gradually absorbed into Communist China, further political problems seem inevitable in the Far East as well. Although North Korea is facing agricultural problems, there is the possibility (probability?) of the building of nuclear bombs there along with the capability to deploy them. Further, there is the ever-present fear worldwide that Iran, other smaller nations, and terrorists will somehow get nuclear weapons too. A growing Japanese assertiveness in Asian and world affairs also seems inevitable because of its typically very strong financial position. Yet the flow of foreign capital from Japan into North America has slowed down. This is probably because Japan has been confronted with its own financial crisis caused by inflated real estate and market values. Also, there would obviously be a strong reaction to any fall in living standards in this tightly knit society. Interestingly, further, the famed Japanese work ethic has become somewhat tarnished by the growing attraction of leisure opportunities.

The situation in Africa has become increasingly grim. Countries south of the Sahara Desert–that is, the dividing line between Black Africa and the Arab world–have experienced extremely bad economic performance in the past two decades. This social influence has brought to a halt much of the continental effort leading to political liberalization while at the same time exacerbating traditional ethnic rivalries. This economic problem has accordingly forced governmental cutbacks in many of the countries because of the pressures brought to bear by the financial institutions of the Western world that have been underwriting much of the development that had taken place. (Note: And now look at the trouble those very institutions are experiencing!) The poor are therefore getting poorer, and health and education standards have in many instances deteriorated even lower than they were previously. At this point one wonders how there ever was thought about the average family ever living "the good life."

America's Position in the 21st Century

Reviewing America's position in the 21st century may help us to get to the heart of the matter about where the so-called "developed world" is heading. For example, we could argue that North Americans do not fully comprehend that their unique position in the history of the world's development will in all probability change radically for the worse in the 21st century. Actually, of course, the years ahead are really going to be difficult ones for all of the world's citizens. However, it does appear that the United States is currently setting itself up "big time" for all kinds of societal difficulties. As the one major nuclear power, Uncle Sam has taken on the ongoing, overriding problem of maintaining large-scale peace. At the turn of the 20th century Teddy Roosevelt, while "speaking softly," nevertheless had his "big stick." The George ("W") Bush administration at the beginning of the 21st century had its "big stick", also, but it didn't give a minute's thought to "speaking softly." The president actually did claim that America's assertive actions are "under God" and are designed for the good of all humanity. This caused various countries, both large and small, to speak out about many perceive as a bullying posture. Some of these countries may or may not have nuclear arms capability already. That is what is so worrisome.

America, despite all of its proclaimed good intentions, may well find that history is going against it in several ways. This means that previous optimism may need to be tempered to shake politicians loose from delusions, some of which persist despite what seems to be commonsense logic. For example, it is troublesome that, despite the presence of the United Nations, the United States has persisted in positioning itself as the world superpower. Such posturing and aggression, often by unilateral action with the hoped-for, belated sanction of the United Nations, has resulted in the two recent United States-led wars in the Middle East and other incursion into Somalia and then Afghanistan for very different reasons. There are also other similar situations on the recent horizon, and I haven't even mentioned the "Vietnam disaster" of the 1960s. And–let's face it! Who knows what the Central Intelligence Agency has been doing lately to make the world safe for American-style democracy. . .? Fidel Castro, after surviving so many assassination-attempts, can now "breathe more easily" as he approaches death from illness.

There is reason. post-George "W" that is, to expect selected U.S. cutbacks brought on by today's excessive world involvement and enormous debt. It appears that many in "the World" do indeed wish President Obama well, but significant retrenchment due to financial debt would inevitably lead to a decline in the economic and military influence of the United States. However, who can argue logically that the present uneasy balance of power is a healthy situation looking to the future? More than a generation ago, Norman Cousins sounded just the right note when he wrote: "the most important factor in the complex equation of the future is the way the human mind responds to crisis." The world culture as we know it today simply must respond adequately and peacefully to the many challenges with which it is being confronted. The societies and nations must individually and collectively respond positively, intelligently, and strongly if humanity as we have known it is to survive.

Additionally, problems and concerns of varying magnitude abound. It seems inevitable that all of the world will be having increasingly severe ecological problems, not to mention the ebbs and flows of an energy crisis. Generally, also, there is a worldwide nutritional problem, and an ongoing situation where the rising expectations of the underdeveloped nations, including their staggering debt, will have to be met somehow. These are just a few of the major concerns looming on the horizon. And, wait a minute, now we find that America has spent so much more "straightening out" the "enemy" that its debt has reached staggering proportions.

In his insightful analysis, *The twilight of American culture* (2000), Morris Berman explained that historically four factors are present when a civilization is threatened with collapse:

> (1) Accelerating social and economic inequality,
> (2) Declining marginal returns with regard to
>   investments in organizational solutions to
>   socioeconomic problems,
> (3) Rapidly dropping levels of literacy, critical
>   understanding,
>   and general intellectual awareness, and
> (4) Spiritual death--that is, Spengler's classicism: the
>   emptying out of cultural content and the freezing (or
>   repackaging) of it in formulas-
>   kitsch, in short. (p. 19).

He then states that all of these factors are increasingly present on the American scene. Question: how did America get itself into this presenting highly precarious situation in regard to the daily lives of its citizens?

The Impact of Negative Social Forces Has Increased.

Keeping our focus on humankind's search for "the good life" in the 21st century, in North America we are finding that the human recreational experience will have to be earned typically within a society whose very structure has been modified. For example,

(1) the concept of the traditional family structure has been strongly challenged by a variety of social forces (e.g., economics, divorce rate);

(2) many single people are finding that they must work longer hours; and

(3) many families need more than one breadwinner just to make ends meet.

Also, the idea of a steady surplus economy may have vanished in the presence of a burgeoning budgetary deficit. What nonessentials do we cut from the debt-overwhelmed budget at a time like this to bring back what might be called fiscal sanity?

Additionally, many of the same problems of megalopolis living described back in the 1960s still prevail and are even increasing (e.g., declining infrastructure, crime rates in multiethnic populated centers, transportation gridlocks, overcrowded school classrooms). Thinking back to 1967 in Canada, Prime Minister Lester Pearson asked Canadians to improve "the quality of Canadian life" as Canada celebrated her 100th anniversary as a confederation. Interestingly, still today, despite all of Canada's current identity problems, some pride can be taken in the fact that Canada has on occasion been proclaimed as the best place on earth to live. Nevertheless, we can't escape the fact that the work week is not getting shorter and shorter, and that the 1960s' prediction about achieving four different types of leisure class are but a distant dream for the large majority of people (Michael).

Further, the situation has developed in such a way that the presently maturing generation is finding (1) that fewer good-paying jobs are available and (2) that the average annual income is declining (especially if we keep a steadily rising cost of living in mind). What caused this to happen is not a simple question to answer. For one thing, despite the rosy picture envisioned a generation ago–one in which we were supposedly entering a new stage for humankind–we are unable today to cope adequately with the multitude of problems that have developed. This situation is true whether inner city, suburbia, exurbia, or small-town living is concerned. Transportation jams and gridlock, for example, are occurring daily as public transportation struggles to meet rising demand for economical transport within the framework of developing megalopolises.

Certainly, megalopolis living trends have not abated and will probably not do so in the predictable future. More and more families, where that unit is still present, need two breadwinners just to survive. Interest rates, although minor cuts are made when economic slowdowns occur, have been reasonable. A truly troubled real estate market now discourages many people from home ownership. Pollution of air and water continues despite efforts of many to change the present course of development. High-wage industries seem to be "heading south" in search of places where lower wages can be paid. Also, all sorts of crime are still present in our society, a goodly portion of it seemingly brought about by unemployment, drug-taking, and rising debt at all levels from the individual to the federal government.

The continuing presence of youth crime is especially disturbing. (This is especially true when homegrown youth turn to terrorism!) In this respect, it is fortunate in North America that municipal, private-agency, and public recreation has received continuing financial support from the increasingly burdened taxpayer. Even here, however, there has been a definite trend toward user fees for many services thereby affecting people's ability to get involved. Life goes on, however, but the question arises in ongoing discussions as to what character we seek for people within a burgeoning population.

What Character Do We Seek for People?

Functioning in a world that is steadily becoming a "Global Village," or a "flat earth" as described by Thomas Friedman, we need to think more seriously than ever before about the character and traits which we should seek to develop in people. Not even mentioning the Third World, people in what we call "developed nations" continue to lead or strive for the proverbial good life. To attain this state, children and young people need to develop the right attitudes (psychologically speaking) toward education, work, use of leisure, participation in government, various types of consumption, and concern for world stability and peace. If we truly desire "the good life," we somehow have to provide an increased level of education for the creative and constructive use of leisure to a greater percentage of the population. As matters stand, there doesn't seem to be much impetus in the direction of achieving this balance as a significant part of ongoing general education. We are simply not ready for a society where education for leisure has a unique role to play on into the indeterminate future. One wonders how such a development might affect the character of our young people?

What are called the "Old World countries" all seem to have a "character"; it is almost something that they take for granted. However, it is questionable whether there is anything that can be called a character in North America (i.e., in the United States? in Canada?). Americans were thought earlier to be heterogeneous and individualistic as a people, as opposed to Canadians. But the Canadian culture–whatever that may be today! –has moved toward multiculturalism quite significantly in the past two decades. Of course, Canada was founded by two distinct cultures, the English and the French. In addition to working out a continuing, reasonably happy relationship between these two cultures, it is now a question because of an aggressive "multicultural approach" of assimilating—as Canadians (!)—people arriving from many different lands. And let's not forget the claims of "first nations" whose 99 entities in British Columbia along claim more territory than exists!

Shortly after the middle of the twentieth century, Commager (1966), the noted historian, enumerated what he believed were some common denominators in American (i.e., U.S.) character. These, he said, were:

(1) carelessness;
(2) openhandedness, generosity, and hospitality;
(3) self-indulgence;
(4) sentimentality, and even romanticism;
(5) gregariousness;
(6) materialism;
(7) confidence and self-confidence;
(8) complacency, bordering occasionally on arrogance;
(9) cultivation of the competitive spirit;
(10) indifference to, and exasperation with laws, rules, and regulations;
(11) equalitarianism; and (
(12) resourcefulness (pp. 246-254).

What about Canadian character as opposed to what Commager stated above for America? Although completed a quarter of a century ago, Lipset (1973) carried out a perceptive comparison between the two countries that has probably not changed significantly in the interim. He reported that these two countries probably resemble each other more than any other two in the world. Nevertheless, he asserted that there seemed to be a rather "consistent pattern of differences between them" (p. 4). He found that certain "special differences" did exist and may be singled out as follows:

Varying origins in their political systems and national identities, varying religious traditions, and varying frontier experiences. In general terms, the value orientations of Canada stem from a counterrevolutionary past, a need to differentiate itself from the United States, the influence of Monarchical institutions, a dominant Anglican religious tradition, and a less individualistic and more governmentally controlled expansion of the Canadian than of the American frontier (p. 5).

Seymour Lipset's findings tended to sharpen the focus on opinions commonly held earlier that, even though there is considerable sharing of values, they are held more tentatively in Canada. Also, he believed that Canada had consistently settled on "the middle ground" between positions arrived at in the United States and England. However, Lipset argued that, although the twin values of equalitarianism and achievement have been paramount in American life--but somewhat less important in Canada--there was now consistent movement in this direction in Canada as well (p. 6). Keeping national aims, value orientations, and character traits in mind as being highly important, of course, as well all of the material progress that has been made by a segment of the population, we are nevertheless forced to ask ourselves if we in Canada are "on the right track heading in the right direction?"

What Happened to the Original Enlightenment Ideal?

The achievement of "the good life" for a majority of citizens in the developed nations, a good life that involves a creative and constructive use of leisure as a key part of general education, necessarily implies that a certain type of progress has been made in society. However, we should understand that the chief criterion of progress has undergone a subtle but decisive change since the founding of the United States republic in North America. This development has had a definite influence on Canada and Mexico as well. Such change has been at once a cause and a reflection of the current disenchantment with technology. Recall that the late 18th century was a time of political revolution when monarchies and aristocracies, and that the ecclesiastical structure were being challenged on a number of fronts in the Western world. Also, the factory system was undergoing significant change at that time.

As Leo Marx (1990, p. 5) reported such industrial development with its greatly improved machinery "coincided with the formulation and diffusion of the modern Enlightenment idea of history as a record of progress..." He explained further that this: "new scientific knowledge and accompanying technological power was expected to make possible a comprehensive improvement in all of the conditions of life–social, political, moral, and intellectual as well as material." This idea did indeed slowly take hold and eventually "became the fulcrum of the dominant American world view" (p. 5). By 1850, however, with the rapid growth of the United States especially, the idea of progress was already being dissociated from the Enlightenment vision of political and social liberation.

By the turn of the twentieth century, "the technocratic idea of progress [had become] a belief in the sufficiency of scientific and technological innovation as the basis for general progress" (Leo Marx, p. 9). This came to mean that if scientific-based technologies were permitted to develop in an unconstrained manner, there would be an automatic improvement in all other aspects of life! What happened–because this theory became coupled with onrushing, unbridled capitalism–was that the ideal envisioned by Thomas Jefferson in the United States has been turned upside down. Instead of social progress being guided by such values as justice, freedom, and self-fulfillment for all people, rich or poor, these goals of vital interest in a democracy were subjugated to a burgeoning society dominated by supposedly more important instrumental values (i.e., useful or practical ones for advancing a capitalistic system).

Have conditions improved? The answer to this question is obvious. The fundamental question still today is, "which type of values will win out in the long run?" In North America, for example, a developing concept of cultural relativism was being discredited as the 1990s witnessed a sharp clash between (1) those who uphold so-called Western cultural values and (2) those who by their presence are dividing the West along a multitude of ethnic and racial lines. This is occasioning strong efforts to promote "fundamentalist" religions and sects–either those present historically or those recently imported. These numerous religions, and accompanying sects, are characterized typically by decisive right/wrong morality. It is just this sort of "progress" that has led concerned people to inquire where we in the developed world are heading. What kind of a future is "out there" for humankind if the world continues in the same direction it is presently heading? We don't know for certain, of course, but a number of different scenarios can be envisioned depending on humanity's response to the present crisis of a society characterized by modernism.

Future Societal Scenarios (Anderson)

In this adventure of civilization, Walter Truett Anderson, then– president of the American Division of the World Academy of Art and Science, postulates four different scenarios for the future of earthlings. In *The future of the self: Inventing the postmodern person* (1997), Anderson argues convincingly that current trends are adding up to an early 21st-century identity crisis for humankind. The creation of the present "modern self," he explains, began with Plato, Aristotle, and with the rights of humans in Roman legal codes.

Anderson argues that the developing conception of self bogged down in the Middle Ages, but fortunately was resurrected in the Renaissance Period of the second half of The Middle Ages. Since then the human "self" has been advancing like a "house afire" as the Western world has gone through an almost unbelievable transformation. Without resorting to historical detail, I will say only that scientists like Galileo and Copernicus influenced philosophers such as Descartes and Locke to foresee a world in which the self was invested with human rights.

"One World, Many Universes." Anderson's "One World, Many Universes" version is prophesied as the most likely to occur. This is a scenario characterized by (1) high economic growth, (2) steadily increasing technological progress, and (3) globalization combined with high psychological development. Such psychological maturity, he predicts, will be possible for a certain segment of the world's population because "active life spans will be gradually lengthened through various advances in health maintenance and medicine" (pp. 251-253). (This scenario may seem desirable, of course, to people who are coping reasonably well at present.)

However, it appears that a problem has developed at the beginning of this new century with this dream of individual achievement of inalienable rights and privileges. The modern self–envisioned by Descartes–a rational, integrated self that Anderson likens to Captain Kirk at the command post of (the original Starship Enterprise–is having an identity crisis. The image of this bold leader (he or she!) taking us fearlessly into the great unknown has begun to fade as alternate scenarios for the future of life on Earth are envisioned.

For example, John Bogle of Vanguard, in his *The Battle for the Soul of Capitalism* (2007) argues that what he terms "global capitalism" is destroying the already uneasy balance between democracy as a political system and capitalism as an economic system. In a world where globalization and economic "progress" seemingly must be rejected because of catastrophic environmental concerns or "demands," the bold-future image could well "be replaced by a postmodern self; de-centered, multidimensional, and changeable" (p. 50).

Captain Kirk, or "Barack Obama" now as he "boldly goes where no man has gone before"–this time to rid the world of terrorists--is facing a second crucial change. As the American Government seeks to shape the world of the 21st century, based on Anderson's analysis, there is another force--the systemic-change force mentioned above--that is shaping the future. This all-powerful force may well exceed the Earth's ability to cope with what happens. As gratifying as such factors as "globalization along with economic growth" and "psychological development" may seem to the folks in Anderson's "One-World, Many Universes" scenario, there is a flip side to this prognosis. This image, Anderson identifies, as "The Dysfunctional Family" scenario. It turns out that all of the "benefits" of so-called progress are highly expensive and available now only to relatively few of the six billion plus people on earth. Anderson foresees this scenario as "a world of modern people relatively happily doing their thing–modern people still obsessed with progress, economic gain, and organizational bigness–along with varieties of postmodern people being trampled and getting angry" [italics added] (p. 51). And, I might add further, as people get angrier, the present-day threat of terrorism in North America could seem like child's play.

What Kind of A World Do You Want for Your Descendants?

What I am really asking here is whether you, the reader of these words, is cognizant of, and approves of, the situation as it is developing today. Are you (and I too!) simply "going along with the crowd" while taking the path of least resistance? Can we do anything to improve the situation by implementing an approach that could help to make the situation more beneficent and wholesome in perspective? *What I am recommending is that the time is ripe for "enlightened countries" to distinguish themselves more aggressively as being on a "different path" than the United States of America.* To do this, however, individually and collectively, we would need to determine what sort of a world we (and our descendants) should be living in.

If you consider yourself an environmentalist, for example, the future undoubtedly looks bleak to you. What can we so to counter the strong business orientation of our society (i.e., being swept along with the "onward and upward" economic and technologic growth of American modernism)? Such is most certainly not the answer to all of our developing problems and issues. We should see ourselves increasingly as "New Agers" working to help our country working to forge its own identity. I grant you, however, some sort of mass, non-religious "spiritual" transformation would have to take place for this to become a reality.

Let me offer one example based on my personal experience where I think any developed nation can make a good beginning in this respect. (Some who read this may wish to hang me in effigy [or literally!] for this assertion). Nevertheless I believe that any concerned nation (i.e., group of citizens therein should strive to hold back the negative influences of America's approach to overly commercial, competitive sport in both universities and the public sector. At present, one country (i.e., Canada) is all too often typically conforming blindly to a power structure in which sport is used largely by private enterprise for selfish purposes. The problem is this: opportunities for participation in all competitive sport--not just Olympic sport--moved historically from amateurism to semi-professionalism, and then on to full-blown professionalism in many instances.

The Olympic Movement, because of a variety of social pressures, followed suit in both ancient times and the present. When the International Olympic Committee gave that final push to the pendulum and openly admitted professional athletes to play in the Games, they may have pleased most of the spectators and all of the advertising and media representatives. But in so doing the floodgates were opened completely. The original ideals upon which the Games were reactivated were completely abandoned. This is what caused Sir Rees-Mogg in Britain, for example, to state that crass commercialism had won the day. This final abandonment of any semblance of what was the original Olympic ideal was the "straw that broke the camel's back." This ultimate decision regarding eligibility for participation has indeed been devastating to those people who earnestly believe that money and sport are like oil and water; they simply do not mix! Their response has been to abandon any further interest in, or support for, the entire Olympic Movement.

The question must, therefore be asked: "What should rampant professionalism in competitive sport at the Olympic Games mean to any given country out of the 200-plus nations involved?" This is not a simple question to answer responsibly. In this present brief statement, it should be made clear that the professed social values of a country should ultimately prevail--and that they will prevail in the final analysis. However, this ultimate determination will not take place overnight. The fundamental values of a social system will eventually have a strong influence on the individual values held by most citizens in that country. If a country is moving toward the most important twin values of equalitarianism and achievement, for example, what implications does that have for competitive sport in that political entity under consideration? The following are some questions that should be asked before a strong continuing commitment is made to sponsor such involvement through governmental and/or private funding:

1. Can it be shown that involvement in competitive sport at one or the other of the three levels (i.e., amateur, semi-professional, professional) brings about desirable social values (i.e., more value than disvalue)?

2. Can it be shown that involvement in competitive sport at one or the other of the three levels (i.e., amateur, semiprofessional, or professional) brings about desirable individual values of both an intrinsic and extrinsic nature (i.e., creates more value than disvalue)?

3. If the answer to Questions #1 and #2 immediately are both affirmative (i.e., that involvement in competitive sport at any or all of the three levels postulated [i.e., amateur, semi-professional, and professional sport] provides a sufficient amount of social and individual value to warrant such promotion), can sufficient funds be made available to support or permit this promotion at any or all of the three levels listed?

4. If funding to support participation in competitive sport at any or all of the three levels (amateur, semiprofessional, professional) is not available (or such participation is not deemed advisable), should priorities—as determined by the expressed will of the people--be established about the importance of each level to the country? Should this not be based on careful analysis of the potential social and individual values that may accrue to the society and its citizens from such competitive sport participation at one or more levels?

Further, as one aging person who encountered corruption and sleaze in the intercollegiate athletic structure of several major universities in the United States, I retreated to a Canadian university where the term "scholar-athlete" still implies roughly what it says. However, I now see problems developing on the Canadian inter-university sport scene as well. Canada has two choices before it. One choice is to do nothing about the "creeping semi–professionalism" that is occurring. This would require no great effort, of course. It can simply go along with the prevailing ethos of a North American society that is using sport to help in the promotion of *social*, as opposed to moral or character traits. In the process, "business as usual" will be supported one way or the other. A postmodern approach, conversely, would be one where specific geographic regions in Canada (the east, the far west. Quebec, and the mid–west) reverse the trend toward semi–professionalism that is steadily developing. The pressure on university presidents and governing boards is increasing steadily. Will they have wisdom and acumen to ward off this insidious possibility?

The reader can readily see where I am coming from with this discussion. I recommend strongly that we take a good look at what is implied when we challenge ourselves to consider what the deliberate creation of a postmodern world might do for the many increasingly multiethnic countries in the world. The hope is, of course, that expanding the elements of postmodernism will have a fighting chance to succeed. In the United States, it appears that one must "forget it'! Nevertheless, if a country is making a solid effort to become a multicultural society, it may already be implementing what may be considered some of the better aspects of the concept of "postmodernism." For better or worse–and it may well be the latter–people in various developed countries must not be so naïve that they can't read the handwriting on the wall about what's happening "the Excited States".

Can We Strengthen the Postmodern Influence?

My review of selected world, European, North American, regional, and local developments occurring in the final quarter of the 20th century may have created both positive and negative thoughts on your part. You might ask how this broadly based discussion relates to a plea for consideration of an increasingly postmodern social philosophy. My response to this question is "vigorous": "It doesn't" and yet "It does." It doesn't relate or "compute" to the large majority of those functioning in the starkly *modern* "North American" world. The affirmative answer–that it does–is correct if we listen to the voices of those in the substantive minority who are becoming increasingly restless with the obvious negatives of the modernism that has spread so rapidly in the modern world.

To help reverse this disturbing development, some wise scholars have recommended that the discipline of philosophy should have some connection to the developing world as it was described above. Richard Rorty (1997), the late philosopher, was termed a eo-pragmatist. He exhorted the presently "doomed liberal Left" in North America to join the fray again. Their presumed shame should not be bolstered by a mistaken belief that only those who agree with the Marxist position that capitalism must be eradicated are "true Lefts." Rorty recommends that philosophy once again become characterized as a "search for wisdom," a search that seeks conscientiously and capably to answer the many pressing issues and problems looming before humankind worldwide.

While most philosophers were "elsewhere engaged," some within the fold considered what has been called postmodernism carefully. For example, in *Crossing the postmodern divide* by Albert Borgmann (Chicago: The University of Chicago Press, 1992), it was refreshing to find such a clear assessment of the present situation. Time and again in discussions about postmodernism, I have encountered what I soon began to characterize as gobbledygook (i.e., planned obfuscation?). This effort by Borgmann was solid, down-to-earth, and comprehensible. However, in the final two pages, he veered to a Roman-Catholic position that he calls *postmodern realism* as the answer to the plight caused by modernism. It is his right, of course, to state his personal opinion after describing the current political and social situation so accurately. However, if he could have brought himself to it–if he had thought it possible for him to do so–it would have been better if he had spelled out several alternative directions for humankind to go in the 21st century. (Maybe we should be thankful that he thought any one might be able to save it!)

With his argument that "postmodernism must become, for better or worse, something other than modernism," Borgmann explains that:

> [postmodernism] already exhibits two distinct tendencies: The first is to refine technology. Here postmodernism shares with modernists an unreserved allegiance to technology, but it differs from modernism in giving technology a hyper-fine and hyper-complex design. This tendency I call hyper-modernism. The alternative tendency is to outgrow technology as a way of life and to put it to the service of reality, of the things that command our respect and grace our life. This I call postmodern realism (p. 82).

At what point could we argue that the modern epoch or era has come to an end? Can we dream realistically that civilization may someday be ready to put hyper-modernism aside and embrace Borgmann's postmodern realism–or any form of postmodernism for that matter? Can we hope to find agreement that the present epoch is approaching closure because a substantive minority of the populace is challenging many of the fundamental beliefs of modernism?

The "substantive minority" may not be large enough yet, but the reader may be ready to agree that indeed the world is moving into a new epoch as the proponents of postmodernism have been affirming over recent decades. Within such a milieu all professions would probably find great difficulty crossing this so-called, postmodern gap (chasm, divide, whatever you may wish to call it). Scholars argue convincingly that many in democracies, under girded by the various rights being propounded (e.g., individual freedom, privacy), have not yet come to believe that they have found a supportive "liberal consensus" within their respective societies.

My contention is that "post-modernists"–whether they recognize themselves as belonging to this group or not–now form a substantive minority that supports a more humanistic, pragmatic, liberal consensus in society. Yet they recognize that present-day society is going to have difficulty crossing any such postmodern divide. Many traditionalists in democratically oriented political systems may not like everything they see in front of them today, but as they look elsewhere they flinch even more. After reviewing where society *has been*, and where *it is now*, two more questions need to be answered. Where is society heading, and–most importantly–where should it be heading?

As despairing as one might be of society's direction today, the phenomenon of postmodernism–with its accompanying deconstructionist analytic technique affirming the idea that the universe is valueless with no absolute–brings one up short quickly. Take your choice: bleak pessimism or blind optimism. The former seems to be more dangerous to humankind's future that that of an idealistic future "under the sheltering arms of a Divine Father." Yet, some argue that Nietzsche's philosophy of being, knowledge, and morality supports the basic dichotomy espoused by the philosophy of being in the post-modernistic position. I can understand at once, therefore, why it meets with opposition by those whose thought has been supported by traditional theocentrism.

A better approach, I recommend, might be one of "positive meliorism" in which humankind is vigorously exhorted to "take it from here and do its best to improve the world situation." In the process we should necessarily inquire: *What happened to the "Enlightenment ideal"?* This was supposed to be America's chief criterion of progress, but it has gradually but steadily undergone a decisive change since the founding of the Republic. That change is at once a cause and a reflection of our current disenchantment with technology.

Post-modernists do indeed subscribe to a humanistic, anthropocentric belief as opposed to the traditional theocentric position. They would probably subscribe, therefore to what Berelson and Steiner in the mid-1960s postulated as *a behavioral science image of man and woman.* This view characterized the human as a creature continuously adapting reality to his or her own ends. Such thought undoubtedly challenges the authority of theological positions, dogmas, ideologies, and some scientific "infallibles".

A moderate post-modernist–holding a position I feel able to subscribe to once I am able to bring it all into focus–would at least listen to what the "authority" had written or said before criticizing or rejecting it. A fully committed post-modernist goes his or her own way by early, almost automatic, rejection of all tradition. Then this person presumably relies simply on a personal interpretation and subsequent diagnosis to muster the authority to challenge any or all icons or "lesser gods" extant in society.

Concluding Statement

In conclusion, it seems obvious that a *moderate* post-modernist would feel most comfortable seeking to achieve his or her personal, professional, and social/environmental goals through the stance that has been described above. This position would be directly opposed to the traditional stifling position of, for example, "essentialist" theological realists or idealists. The world is changing. It has changed! These conflicting "world religions" are getting in the way of civilization's progress. The conflicts they cause could destroy humankind. A more pragmatic "value-is-that-which-is proven-through-experience" orientation that could emerge as one legacy of postmodernism would leave the future open-ended.

That is the way it ought to be for the future on this "speck" called Earth in what appears to be an infinite universe.

Part Two: The Status of Physical (Activity) Education and Educational Sport

Selection #4
American Physical Education History:
A Historical Summary

According to Norma Schwendener (1942), the history of physical education in the United States was divided into four distinct periods: (1) The Colonial Period (1609-1781); (2) The Provincial Period (1781-1885); (3) The Period of the Waning of European Influence (1885-1918); and (4) The Period of American Physical Education (1918-). Although this classification will not be followed here, the reader can get some perspective from Schwendener's earlier outline.

The Colonial Period

Living conditions in the American colonies in the 17th and 18th centuries were harsh, the finer elements of then civilized life being possible for only a relatively few wealthy individuals. The culture itself had been transported from Europe with its built-in class distinctions. The rules of primogeniture and entail served to strengthen such status. Slavery, and near-slavery, were general practice, especially in the South, and the right to vote was typically restricted to property owners. Cultural contrasts were marked. Religion was established legally. Geography, differences between the environment in the North and South, had a great deal to do with many differences that were evident. Actually, there was even considerable feeling against democratic principles both from a political and social standpoint. Any consideration of educational practice must, therefore, be viewed in the light of these conditions.1

Most of the American colonies established between 1607 and 1682 were guided in their educational outlook and activities by England's contemporary practices, the influence of other European countries being negligible at first. Education was thought to be a function of the Church, not the State. By today's standards, the provisions made for education were extremely inadequate. In a pioneer country struggling with a hazardous physical environment, the settlers were engaged in a daily struggle for their very existence. Early colonists migrated into different regions relatively close to the eastern coastline almost by chance. These differing environments undoubtedly influenced the social order of the North and the South; yet, for several generations there were many points of similarity in the traditions and experiences of the people as a whole. They all possessed a common desire for freedom and security, hopes that were to be realized only after a desperate struggle.

The church was the institution through which the religious heritage, and also much of the educational heritage, was preserved and advanced. The first schools can actually be regarded as the fruits of the Protestant revolts in Europe. The settlers wanted religious freedom, but the traditionalists among them insisted that a knowledge of the Gospel was required for personal salvation. The natural outcome was the creation of schools to help children learn to read; thus, it was the dominant Protestant churches that brought about the establishment of the elementary schools.

Three types of "attitude" developed toward education. The first was the compulsory-maintenance attitude of the New England Puritans, who established schools by colony legislation of 1642 and 1647. The second attitude was that of the parochial school, and this was best represented by Pennsylvania where private schools were made available for those who could afford it. The pauper-school, non-State-interference attitude was the third. It was best exemplified by Virginia and the other southern colonies. Many of these people had come to America for profit rather than religious freedom, the result being that they tended to continue school practice as it had existed in England. In all these schools, discipline was harsh and sometimes actually brutal. The curriculum consisted of the three R's and spelling, but the books were few and the teachers were generally unprepared.

The pattern of secondary education had been inherited from England too. In most of the colonies, and especially in New England, so-called Latin grammar schools appeared. Also, higher education was not neglected. Nine colleges were founded mainly through the philanthropy of special individuals or groups. In all of these institutions, theology formed an important part of the curriculum. A notable exception that began a bit later was the Academy and College of Philadelphia where Benjamin Franklin exerted a strong influence.

Early Games, Contests, and Exercise

What about physical training and play for the young? What were the objectives for which people strove historically in what later was called physical education in the United States? We will now take a look at the different roles that such development physical activity played (or didn't play!) in the educational pattern of the States over a period of several centuries down to the present day. This entire time period covering the history of physical education in the United States could be divided logically into four distinct periods: the Colonial Period (1609-1781); the Provincial Period (1781-1885); the Period of the Waning of European Influence (1885-1918); and the Period of American Physical Education (1918-....).

Because the population of the colonial United States was mostly rural, one could not expect organized gymnastics and sports to find a place in the daily lives of the settlers. Most of the colonies, with the possible exception of the Puritans, engaged in the games and contests of their motherlands to the extent that they had free time. Even less than today, the significance of play and its possibilities in the educative process were not really comprehended; in fact, the entire educational system was opposed to the idea of what would be included in a fine program of sport and physical education today.

The 18ᵗʰ Century

With the advent of the 18th century, the former religious interest began to slacken. The government gradually developed more of a civil character with an accompanying tendency to create schools with a native vein or character. This was accompanied by a breakdown in some of the former aristocratic practices followed by a minority. The settled frontier expanded, new interests in trade and shipping grew, and the population increased. An evident trend toward individualism characterized this period as well. Several American industries date back to this time, the establishment of iron mills being most noteworthy.

Although the colonists were typically restricted by the financial practices placed by the English on the use of money, there was sufficient prosperity to bring about a change in the appearance of the established communities. An embryonic class structure began to form, with some colonials achieving a certain amount of social status by the holding of land and office. However, there were other concerns such as a series of small wars with the Spanish and the French extending from 1733 to 1763. These struggles were interspersed by period of cold war maneuvering. What was called the Seven Years' War (1755-1763) ended with the colonies as a fairly solid political and economic unit. However, the British method of governance over the colony was a constant source of annoyance and serious concern with the result that a strong nationalistic, separatist feeling emerging about 1775.

Beginning in the third decade of the eighteenth century, a revival of religious interest was apparent. This occasioned a recurring strong emphasis on religious education in the elementary schools. However, with the stirring of economic, political, and nationalistic forces from approximately 1750 onward, a period of relative religious tolerance resulted. This was accompanied by a broader interest in national affairs by many. The result was a lesser emphasis on the earlier religious domination of the elementary curriculum.

Secondary education was still provided by the grammar schools. These schools, generally located in every large town, were supported by the local government and by private tuition. The curricula were non-utilitarian and were designed to prepare boys for college entrance. Insofar as higher education was concerned, the pattern had been established from the beginning (Harvard College in 1636) after the European university type of liberal arts education with a strong emphasis on mental discipline and theology.

Despite the above, the reader should keep in mind that there were still very few heavily populated centers. In the main, frontier life especially, but also life in small villages, was still most rigorous. Such conditions were simply not conducive to intellectual life with high educational standards. Educational theorists had visions of a fine educational system, of course, but state constitutional provisions regarding education were very limited, and the federal constitution didn't say anything about educational standards at all. The many new social forces at work offered some promise, but with the outbreak of the War of Independence formal education came to almost a complete standstill.

The last 25 years of the 18th century saw a great many changes in the life of the United States. In the first place, many of the revolutionaries who started the war lived to tell about it and to help in the sound reconstruction of the young nation. State and federal constitutions had to be planned, written, and approved. Also, it was very important to the early success of the country that commerce be revived, a process that was accomplished sooner by the South because of the nature of the commodities they produced. New lines of business and trade were established with Russia, Sweden, and the Orient. The Federal Convention of 1787 managed to complete what has turned out to be possibly the most successful document in all of history, the Constitution of the United States of America. Then George Washington's administration began, and it was considered successful both at home and abroad. Interestingly, the concurrent French Revolution became an issue in American politics, but Washington persuaded his government to declare a position of neutrality (although he was hard pressed to maintain it).

As soon as the War of Independence in the U.S. was over, considerable attention was turned to education with the result that higher and secondary education improved. The colleges of the North took longer to recover from the War than those in the South where soon an imposing list of both private, religiously endowed, and state-sponsored institutions were founded.

Early Support for Physical Training

At the secondary level, the institutions that succeeded the Latin grammar schools became known as the academies. Their aim was to prepare youth to meet life and its many problems, a reflection of the main influences of the Enlightenment in America. With such an emphasis, it is natural that the physical welfare of youths gradually was considered to be more important that it had been previously. Some of the early academies, such as Dummer, Andover, Exeter, and Leicester, were founded and incorporated before 1790. This movement reached its height around 1830 when there was said to be approximately 800 such schools throughout the country.

Many of the early American educators and statesmen supported the idea that both the body and the mind needed attention in our educational system. Included among this number were Benjamin Franklin, Noah Webster, Thomas Jefferson, Horace Mann, and Henry Barnard. Further support came from Captain Alden Partridge, one of the early superintendents of the United States Military Academy at West Point, who crusaded for the reform of institutions of higher education. He deplored the entire neglect of physical culture.

The 19th Century

With the stage set for the United States to enter a most important period in her history, the 19th century witnessed steady growth along with a marked increase in nationalism. There was a second war with Great Britain, the War of 1812. In the ensuing nationalist era, many political changes or "adjustments" were carried out in relations with Britain and other nations where necessary. The Monroe Doctrine declared to the world that countries in this hemisphere should be left alone to develop as they saw fit and were not to be used by outside powers for colonization. However, at home dissent was growing as the North and the South were being divided. The North was being changed by virtue of the Industrial Revolution taking place, along with many educational and humanitarian movements. The South, conversely, continued to nurture a different type of society regulated by what has been called a slave and cotton economy.

In the realm of education, the first 50 years of the new national life was a period of transition from the control of the church to that of the State. State control and support gradually seemed more feasible, although the change was seemingly slow in coming. Political equality and religious freedom, along with changing economic conditions, finally did make education for all a necessity. By 1825, therefore, a tremendous struggle for the creation of the American State School was underway. In the field of public education, the years from 1830 to 1860 have been regarded by some educational historians as "The Architectural Period."

North American Turners. In the early 19th century German gymnastics (Turnen) came to the United States through the influx of such men as Charles Beck, Charles Follen, and Francis Lieber. However, the majority of the people were simply not ready to recognize the possible values of these activities imported from foreign lands. The Turnverein movement (in the late 1840s) before the Civil War was very important for the advancement of physical training. The Turners advocated that mental and physical education should proceed hand in hand in the public schools. As it developed, they were leaders in the early physical education movement around 1850 in such cities as Boston, St. Louis, and Cincinnati.

Other leaders in this period were George Barker Win(d)ship and Dioclesian Lewis. Windship was an advocate of heavy gymnastics and did much to convey the mistaken idea that great strength should be the goal of all gymnastics, as well as the notion that strength and health were completely synonymous. Lewis, who actually began the first teacher training program in physical education in the country in 1861, was a crusader in every sense of the word; he had ambitions to improve the health of all Americans through his system of light calisthenics--an approach that he felt would develop and maintain flexibility, grace, and agility as well. His stirring addresses to many professional and lay groups did much to popularize this type of gymnastics, and to convey the idea that such exercise could serve a desirable role in the lives of those who were weaker and perhaps even sickly (as well as those who were naturally stronger).

The Civil War between the North and the South wrought a tremendous change in the lives of the people. In the field of education, the idea of equality of educational opportunity had made great strides; the "educational ladder" was gradually extending upward with increasing opportunity for ever more young people. For example, the number of high schools increased fivefold between 1870 and 1890. The state was gradually assuming a position of prime importance in public education. In this process, state universities were helpful as they turned their attention to advancing the welfare of the individual states. The Southern states lagged behind the rest of the country due to the ravages of War with subsequent reconstruction, racial conflict, and continuing fairly "aristocratic theory" of education. In the North, however, President Eliot of Harvard called for education reform in 1888. One of his main points was the need for greatly improved teacher training.

After the Civil War, the Turners through their societies continued to stress the benefits of physical education within public education. Through their efforts it was possible to reach literally hundreds of thousands of people either directly or indirectly. The Turners have always opposed military training as a substitute for physical education. Further, the modern playground movement found the Turners among its strongest supporters. The Civil War had demonstrated clearly the need for a concerted effort in the areas of health, physical education, and physical recreation (not to mention competitive sports and games). The Morrill Act passed by Congress in 1862 helped create the land-grant colleges. At first, the field of physical education was not aided significantly by this development because of the stress on military drill in these institutions. All in all, the best that can be said is that an extremely differentiated pattern of physical education was present in the post-Civil War of the country.

Beginning of Organized Sport

The beginning of organized sport in the United States as we now know it dates back approximately to the Civil War period. Baseball and tennis were introduced in that order during this period and soon became very popular. Golf, bowling, swimming, basketball, and a multitude of other so-called minor sports made their appearance in the latter half of the nineteenth century. American football also started its rise to popularity at this time. The Amateur Athletic Union was organized in 1888 to provide governance for amateur sport. Unfortunately, controversy about amateurism has surrounded this organization almost constantly ever since. Nevertheless, it has given invaluable service to the promotion of that changing and often evanescent phenomenon that this group has designated as "legitimate amateur sport."

The Young Men's Christian Association

The YMCA traces its origins back to 1844 in London, England, when George Williams organized the first religious group. This organization has always stressed as one of its basic principles that physical welfare and recreation were helpful to the moral well-being of the individual. Some of the early outstanding physical education leaders in the YMCA in the United States were Robert J. Roberts, Luther Halsey Gulick, and James Huff McCurdy.

Early Physical Activity at the College Level

It was toward the middle of the 19th century that the colleges and universities began to think seriously about the health of their students. The University of Virginia had the first real gymnasium, and Amherst College followed in 1860 with a two-story structure devoted to physical education. President Stearns urged the governing body to begin a department of physical culture in which the primary aim was to keep the student in good physical condition. Dr. Edward Hitchcock headed this department for an unprecedented period of fifty years until his death in 1911. Yale and Harvard erected gymnasiums for similar purposes in the late 1800s, but their programs were not supported adequately until the early 1900s. These early facilities were soon followed elsewhere by the development of a variety of "exercise buildings" built along similar lines.

Harvard was fortunate in the appointment of Dr. Dudley Allen Sargent to head its now-famous Hemenway Gymnasium. This dedicated physical educator and physician led the university to a preeminent position in the field, and his program became a model for many other colleges and universities. He stressed physical education for the individual. His goal was the attainment of a perfect structure--harmony in a well-balanced development of mind and body.

From the outset, college faculties had taken the position that games and sports were not necessarily a part of the basic educational program. Interest in them was so intense, however, that the wishes of the students, while being denied, could not be thwarted. Young college men evidently strongly desired to demonstrate their abilities in the various sports against presumed rivals from other institutions. Thus, from 1850 to 1880 the rise of interest in intercollegiate sports was phenomenal. Rowing, baseball, track and field, football, and later basketball were the major sports. Unfortunately, college representatives soon found that these athletic sports needed control as evils began to creep in and partially destroy the values originally intended as goals.

An Important Decade for Physical Education

The years from 1880 to 1890 undoubtedly form one of the most important decades in the history of physical education in the United States. The colleges and universities, the YMCAs, the Turners, and the proponents of the various foreign systems of gymnastics made contributions during this brief period. The Association for the Advancement of Physical Education (now AAHPERD) was founded in 1885, with the word "American" being added the next year. This professional organization was the first of its kind in the field and undoubtedly stimulated teacher education markedly. An important early project was the plan for developing a series of experiences in physical activity--physical education--the objectives of which would be in accord with the existing pattern of general education. The struggle to bring about widespread adoption of such a program followed. Early legislation implementing physical education was enacted in five states before the turn of the 20th century.

The late 19th century saw the development also of the first efforts in organized recreation and camping for children living in underdeveloped areas in large cities. The first playground was begun in Boston in 1885. New York and Chicago followed suit shortly thereafter, no doubt to a certain degree as a result of the ill effects of the Industrial Revolution. This was actually the meager beginning of the present tremendous recreation movement in our country. Camping, both that begun by private individuals and organizational camping, started before the turn of the century as well; it has flourished similarly since that time and has been an important supplement to the entire movement.

Although criticism of the educational system as a whole was present between 1870 and 1890, it really assumed large scale proportions in the last decade of the 19th century. All sorts of innovations and reforms were being recommended from a variety of quarters. The social movement in education undoubtedly had a relationship to a rise in political progressivism. Even in the universities, the formalism present in psychology, philosophy, and the social sciences was coming under severe attack. Out in the public schools, a different sort of conflict was raging. Citizens were demanding that the promise of American life should be reflected through change and a broadening of the school's purposes. However, although the seeds of this educational revolution were sown in the 19th century, the story of its accomplishment belongs to the present century.

The 20th Century

The tempo of life in the United States seemed to increase in the 20th century. The times were indeed changing as evidenced, for example, by one war after another. In retrospect there were so many wars--World War I, World War II, the Korean War, the Vietnam War, and the seemingly ever-present "cold war" after the global conflict of the 1940s. They inescapably had a powerful influence of society along with the worldwide depression of the 1930s. Looking back on 20th century history is frightening; so much has happened, and it has happened so quickly. The phenomenon of change is as ubiquitous today as are the historic nemeses of death and taxes.

In the public realm, social legislation and political reform made truly significant changes in the lives of people despite the leavening, ever-present struggle between conservative and liberal forces. Industry and business assumed gigantic proportions, as did the regulatory controls of the federal government. The greatest experiment in political democracy in the history of the world was grinding ahead with deliberate speed, but with occasional stopping-off sessions while "breath was caught." The idealism behind such a plan that amounted to "democratic socialism" was at times being challenged from all quarters. Also, wars and financial booms and depressions (or later recessions) weren't the types of developments that made planning and execution simple matters. All of these developments mentioned above have had their influence on the subject at hand-- education (and, of course, physical education and sport).

In the early 20th century, United States citizens began to do some serious thinking about their educational aims or values. The earliest aim in U.S. educational history had been religious in nature, an approach that was eventually supplanted by a political aim consistent with emerging nationalism. But then an overwhelming utilitarian, economic aim seemed to overshadow the political aim. The tremendous increase in high school enrollment forced a reconsideration of the aims of education at all levels of the system. Training for the elite was supplanted by an educational program to be mastered by the many. It was at this time also that the beginnings of a scientific approach to educational problems forced educators to take stock of the development based on theory and a scholarly rationale other than one forced on the school simply because of a sheer increase in numbers.

Then there followed an effort on the part of many people to consider aims and objectives from a sociological orientation. For the first time, education was conceived in terms of complete living as a citizen of an evolving democracy. The influence of John Dewey and others encouraged the viewing of the curriculum as child-centered rather than subject-centered--a rather startling attempt to alter the long-standing basic orientation that involved the rote mastery of an amalgam of educational source material. The Progressive Education Movement placed great emphasis on individualistic aims. This was subsequently countered by a demand for a theory stressing a social welfare orientation rather than one so heavily pointed to individual development.

The relationship between health education and physical education grew extensively during the first quarter of the 20th century, and this included their liaison with the entire system of education. Health education in all its aspects was viewed seriously, especially after the evidence surfaced from the draft statistics of World War I. Many states passed legislation requiring varying amounts of time in the curriculum devoted to the teaching of physical education. National interest in sports and games grew at a phenomenal rate in an era when economic prosperity prevailed. The basis for school and community recreation was being well-laid.

Simultaneously with physical education's achievement of a type of maturity brought about legislation designed to promote physical fitness and healthy bodies, the struggle between the inflexibility of the various foreign systems of gymnastics and the individual freedom of the so-called "natural movement" was being waged with increasing vigor. Actually the rising interest in sports and games soon made the conflict unequal, especially when the concept of "athletics for all" really began to take hold in the second and third decades of the century.

Conflicting Educational Philosophies

Even today the significance of play and its possibilities in the educative process have not really been comprehended. In fact, until well up in the 1800s in the United States, the entire educational system was opposed to the entire idea of what would be included in a fine program of sport and physical education today. It was the organized German-American Turners primarily, among certain others, who came to this continent from their native Germany and advocated that mental and physical education should proceed hand in hand in the public schools. The Turners' opposition to military training as a substitute for physical education contributed to the extremely differentiated pattern of physical education in the post-Civil War era. Their influence offset the stress on military drill in the land-grant colleges created by Congress passing the Morrill Act in the United States in 1862. The colleges and universities, the YMCAs, the Turners, and the proponents of the various foreign systems of gymnastics made contributions during the last quarter of the 19th century. The beginning of U.S. sport as we know it also dates to this period. However, from the outset college faculties took the position that games and sport were not a part of the basic educational program.

In the early 20th century Americans began to do some earnest thinking about their educational aims and values. Whereas the earliest aim in U.S. educational history had been religious in nature, this was eventually supplanted by a political aim consistent with emerging nationalism. But then an overwhelming utilitarian, economic aim seemed to overshadow the political aim. It was at this time also that the beginnings of a scientific approach to educational problems forced educators to take stock of the development based on a rationale other than the sheer increase in student enrollment.

Then there followed an effort to consider aims and objectives from a sociological orientation. For the first time, education was conceived in terms of complete living as a citizen in an evolving democracy. The influence of John Dewey and others encouraged the viewing of the curriculum as child-centered rather than subject-centered. Great emphasis was placed on individualistic aims with a subsequent counter demand for a theory stressing more of a social welfare orientation.

The relationship between health and physical education and the entire system of education strengthened during the first quarter of the 20th century. Many states passed legislation requiring physical education in the curriculum, especially after the damning evidence of the draft statistics in World War I (Van Dalen, Bennett, and Mitchell, 1953, p. 432). Simultaneous with physical education's achievement of a type of maturity through such legislation, the struggle between the inflexibility of the various foreign systems of gymnastics and the individualistic freedom of the so-called "natural movement" was being waged with increasing vigor. Actually the rising interest in sports and games soon made the conflict unequal, especially when the concept of athletics for all really began to take hold in the second and third decades of the century.

The natural movement was undoubtedly strengthened further by much of the evidence gathered by many natural and social scientists. A certain amount of the spirit of Dewey's philosophy took hold within the educational environment, and this new philosophy and accompanying methodology and techniques did appear to be more effective in the light of the changing ideals of an evolving democracy. Despite this pragmatic influence, however, the influence of idealism remained strong also, with its emphasis on the development of individual personality and the possible inculcation of moral and spiritual values through the transfer of training theory applied to sports and games.

Embryonic Emergence of the Allied "Professions"

School health education was developed greatly during the period also. The scope of school hygiene increased, and a required medical examination for all became more important. Leaders were urged to conceive of school health education as including three major divisions: health services, health instruction, and healthful school living. The need to expansion in this area was gradually accepted by educator and citizen alike. For example, many physical educators began to show a concern for a broadening of the field's aims and objectives, the evidence of which could be seen by the increasing amount of time spent by many on coaching duties. Conversely, the expansion of health instruction through the medium of many public and private agencies tended to draw those more directly interested in the goals of health education away from physical education.

Progress in the recreation field was significant as well. The values inherent in well-conducted playground activities for children and youths were increasingly recognized; the Playground Association of America was organized in 1906. At this time there was still an extremely close relationship between physical education and recreation, a link that remained strong because of the keen interest in the aims of recreation by a number of outstanding physical educators. Many municipal recreation centers were constructed, and it was at this time that the use of some--relatively few, actually--of the schools for "after-hour" recreation began. People began to recognize that recreational activities served an important purpose in a society undergoing basic changes. Some recreation programs developed under local boards of education; others were formed by the joint sponsorship of school boards and municipal governments; and a large number of communities placed recreation under the direct control of the municipal government and either rented school facilities when possible, or gradually developed recreational facilities of their own.

Professional Associations Form an Alliance

The American Association for Health, Physical Education, and Recreation (now the American Alliance for Health, Physical Education, Recreation, and Dance) has accomplished a great deal in a strong united effort to coordinate the various allied professions largely within the framework of public and private education. Despite membership losses during the 1970s, its success story continues with those functions that properly belong within the educational sphere. The Alliance should in time also gradually increase its influence on those seeking those services and opportunities that we can provide at the various other age levels as well.

Of course, for better or worse, there are many other health agencies and groups, recreational associations and enterprises, physical education associations and "splinter" disciplinary groups, and athletics associations and organizations moving in a variety of directions. One example of these is the North American Society for Sport Management that began in the mid-1980s and has grown significantly since. Each of these is presumably functioning with the system of values and norms prevailing in the country (or culture, etc.) and the resultant pluralistic educational philosophies extant within such a milieu.

We have seen teacher education generally, under which physical education has been bracketed, and professional preparation for recreational leadership also, strengthened through self-evaluation and accreditation. The dance movement has been a significant development within the educational field, and those concerned are still determining the place for this movement within the educational program at all levels. A great deal of progress has been made in physical education, sport, and (more recently) kinesiology research since 1960.

Achieving Some Historical Perspective

It is now possible to achieve some historical perspective about the second and third quarters of the 20th century as they have affected physical education and sport, as well as the allied professions of health education, recreation, and dance education. The Depression of the 1930s, World War II, the Korean War, and then Vietnam War, and the subsequent cold war with the many frictions among countries have been strong social forces directly influencing sport, physical education, health education, recreation, and dance in any form and in any country. Conversely, to what extent these various fields and their professional concerns have in turn influenced the many cultures, societies, and social systems remains yet to be accurately determined.

It would be simplistic to say that physical educators want more and better physical education and intramural-recreational sport programs, that athletics-oriented coaches and administrators want more and better athletic competition, that health and safety educators want more and better health and safety education, that recreation personnel want more and better recreation, and that dance educators want more and better dance instruction--and yet, this would probably be a correct assessment of their wishes and probably represents what has occurred to a large degree.

Professional Preparation and Disciplinary Specialization in American Physical Education and Kinesiology

In 1988, Zeigler (pp. 177-196) reported the results of a comparative investigation of the undergraduate professional preparation programs in physical education in the United States and Canada based on his own investigation of both the theoretical and the practical aspects of training programs in both countries. Hypothesizing that there have been significant changes, some similar and others in markedly different directions in the past quarter century (from approximately 1960 to 1985), he further hypothesized that, if and when changes did occur, they tended to come about in the United States first. This latter hypothesis was based on the author's personal experience in both countries, and was reinforced by the results of a study by Lipset (1973). Lipset had pointed out that there has been reluctance on the part of Canadians "to be overly optimistic, assertive, or experimentally inclined." Based on the results of this investigation, however, such has not necessarily been the case in the field of physical education and sport (see also Zeigler, 1980).

To report more accurately on this subject for the 1980s, and also to gain a better perspective on the United States' scene, seven members of the American Academy of Physical Education, distributed geographically across the country, each who have been involved in professional preparation for periods up to 40 years, were asked to describe what they believe took place in the United States over three different time periods (i.e., during the 1960s, the 1970s, and the 1980s). What follows here, then, is delimited to their responses for the period covering the 1980s and also to the investigation and analysis carried out personally by the author.

Five problems, phrased as questions, were included in the questionnaire as follows: (1) what have been the strongest social influences during the current decade? (2) what changes have been made in the professional curriculum? (3) what developments have taken place in instructional methodology? (4) what other interesting or significant developments have occurred (typically within higher education)? (5) what are the greatest problems in professional preparation currently?

Strongest Social Influences

During the 1980s, a number of strong social influences were indicated on the United States scene. Worldwide communication was improving greatly as ever more satellites were put into service. Nevertheless, the seemingly ever-present concern with the several violently conflicting world ideologies remained at a high level of intensity as the decade began. The Reagan administration displayed an aggressive "proud to be American" leadership style, along with emphasis on strong offensive and defensive military concerns, in an ongoing struggle to combat spreading communism at numerous points around the globe. Others were worried that the United States was overextending itself through "imperial overstretch" in its zeal to make the world safe for democracy (Kennedy, 1987, p. 515).

A variety of new and continuing problems and issues were apparent on the home front as well, some having both positive and negative implications for the future. The impact of high technology (e.g., computers, software--the entire "knowledge industry" for that matter) was felt increasingly. Certain large industries were suffering greatly from cheaper foreign competition (e.g., steel production), but fortunately the North American car market held up (to some extent through wise partial mergers with foreign competitors).

The cost of education soared at all educational levels, while concurrently funding from the federal level was decreasing. Greater cooperation between the public schools and higher educational institutions was apparent. With an enrollment decline beginning to have an effect on many colleges and universities, there was increased competition for top students. A presidential task force on the state of education was proclaiming a "prevalence of mediocrity" in the secondary schools. This demand for accountability at a very high level brought about a steady call throughout the decade for a "back to basics" movement in education. It was argued that "teachers can't teach," but others were promoting the idea of "mastery teaching" (an idea that makes sense upon first examination). However, some wanted students promoted anyhow because age differentials were creating more disciplinary problems. Developments that impacted on physical education were (1) the federal government easing off on Title IX enforcement that took some pressure off state legislatures to provide equal opportunity for girls and women in sport, and (2) there was evidence that less than one-third of the total school population (ages 10-17) received daily physical education.

The Physical Education/Kinesiology Curriculum

Along with the continued expansion of non-teaching options or areas of concentration within the physical education/kinesiology major program, there was a concurrent decline of interest in under-girding liberal education and an evident increase in the importance of job orientation. Many felt there was a need to eliminate what they regarded as superfluous courses, while stressing the need for improved scholarship within those that remained. The feeling was that students were typically more serious and goal-oriented, but the concern and pressure for high numerical grades was disconcerting to some observers.

Interestingly, and unfortunately, there was an increased number of students with relatively poor physical skills in the professional-disciplinary programs. Whether this trend was counteracted by an improvement in theoretical understanding remain debatable, however. In the final analysis, however, it should be recognized that each university can't be "all things to all people" with its program offerings.

The 1980s witnessed also a new emphasis on special physical education because of state legislation, but such specialization within professional preparation programs was still not sufficiently available. There was also continued concern, but not much concrete action, for improved standards as evidenced by state certification for alternate career graduates and/or voluntary national accreditation for such programs related to ongoing teacher education programs. One promising note was the establishment of a National Association for Sport and Physical Education (NASPE) Task Force working on a revision of accreditation standards for undergraduate physical education teacher preparation.

Along with declining enrollment in professional curricula, there was a need to generate increased revenue. Faculty positions were being lost due to inadequate funding, and intra-institutional research funding was drying up.

Instructional Methodology

Several definite observations can be safely made in connection with instructional methodology. The weakening financial situation brought about a collapsing of course sections into larger lecture groups. This created a problem, however, because there was also been continued concern for teacher/coach effectiveness. Many faculty members began to take their teaching responsibilities more seriously, and there appeared to be an improved level of innovation and creativity in their efforts. This trend was accompanied by the retooling of certain faculty members to improve their instructional competency, thereby making them more valuable to their faculty units. There is no doubt but that course content has been based somewhat more on research findings and improved theory. Computer instruction is gradually being incorporated into the instructional pattern in a variety of ways, as is increased use of videotaping. The need to somehow streamline the learning experiences was expressed, as was a concern that there be greater stress on education for "human fulfillment" with the teacher as facilitator.

Other Campus Developments

At the beginning of the 1980s, the continuing, bleak financial picture brought about a considerable degree of faculty pessimism and cynicism. Requirements for promotion and tenure were ever more stringent, while at the same time faculty positions were threatened because of continued economic pressures. Salary schedules did not keep pace with many other professions and occupations.

Sub-disciplinary specialization of faculty members increased steadily in the larger universities. This broadly based approach involved more research and publication, but also involved heavier teaching/coaching workloads. Thus, prevailing dictum seemed to be: Get the research grant no matter whether there is time to complete the project. Early retirement schemes appeared, but they were often not sufficiently creative or rewarding to encourage faculty departure. All in all, there was the feeling that the environment was too stressful.

**The Greatest Problems or Needs
in Professional Preparation
and Disciplinary Specialization**

As the field entered the final decade of the 20th century, a number of problems expressed as needs were identified as follows:

1. Need to develop consensus about a disciplinary
definition from which should evolve a more unified,
much less fractionated curriculum (i.e., a greater
balance among the bio-scientific aspects, the social-science
& humanities aspects, and the "professional aspects" of our field).

2. Need to develop a sound body of retrievable knowledge
in all phases of the profession's work.

3. Need to implement the educational possibilities
of a competency approach within the professional
preparation curriculum.

4. Need to develop a variety of sound options for
specialization within a unified curriculum
(extending to a 5th year of offerings?). This
involves the expansion of alternate career
options in keeping with the profession's goal of
serving people of all ages and all abilities.

5. Need to develop a format whereby regular
future planning between staff and students
occurs.

6. Need to graduate competent, well-educated,
fully professional physical educator/coaches
who have sound personal philosophies embodying
an understanding of professional ethics.

7. Need to seek recognition of our professional

endeavors in public, semi-public, and private
agency work through certification at the state
level and voluntary accreditation at the national level.

8. Need to help control or lessen the impact of
highly competitive athletics within the
college and university structure so that a
finer type of professional preparation program
is fostered.

9. Need to recognize the worth of intramural
recreational sports in our programs, and to
make every effort to encourage those
administering these programs to maintain
professional identification with the National
Association for Sport and Physical Education.

10. Need to continue the implementation of
patterns of administrative control in educational institutions
that are fully consonant with individual freedom within the
society.

11. Need to work for maintenance of collegiality
among faculty members despite the inroads of
factors that are tending to destroy such a
state: lack of adequate funding, faculty
unionization, pressure for publication and the
obtaining of grants, and extensive
intra-profession splintering.

12. Need to develop an attitude that will permit
us to "let go of obsolescence." Somehow we
will have to learn to apply new knowledge
creatively in the face of an often discouraging
political environment.

13. Need to work to dispel any malaise present
within our professional preparation programs
in regard to the future of the profession.
If we prepare our students to be certified and
accredited professionals in their respective
options within the broad curriculum, we will
undoubtedly bring about a service profession
of the highest type within a reasonable period
of time (Zeigler, 1986).

Concluding Statement

As these words are being written, there is obviously a continuing value struggle going on in the United States that results in distinct swings of the educational pendulum to and fro. It seems most important that a continuing search for a consensus be carried out. Fortunately, the theoretical struggle fades a bit when actual educational practice is carried out. If this were not so, very little progress would be possible. If we continue to strive for improved educational standards for all this should result in the foreseeable future in greater understanding and wisdom on the part of the majority of North American citizens. In this regard science and philosophy can and indeed must make ever-greater contributions. All concerned members of the allied fields in both the United States and Canada need to be fully informed as they strive for a voice in shaping the future development in their respective countries. It is essential that there be careful and continuing study and analysis of the question of values as they relate to sport, exercise, dance, and play. Such study and analysis is, of course, basic as well to the implications that societal values and norms have for the allied fields of health and safety education, recreation, dance, and sport management.

Note

1. The information about the United States has been adapted from several sources, sections or parts of reports or books written earlier by the author. See Zeigler, 1951, 1962, 1975, 1979, 1988a, 1988b, 1990, 2003, 2005

References and Bibliography

American Alliance for Health, Physical Education, Recreation and Dance (1962) *Professional preparation in health education, physical education, recreation education. Report of national conference.* Washington, DC: Author.

American Alliance for Health, Physical Education, Recreation and Dance. (1974). *Professional preparation in dance, physical education, recreation education, safety education, and school health education.* Report on national conference. Washington, DC: Author.

Bennett, B.L. (1962). Religion and physical education. Paper presented at the Cincinnati Convention of the AAHPER, April 10.

Bookwalter, K.W., & Bookwalter, C.W. (1980). *A review of thirty years of selected research on undergraduate professional preparation physical education programs in the United States.* Unionville, IN: Author.

Brubacher, J.S. (1966). *A history of the problems of education* (2nd ed.). New York: McGraw-Hill.

Brubacher, J.S. (1969). *Modern philosophies of education* (4th ed.). New York: McGraw-Hill.

Bury, J.B. (1955). *The idea of progress.* New York: Dover.

Butts, R.F. (1947). *A cultural history of education.* New York: McGraw-Hill.

Commager, H.S. (1961). A quarter century--Its advances. *Look*, 25, 10 (June 6), 80-91.

Conant, J.B. (1963). *The education of American teachers* (pp. 122-123). New York: McGraw-Hill.

Elliott, R. (1927). *The organization of professional training in physical education in state universities.* New York: Columbia Teachers College.

Flath, A.W. (1964). *A history of relations between the National Collegiate Athletic Association and the Amateur Athletic Union of the United States (1905-1963).* Champaign, IL: Stipes. (Includes a Foreword by E.F. Zeigler entitled "Amateurism, semiprofessionalism, and professionalism in sport: A persistent historical problem.")

Hayes, C. (1961). *Nationalism: A religion.* New York: Macmillan.

Heilbroner, R.L. (1960). *The future as history.* New York: Harper & Row.

Hershkovits, M.J. (1955). *Cultural anthropology* (pp. 33-85). New York: Knopf.

Hess, F.A. (1959). *American objectives of physical education from 1900 to 1957 assessed in light of certain historical events.* Doctoral dissertation, New York University.

Johnson, H.M. (1969). The relevance of the theory of action to historians. *Social Science Quarterly*, (June), 46-58.

Kennedy, P. (1987). *The rise and fall of the great powers.* NY: Random House.

Kennedy, J.F. (1958). Address by the President in Detroit, Michigan. (At that time he was a U.S. Senator.)

Leonard, F.E., & Affleck G.B. (1947). *The history of physical education* (3rd ed.). Philadelphia: Lea & Febiger.

Lipset. S. M. (1973). National character. In D. Koulack & D. Perlman (Eds.), *Readings in social psychology: Focus on Canada.* Toronto: Wiley.

McCurdy, J.H. (1901). Physical training as a profession. *American Physical Education Review*, 6, 4:311-312.

Morris, V.C. (March, 1956). Physical education and the philosophy of education. *Journal of Health, Physical Education and Recreation*, (21-22, 30-31.

Muller, H.J. (1954). *The uses of the past.* NY: New American Library.

Murray, B.G. Jr. (1972). What the ecologists can teach the economists. *The New York Times Magazine*, December 10, 38-39, 64-65, 70, 72.

Naisbitt, J. (1982). *Megatrends.* NY: Warner

Nevins, A. (1962). The gateway to history. Garden City, NY: Doubleday.

Oberlin College Catalogue (1894).

Reisner, E.H. (1925). *Nationalism and education since 1789.* New York: Macmillan.

Sigerist, H.E. (1956). *Landmarks in the history of hygiene.* London: Oxford University Press.

Sparks, W. (1992). Physical education for the 21st Century: Integration, not specialization. *NAPEHE: The Chronicle of Physical Education in Higher Education*, 4, 1:1-10-11.

Wellesley College Catalogue (1910).

Zeigler, E.F. (1951). *A history of undergraduate professional preparation in physical education in the United States, 1861-1948.* Eugene, OR: Oregon Microfiche.

Zeigler, E.F. (1962). A history of professional preparation for physical education in the United States (1861-1961). In *Professional preparation in health education, physical education, and recreation education* (pp. 116-133). Washington,, DC: The American Association for Health, Physical Education, and Recreation.

Zeigler, E.F. (1968). *Problems in the history and philosophy of physical education and sport.* Englewood Cliffs, NJ: Prentice-Hall.

Zeigler, E.F. (Ed. & author). (1973). *A history of physical education and sport to 1900.* Champaign, IL: Stipes.

Zeigler, E.F. (1975). Historical perspective on contrasting philosophies of professional preparation for physical education in the United States. In *Personalizing physical education and sport philosophy* (pp. 325-347). Champaign, IL: Stipes.

Zeigler, E.F. (Ed. & author). (1975). *A history of physical education and sport in the United States and Canada.* Champaign, IL: Stipes.

Zeigler, E.F. (1979). The past, present, and recommended future development in physical education and sport in North America. In *Proceedings of The American Academy of Physical Education* (G.M. Scott (Ed.), Washington, DC: The American Alliance for Health, Physical Education, Recreation, and Dance.

Zeigler, E.F. (1980). An evolving Canadian tradition in the new world of physical education and sport. In S.A. Davidson & P. Blackstock (Eds.), *The R. Tait McKenzie Addresses* (pp. 53-62). Ottawa, Canada: Canadian Association for Health, Physical Education and Recreation.

Zeigler, E.F. (1983a). Relating a proposed taxonomy of sport and developmental physical activity to a planned inventory of scientific findings. *Quest*, 35, 54-65.

Zeigler, E.F. (1986). Undergraduate professional preparation in physical education, 1960-1985. *The Physical Educator*, 43 (1), 2-6.

Zeigler, E.F. *et al.* (1988a). *A history of physical education and sport.* Champaign, IL: Stipes. See the excellent chapter on American physical Education and sport by R.K. Barney, pp. 173-219).

Zeigler, E.F. (1988b). A comparative analysis of undergraduate professional preparation in physical education in the United States and Canada. In Broom, E., Clumpner, R., Pendleton, B., & Pooley, C. (Eds.), *Comparative physical education and sport*, Volume 5. Champaign, IL: Human Kinetics.

Zeigler, E.F. (1990). *Sport and physical education: Past, present, future.* Champaign, IL: Stipes.

Zeigler, E.F. (2003). *Socio-Cultural Foundations of Physical Education and Educational Sport.* Aachen, Germany: Meyer & Meyer Sports.

Zeigler, E.F. (2005) *History and Status of American Physical Education and Educational Sport.* Victoria, Canada: Trafford.

Selection #5
Guiding Professional Students to Literacy in Physical Activity Education

"There was a field called physical education.
With so many names it writhed in frustration.
Still it dithered and blathered while peregrinating,
and finally died silently while still ruminating."

It would be neither wise nor kind at this time to criticize--or perhaps even make a bit of fun of, as was done immediately above--earlier leaders in the field of physical education for the present plight the field faces. In fact it would be very difficult to say precisely where and when the field "went wrong" during the twentieth century. For example, was there a critical incident at which point the die was cast? Suffice it to say that there are now well over 200 different, multi-faceted titles presumably describing what is intended to be the subject-matter composition of these present-day educational units--professional and/or disciplinary--at the college and university levels in the United States of America.

Although the development of the concept of "the allied professions" began early in the 20th century, a critical incident in the development of the field of physical education as a so-called profession was the decision of the American Academy of Physical Education (AAPE) to change its name to the American Academy of Kinesiology and Physical Education (AAKPE). A full explanation of the reasons behind this change will not be presented here. Subsequently--with the guidance of Editor Janet C. Harris of *Quest* and Karl M. Newell's argument that use of the term *kinesiology* would help to bring "chaos out of order--the entire issue of *Quest* (Vol. 42, No. 3, December, 1990) was devoted to a discussion of this development by various theorists in the field. In that issue Daryl Siedentop stated (pp. 320-321) "Newell and I disagree fundamentally on the nature of the field. I believe it to be a professional field. I believe persons who want to serve in the field need to be prepared in a professional program. . . ." To this author the intent of Siedentop's statement is crucial to the future development of a profession that should be called *physical activity education*. What follows here is an effort to explain how those who now call themselves "physical educators" at heart and in practice might recover from this present plight. The question is asked whether they can ever fulfill what was intended to be their original mission, thereby becoming vital to the provision of healthful, developmental physical activity for the country's population.

This halcyon state could possibly be achieved if those responsible for professional preparation guided *qualified* professional students to full literacy in a discipline called *developmental physical activity* while at the same time preparing them *professionally* in *physical activity education*. If this were to become the norm, and these graduates were imbued with a life purpose to provide people of all ages and conditions with purposeful, developmental physical activity, physical activity educators could create a nation of healthy, vigorous people that would set an example for the world.

Definitions

1. The meaning used for the term "literacy" here is *the second one* provided in the *ENCARTA World English Dictionary*, 1999, p. 1052)-- i.e., "knowledge of, or training in, a particular subject or area of activity." (The first definition given is "the ability to read and write to a competent level.") Further, the meaning of the term in this analysis has been broadened to mean *professional* literacy--*i.e., the expert knowledge and competencies held by the professional practitioner.*

2. The term *"developmental physical activity"* is defined as the discipline or body of knowledge about human movement in exercise, sport, and physical recreation.

3. The term *"physical activity education"* is defined as the knowledge, competencies, and skills relating to exercise, sport, and physical recreation that can be taught to children and young people in educational institutions, as well as to adults of all ages throughout their lives in various situations and environments.

4. The term *"physical activity educator"* is defined as that person who uses the knowledge and competency available about developmental physical activity to teach a planned program of physical activity education either in the educational system or in society at large.

Cultural Literacy

The reader may wonder why the terms "literacy" and now "cultural literacy" are being introduced into this discussion. The reason is that clarification of the full meaning of the terms is needed. Actually, part of the problem that the field of physical education has faced is that many people feel that its professional practitioners themselves often have not achieved full literacy--literacy based on the *first* definition of the term in a dictionary (see "Definitions" immediately above). Whether physical educators are good readers and writers--as all professional people should be--is not the primary concern of this discussion at the moment, however. What is needed now is to explain that the "literacy" needed for profession practitioners is provided in the second definition provided above under "Definitions"--i.e., the expert knowledge *and competency* desired for the physical activity educator. Such "literacy" would be "professional literacy" that is over and above the "cultural literacy" recommended for all Americans by Prof. E. D. Hirsch in the late 1980's (1988, 1991).

Before discussing expert knowledge and professional competency further, however, it is important to clarify the subject of cultural literacy somewhat further. Hirsch believes that it is their common knowledge or collective memory that "allows people to communicate, to work together, and to live together," and that "if it is shared by enough people, it is a distinguishing characteristic of a national culture," "one that makes each national culture unique" (p. ix). After publishing *Cultural literacy*, a book in which he explained his conception, he took the next logical step, with associates Joseph Kett and James Trefil, to publish *The dictionary of American literacy* in 1988. The "cultural knowledge" included in this unique volume was stated to be what every literate American of the late 20th century ought to know, or at least be familiar with if not known fully and precisely. Such cultural knowledge is simply that mass of information that is to be preserved along with any additional information meeting the definition that is constantly being added to the "mass" as time passes.

If this cultural literacy is "the foundation of our public discourse," and it is "what makes Americans American," then the authors had to establish certain rules that would apply to this assemblage of information. First, they decided not to include specialized information that would be known only by experts, while at the same time leaving out basic information that was "below" what they termed necessary cultural literacy. Second, they decided to include only that information or item that would presumably be known by a majority of *literate* Americans. Finally, they did not include current events that would not have enduring significance to the society, or at least a strong possibility of achieving such status. These exclusions and inclusions, they felt, would give cultural literacy a "lasting significance" (p. x). Interestingly, and disturbingly, the authors decided that what happened in competitive sport, plus what they called "entertainment," in America was too "ephemeral" to include--with notable exceptions (e.g., Lou Gehrig, Babe Ruth). (This decision appears to be most unfortunate because, if art, music, and dance have been included under "Fine Arts" as cultural forces--which they should be, of course--then, for better or worse, sport too has become a very strong cultural influence in America. It is now possibly even too strong a social force; so, its omission would seem to be an error in judgment, made possibly through bias.)

Hirsch and his colleagues have certainly given all of us interested in general education something to think about. When the declining statistics of such basic information are known, how can anyone argue with the proposition that "achieving high universal literacy ought to be a primary focus of educational reform in this country"? (p. xi). They argue that what they call "true functional literacy" is fundamental to a successful society because it is what "is holding the social fabric of the nation together." The authors assert also that "true literacy depends on a knowledge of the *specific* information that is taken for granted in our public discourse." They insist that true literacy involves "acts of communication" that "requires a knowledge of shared, taken-for-granted information" that lies "below" the written page. On the surface of things, their rationale provides a strong argument for attempting to counteract the decline in what is called "national literacy" in their discussion (p. xi).

The authors explain further why there is a "high correlation between reading ability and learning ability." They stress how important is that a reader be able to comprehend various types of writing. They argue that "to have a good *general* reading ability, the student needs to know about a lot of things." Taking this argument still further, they state that "language arts are also knowledge arts." Having pointed out that "high reading ability is a multiplex skill that requires knowledge in a wide range of subjects," Hirsch et al. declare that the same thing can be said about *learning* ability. If we can associate something new with something that we learned previously, we are literally combining the new idea with similar older ideas or concepts already mastered. All of this--learning more and more about the world in which we live--adds up to the need for people to have as broad a background knowledge as possible.

It was important to explain what cultural literacy is meant to be and where it fits into the educational scheme provided for the literate citizen. Cultural literacy is general information that helps us communicate with friends, business associates, and strangers alike. However, professional literacy in what is here being called physical activity education is the main topic for consideration in this investigation.

Physical Activity Education

Throughout this volume the author will argue that the term *physical activity education* would be a better term for a field that wishes to become a full-fledged profession--one that serves people of all ages and conditions in twenty-first century schools and communities. The following are three basic reasons for this assertion:

> 1. It has long been argued that the term physical education implies a tri-partite division of the human organism. Educational essentialists were said to believe in education OF the physical dimension of a person, whereas educational progressivists countered with an "education **THROUGH** the physical" argument. The latter approach now coincides with the belief in psychology that the human organism is indivisible. Nevertheless, this quibbling between factions in the field made it very difficult for physical education to make its case in the educational hierarchy throughout the twentieth century. Unfortunately this opprobrium against physical education still exists today in many quarters both within the educational milieu and in the public domain.
>
> 2. The term "physical education" has somehow become identified with a learning experience that takes place in a gymnasium in an educational institution only. As such it has often been associated in people's minds with dull,

routine-like exercises and similar uninteresting experiences that they don't want to repeat for the rest of their lives after school years are over.

3. For several years the term "physical activity" has been used by various professional and disciplinary groups instead of the term "exercise," the assumption being that people don't like being told that they *have* to exercise. For example, *Physical Activity Today* is a publication put out by the Research Consortium of the American Alliance for Health, Physical Education, Recreation, and Dance. Also, the Presidents Council on Physical Fitness and Sport has substituted the term "physical activity" for "exercise." Further, Health Canada, a governmental group, in collaboration with ALCOA (Active Living Coalition for Older Adults) and CSEP (Canadian Society for Exercise Physiology) publishes *Canada's Physical Activity Guide* and makes it available free of charge. Thus, physical activity implies a variety of activities such as walking, exercising, sports, and types of physical recreation. It now seems, therefore, that physical activity education, may well be the most desirable term to take the place of physical education.

If this proposal were accepted generally, the professional preparation program or curriculum in a university would be designed to prepare a physical activity educator as a qualified professional practitioner. Depending on the standards set, this person could also qualify for subsequent certification or licensing by the state or province (1) as a teacher in the public schools, (2) as a professional physical activity educator in private practice, or (3) as a professional physical activity educator in a private, semi-public, or public agency.

Such achievement would constitute a guarantee to the public and other hiring officials that the graduating professional student had completed a thoroughgoing, competency-based, physical-activity education program in which:

(1) professional functions and needs were ascertained,
(2) individual competencies were specified,
(3) necessary performance levels were determined,
(4) program content and instructional methodology were defined, and
(5) competency attainment, as specified at the outset, was carefully evaluated.

Professional Preparation Development of the Physical (Activity) Educator

Down through the years of the 20th century many educators urged that there should be a stronger "cultural" component in the professional curriculum of the physical education teacher. However, although some progress was made, the demands for strengthening in the other curriculum areas (i.e., foundation arts and sciences, professional education requirements, health education courses) limited the extent to which this objective could be reached. A number of studies indicated also a lack of standardization in course terminology within the developing specializations of the overall field of health education, physical education, and recreation (Zeigler, 1962)

There were many attempts to improve the *quality* of professional preparation through studies, surveys, research projects, national conferences, and accreditation plans. A significant text recommending a "competency approach" to the preparation of teachers was published (Snyder and Scott, 1954). The field had been continuing to move toward ongoing self-evaluation and improvement. The American Association for Health, Physical Education, and Recreation (subsequently "the Alliance") was a great influence in this historic development. It was aided significantly by such affiliated groups as the College Physical Education Association (later the NCPEAM) and the National Association of Physical Education for College Women (NAPECW), both of which merged to form the National Association for Physical Education in Higher Education.

The American Alliance for Health, Physical Education, Recreation, and Dance has long since fully recognized that each of the terms in its name represents separate professions (or fields of endeavor) that are nevertheless also almost inextricably allied. Interestingly, the International Council for Health, Physical Recreation, Sport and Dance has recently added the term "sport" to its title as well. The term "physical education" has also been joined with the word "sport" for some time in the National Association for Sport and Physical Education within the Alliance, but the Alliance's name remains unchanged. Interestingly, although PHE Canada (formerly the Canadian Association for Health, Physical Education, Recreation and Dance) has followed the lead of its counterpart in the United States.. However, physical and health education remain closely intertwined; in fact, PHE Canada's publication is called *Physical and Health Education Journal.* Dance educators are also active within **PHE Canada**).

What has been a most significant development in both countries is the inauguration in the 1960's of a great variety of separate sub disciplinary and "sub professional" societies in each country that are often conjoined as North American societies (e.g., the North American Society for Sport History). For better or worse, a large majority of the scholars trained in physical education graduate programs originally have now transferred their primary allegiance to these more broadly North American societies as well. Also, a devastating blow to the field of physical education was the fracture in the relationship between the Alliance (AAHPERD) and the American Academy for Kinesiology and Physical Education (AAKPE), a move caused by a perceived need to separate the discipline from the profession. However, it can be argued that it occurred also because of certain state legislators' concern about the term "education" in the school curriculum and possible personality conflicts within the Alliance and the Academy. These two organizations (AAHPERD and AAKPE) had historically met annually in a conjoint fashion to the great benefit of both groups. Meeting separately now means that upwards of 100 of the field's finest scholars and researchers are to all intents and purposes removed from the strong *professional* milieu of the Alliance. Funds for professional travel can only be stretched so far.

These developments described immediately above have taken place largely within the last half of the 20th century, although some of the "subdivision" that has occurred within what was earlier known as *physical education only* started earlier (e.g., health education, recreation). *What is significant in all of these individual movements, of what may be called either a professional or "sub disciplinary" nature (e.g., recreation or sport psychology, respectively) is that they were efforts by professional people and/or scholars and researchers to specialize in the related fields of study (i.e., the sub disciplinary and sub professional components of the field)..*

This movement of professionals and scholars, either within the Alliance or outside of it, has left the field of physical education in a precarious, untenable situation. To be a qualified physical educator in the eyes of one of more groups or jurisdictions, the prospective teacher was confronted with a number of difficult hurdles. In fact, the difficulty of overcoming these "obstacles" became apparent to this author when completing an unpublished master's degree study on the topic more than 60 years ago. He concluded that a five-year program of study was needed instead of the four typically required for state certification. It was found that it was simply impossible to guarantee (1) a broad general education, (2) a creditable major in physical education including foundation subjects, (3) an acceptable minor in a related teaching area, and (4) the requisite number of professional education courses (including student teaching) in a four-year curriculum.

A Need for Redirection and Rejuvenation

Diagnosis of the present situation indicates that the field known as physical education throughout the 20th century needs *redirection* and *rejuvenation* as the field enters this new century. As difficult as it may be, the field should come to grips with the fact right now that physical educators are still typically "jacks-of-all-trades and masters of none!" This is what they have been, and this is what they are presently. Can it possibly be argued that this a good thing, or is it bad and should such a casual description of the field be changed? After many years of involvement, the author has now come to believe that the profession--is it truly one, technically speaking, or is it a segment of the education profession?--has a duty and responsibility to work its way through to an appropriate name and a consensual taxonomy of required knowledge and competencies for its work. Every self-respecting profession has a body of knowledge that practitioners should (must?) master to practice effectively. What is the body of knowledge in physical education? What are the specific competencies and skills this person should possess? Where is all of this explained?

Agreement about a name for the field, a complete taxonomy for its subject matter, the steady, ongoing development of an under girding body of knowledge, and a list of the required competencies needed would reasonably soon place the field in a position where a professional practitioner would be recognized as a "such-and-such" no matter what type of position that person held within the field--or for that matter in which state or territory such professional service was carried out. Reaching consensus will undoubtedly be "horrendously difficult." However, it is now absolutely essential that the field strive for such an objective. Right now one is continually forced to the conclusion that physical educators have over the decades become "jacks of all trades, masters of none." Frankly, something must be done about it! The time has come to bring the field's image into sharper focus for the sake of the futures of professional students, not to mention the public at large (Zeigler, 1997).

The author might as well "climb further out on a limb" by stating his own position about what it is for which we should be responsible. We could call ourselves human motor performance, but this may not sound sufficiently complete and accurate. "Movement arts and science" has possibilities as a disciplinary title suitable for acceptance at a university. The term "kinesiology" has been in the dictionary for decades, but its definition is too narrow and is also unclear to the public. It is not completely accurate either! The late Elizabeth Halsey recommended "developmental physical activity" in the 1950's. This was actually a very good prospect for consideration because the field had been largely involved with developmental physical activity in sport, exercise, and related expressive movement. However, in the 1950s the field was not yet ripe for its acceptance.

Obviously, the profession should be promoting such developmental physical activity, or physical activity education, for people of all ages. Further, teachers should be "professing" their theoretical and applied knowledge on behalf of normal, accelerated, and special populations in society. Then, in addition to what happens within educational circles, to become a profession the field should have a "womb to tomb" responsibility for all citizens throughout their lives. Yet we do not find physical educators serving as such–and accordingly called by some title such as physical activity educators–serving the public outside of their work in educational institutions.

Today's physical educators are not typically qualified to be *recreation directors,* nor are they *health specialists* or *dance specialists* with undergraduate and graduate degrees in either of these three fields. Yet, it is true that professional students may have minors or areas of concentration in one or more of these areas. However, by now it should be well recognized that these allied professions are too highly specialized for physical educators to think that there can be *one* professional *association* for all four fields. What present-day physical educators do understand quite well is *physical* recreation only, some of the "health aspects" of physical activity, and occasionally some of the social and traditional dances.

A Taxonomy for a Curriculum
Termed Physical Activity Education

What then should be the composition of the curriculum in physical activity education? In the late 1970s the author began to deplore the rift that had seemingly inevitably developed in the field since the mid-1960's between the so-called scholars and the so-called practicing professionals. The reader may remember what happened--that is, the rift between the people who were not ashamed to be called "physical educators" and those who were. As time has shown, there are now the self-proclaimed kinesiologists or "human kineticists" seeking academic respectability in our universities by calling themselves "what they ain't!" Typically they can't truly analyze human movement! Those anxious to accept the term "kinesiology" for use as the name of the former physical education unit on college and university campuses should move slowly and cautiously before changing their department's name. Somehow very few graduating physical education/kinesiologists end up being able to analyze movement kinematically, much less kinetically. And yet this is what the term "kinesiology" means literally--the study of movement! In addition, as it has turned out, the offerings of various departments and schools of kinesiology differ significantly. One school of kinesiology (unnamed!) offers, for example, a variety of areas of concentration: health and physiological science, human/factors/ergonomics, active health, and biomedical engineering. Interestingly, many of these units designated as kinesiology are more than meeting their admission quotas. It is true, also, that certain people in these departments of kinesiology have been deprecating those old-fashioned units at other universities still adhering to the name "physical education." Yet do we really know what their students specializing in kinesiology do after they graduate?

We can grant that "a rose by any name smells the same." The term "kinesiology" is from the Greek language and does indeed mean "the study of movement." Although this may be technically correct, the advocates of this name change in lieu of "physical education"--at the university level at least--evidently don't know (or care?) that the verb *kineo* is also a very common Greek verb that describes the movements of sexual intercourse. And the husband's name in Aristophanes' famous *Lysistrata*, the comedy where the women of Athens go on a sex strike to get their husbands to end a war--you guessed it--was *Kinesias*. Further, to "add insult to injury," those units that have adopted the term "human kinetics" should keep in mind that kinetics is actually a subdivision of another department on campus--the department of physics!

The author recalls the words of the great C. H. McCloy, State University of Iowa, written to the author more than a half century ago. He said, "The name 'physical education' is now so solidly entrenched that changing it would be akin to rolling back Niagara Falls." However, this feat has indeed now been accomplished on occasion. Where does that now leave a field called "physical education." What does all of this add up to? If physical education doesn't take positive steps to rectify this ongoing decline and continuing trend, it will continue to lose "professional ground."

What can possibly be done about these myriad problems? One approach would be to develop a taxonomy including both the professional and the scholarly dimensions of the field. Accordingly, it was postulated that a "balanced approach" between the *sub disciplinary* areas of the field and what might be identified as the *sub professional* or concurrent professional components. By this was meant that what many have called scholarly professional writing (e.g., in curriculum theory, management thought and practice) will be regarded as scholarly endeavor if done well, just as what many have considered to be scholarly, scientific endeavor (e.g., in the exercise sciences) if done well should indeed be regarded as professional writing too (i.e., writing that should ultimately serve the profession).

As part of an effort to close what was regarded as a debilitating, fractionating rift within the field, a taxonomical table was developed to explain the proposed areas of scholarly study and research using nomenclature from the field (physical activity terms only) along with the accompanying disciplinary and professional aspects. There was agreement on eight areas of scholarly study and research that are correlated with their respective sub disciplinary and sub professional aspects in Table 1 below.

Please see Table 1 on the following page.)

Table 1
DEVELOPMENTAL PHYSICAL ACTIVITY IN SPORT, EXERCISE, AND RELATED EXPRESSIVE MOVEMENT

Areas of Scholarly Study & Research	Sub disciplinary Aspects	Sub professional Aspects
I. BACKGROUND, MEANING, & SIGNFICANCE	-History -Philosophy	-International Relations -Professional Ethics -Intern.& Compar. Study
II. FUNCTIONAL EFFECTS OF PHYSICAL ACTIVITY	-Exercise Physiology -Anthropometry & Body Composition	-Fitness & Health Appraisal -Exercise Therapy
III. SOCIO-CULTURAL & BEHAVIORAL ASPECTS	-Sociology -Economics -Psychology (individ. & social) -Anthropology -Political Science -Geography	-Application of Theory to Practice
IV. MOTOR LEARNING & CONTROL	-Psycho-motor Learning -Physical Growth & Development	-Application of Theory to Practice
V. MECHANICAL & MUSCUL. ANALYSIS OF MOTOR SKILLS	-Biomechanics -Neuro-skeletal Musculature	-Application of Theory to Practice
VI. MANAGEMENT THEORY & PRACTICE	-Management Science -Business Admin.	-Application of Theory to Practice
VII. PROGRAM DEVELOPMENT	-Curriculum Studies	-Application of Theory/Practice

(General education; professional preparation; intramural sports and physical recreation; intercollegiate athletics; programs for special populations--e.g., handicapped--including both curriculum and instructional methodology)

VIII. EVALUATION & MEASUREMENT	-Measurement Theory	-Application of Theory to Prac.

The Field Should Develop and Promote
Its Own Discipline and Its Own Field of Study

The position being taken here is that the field should promote and develop *its own discipline* of developmental physical activity and *its own field* of physical activity education taught by physical activity educators as described above. At the same time the practitioners in physical activity education should be working cooperatively with their related disciplines and allied professions (to the extent that such cooperation is possible and useful in relation to the problems jointly faced).

There is an important point to be made at this juncture. Continuing to speak of *sociology* of sport, *physiology* of exercise, etc., is making these other disciplines and professions awaken to the importance of what physical educators in the past believed to be *their* professional task (i.e., the gathering and dissemination of knowledge about developmental physical activity through the media of sport, exercise, and related expressive movement, and the promotion of it to the extent that such promulgation is socially desirable).

Such "awakening" by people in the related disciplines and allied professions is necessarily not a bad thing, of course. For example, it happened in the historical aspects of the field when it was reported in the *Chronicle of Higher Education* in the 1970's that sport history had been discovered. As a matter of fact, as of 1969 there were already 54 physical education doctoral studies and hundreds of master's theses on *purely* sport history (Adelman, 1971). Additionally, there have been literally thousands of physical education theses and dissertations with a historical orientation over the past 50 years! Further, the North American Society for Sport History has held conferences and published a scholarly journal since the early 1970's, and there was also a fine *Canadian Journal of Sport History*. This encroachment on what was considered to be its domain should cause the field of physical education no concern, however, if its primary emphasis were to shift to what is known about *developmental physical activity* and how this knowledge may be used effectively and efficiently in *physical activity education*!

The reader can certainly understand, however, that there is a different serious concern being expressed here. The end result of a continuation of this splintering of the so-called profession of (sport and) physical education is bound to result in a "mish-mash" of isolated findings by well-intentioned, scholarly people not in a position to fully understand the larger goal toward which the profession has been striving. It can be argued that the field is gradually becoming doomed to perpetual *trade* status--not *professional* status--composed of perennial "jacks-of-all-trades, masters of none." The field is being outflanked by so many different specialists and specialties--including kinesiology (or human kinetics)--that one hardly knows in what area physical education as a self-described profession can speak authoritatively. If physical educators don't take positive steps to rectify this continuing trend in their field's development by changing their image, it will continue to lose "professional ground" while functioning with a subject matter still considered an unimportant, expendable part of the educational curriculum.

It doesn't have to be this way. However–and this is vital–the situation would change dramatically if the present field of sport and physical education (NASPE's designation) were subdivided and the physical education segment were to become physical activity education (e.g., from NASPE to NAPAE). (Here it is being assumed that there would [or could] be a separate association for sport and/or sport education.) *A separate profession known as physical activity education has the inherent potential to serve the high goal of enriched living and wellbeing for all people.* It can provide an opportunity for the improvement of the quality of life and, additionally, there is now evidence that regular exercise throughout one's life will lengthen one's lifespan as well. These are tremendously important reasons for every man, woman, and child to want to strive for an ongoing state of physical wellbeing. No other professions can make such a claim, but a profession called physical activity education could do this best for people of all ages and conditions with the accompanying help of its allied professions and related disciplines. Moreover, no other profession or discipline will (or can) do this for what is now called physical education! However, because of physical education's inability or unwillingness, other professions and trades are arguably now fulfilling some of its duties and responsibilities--*but in a piecemeal fashion!* This can only result in sporadic, incomplete knowledge, competencies, and skills coming belatedly and ineffectively to help people improve the quality of their lifestyles.

An Inventory of Scientific Findings About Developmental Physical Activity Is Needed Right Now

What is needed right now, and is not presently available, is a steadily growing, categorized inventory of scientific findings about *developmental physical activity* in exercise, sport, physical recreation, and expressive movement arranged as *ordered generalizations* to help professional practitioners *in physical activity education* in their daily work. Physical activity education, as it is being called here, does not have this knowledge and information readily available for daily use by its practitioners. Such emerging knowledge is fundamental for the finest level of professional practice for teachers, coaches, scholars, laboratory researchers, managers, supervisors, performers, and others engaged in positions of a public, semipublic, or private nature (e.g., YMCAs and commercial fitness establishments).

Ordered Principles or Generalizations

To make these ordered generalizations available and current, the professional association should devise and develop a series of ordered generalizations about developmental physical activity in sport, exercise, and related expressive movement and make them available to professionals both online and in the form of a loose-leaf, expandable handbook. What exactly are *ordered principles* or *generalizations?*

Ordered principles or generalizations are simply important and verified findings about (1) what we really know, (2) what we nearly know, (3) what we think we know, and (4) what we claim to know. These principles or generalizations are arranged in an ordered, 1-2-3-4 arrangement--*and in as plain English as is possible!*

As an example, taken from the field of management theory (one of the sub-professional divisions of developmental physical activity explained in Table 1 above), the following findings about "the organization," arranged as *ordered* principles or generalizations have been extracted from Berelson & Steiner (1964, pp. 365-373):

The Organization.
A1   The larger, the more complex, and the more heterogeneous the society, the greater the number of organizations and associations that exist in it.

   A1.1   Organizations tend to call forth organizations: if people organize on one side of an issue, their opponents will organize on the other side.

   A1.2   There is a tendency for voluntary organizations to become more formal.

A2   There is always a tendency for an organization (of a non-profit character) to turn away, at least partially, from its original goals.

   A2.1   Day-to-day decisions of an organization tend to be taken   as commitments and precedents, often beyond the scope for which they were initially intended, and thus affect the character of the group.

      A2.1a The very effort to measure organizational efficiency, as well as the nature of the yardstick used, tends to determine organizational procedures.

A3   The larger the organization becomes, the more ranks of personnel there will tend to be within it. [Etc.--keeping in mind practical limitations, of course.]

A Plan Leading To An Ever-Expanding Body of Knowledge Through The Implementation Of A System Approach

An initial effort has been made above to present the "why" and "what" of a proposed online inventory of scientific findings covering developmental physical activity as it relates to the field, but now it is time to discuss the "how" in relation to the way in which this proposed development can be effected. It has been recommended further that such an inventory be based on a revised taxonomy including both the sub disciplinary and the sub professional aspects of the profession.

The first such inventory of ordered principles or generalizations would assuredly have certain gaps or deficiencies caused obviously by present inadequacy. Such an inventory of the discipline of *developmental physical activity* or the proposed profession of *physical activity education* should be arranged primarily for *"our own"* use. The basic difference between what is presently available through several sources (e.g., SIRC) is that, in addition to bibliographic data, articles, etc., it would provide the *first* version of an ordered set of generalizations as described in the example immediately above. This version would have obviously leave much to be desired. There would be no need for apology, however, because such an effort would represent a meager beginning compared to what may be possible in 10, 20, or 50 years. However, this development will not come about unless substantive change in present practice occurs .

To this end, a recommendation is being made here for the gradual implementation of a systems approach, so that (1) university personnel relating to the discipline, (2) professional practitioners in the field, (3) scholars and researchers in other disciplines and professions, and (4) the general public could visualize the scope of the development needed to make available a sound, complete body of knowledge about developmental physical activity. This service is needed *right now* and should be made available as soon as possible in such a way that it can be called up instantaneously--either as a bibliographic listing, an abstract, a complete article, *or as a series of ordered generalizations indicating where this new knowledge coincides or clashes with present understanding.*

Along with many other fields, those scholars relating to developmental physical activity, and those teaching physical activity education, do not yet appreciate the need to promote and subsequently implement a "total system" concept. There are many urgent reasons why the field must take a holistic view if the discipline and most closely related profession hope to merit increased support in the future. The promotion of this "evolving entity" of developmental physical activity, characterized as it is with so many dynamic, interacting, highly complex components, would require the cooperation of innumerable local, state or provincial, national, and international scholarly and professional associations and societies. In this way full support for the total professional effort could be provided.

The model presented here to help achieve a common purpose for developing and using theory and research (Figure 1) explains a system with interrelated components that could be functioning as a unit--admittedly with constraints--much more effectively than it is at present! Although in practice the execution of such an approach would be complex, the several components of the model being recommended are basically simple. As can be observed from Figure 1, the cycle progresses from *input to thruput to output* and then, after sound consumer reaction is obtained and possible corrective action is taken, moves back to input again (possibly with altered demand or resources) as the cycle is renewed (Zeigler, 1990, p. 218a).

Taking the first step toward the development of an inventory of scientific findings, one designed to meet the needs of North Americans primarily, would also have relevance for practitioners and scholars anywhere in the world. As mentioned above, it could be used:

(1) for students during their period of professional training,
(2) for mature students preparing for comprehensive examinations at the graduate level,
(3) for professional practitioners on the job on a daily basis,
(4) for non-professionals wishing to round out their general education, and, last but not least,
(5) in concert with a planned, graduated set of laboratory experiences from which would result the competencies and skills necessary to perform as a successful professional practitioner.

(It could also be studied profitably in an ancillary manner by students wishing to specialize in either health and safety education or recreation and park administration. However, it has not been designed to meet the needs as an introduction to either of these developing professions. Moreover, students intending to specialize in sport coaching or dance education as developing professions could use it to advantage as an introduction to developmental physical activity because the focus should be on human movement in exercise, sport, physical recreation, and expressive movement.)

In any analysis of this emerging field that traces the developments of the twentieth century, three categories or subdivisions of the field should be investigated: (1) the growing and potential body of knowledge being created by researchers and scholars drawing upon research methods and techniques of the sub disciplinary areas; (2) the similar development of knowledge emanating from the concurrent professional components of the developing field (as exist in all subject-matter fields to a greater or lesser extent); and (3) the knowledge becoming available from what may be called the allied professions.

:

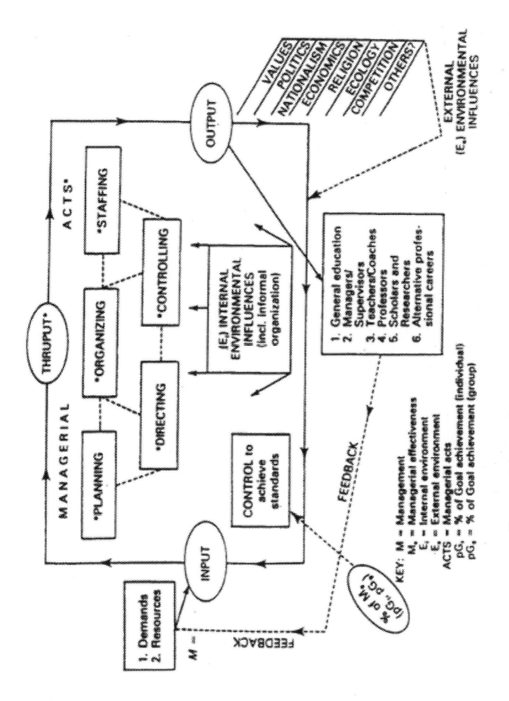

Figure 6. A System Analysis Model for Managerial Effectiveness in a Professional Preparation Program for Sport & Physical Activity Managers

Competencies and Skills Required
for Achievement of Professional Literacy

It should be made crystal-clear at this point that, *in addition to mastery of the necessary knowledge base*--in a thoroughgoing competency-based approach should be employed throughout the professional program so that the competencies, and skills deemed necessary are acquired sufficiently. This experiential approach represents one more effort to direct professional preparation away from the stereotypical *"mastery of the textbook approach"* employed throughout the twentieth century. (In addition to making available a *broadly based* knowledge component that--through textbooks, lectures, and related literature--should be mastered prior to receiving a baccalaureate degree, such an evolving body of information should also be available on-line in the form of *ordered generalizations* for qualified, registered professionals in the field wherever they might be located.)

What follows will seek to explain how the author and his colleague (Gary Bowie) deviated from "the standard approach" in relation to one subject-matter area of the eight displayed in the model for the discipline proposed in Table 1 above--i.e., management theory and practice related to physical education and (educational) sport (Zeigler and Bowie, 1995). (It should be made clear that this same *experiential* or *laboratory* approach is being recommended for learning in *each* of the other seven categories displayed in Table 1 above (e.g., functional effects of physical activity, curriculum theory & program development) of the overall discipline designated as developmental physical activity.) The authors proceeded on the assumption that the time was past due to develop a text that truly related to management *competency* development for trainees who would later themselves be administering programs in physical activity education. What resulted was unique in that it was the first time that an "experiential" or laboratory approach had been employed throughout an *entire* administration text in the field. The result was a workbook or manual that could be used *independently* or even in conjunction with what was considered a standard text (i.e., one that had little or no *practical* exercises in it). Thus, the instructor was in a position to involve the students in "laboratory experiences" that were developed from well over 100 desirable experiences tabulated under five broad management competency categories.

The five broad competency categories for use in the experiential approach were determined after a comprehensive analysis of management science literature. From many sources the predominant thought was that there was a need to introduce a step-by-step plan for management competency or skill attainment. In doing so in connection with this investigation, a decision was made to build on Katz's (Harvard) tri-partite categorization (1974). The end result included five subdivisions in which the *personal* attributes needed for the administrator of physical activity education, as well as those *"conjoined"* skills gained through a "combinatorial" process that the individual is often required to employ on the job. What Katz called *human* skills, were now called *interpersonal* skills so as to distinguish them from personal skills (# 1 below). These subdivisions or categories of administrative skills are as follows:

1. *Personal skills* (or developing one's own individual competencies prior to concentrating on the managerial task).
2. *Interpersonal skills* (or acquiring the skills needed to influence people positively to work accomplishment of organizational objectives and goals).
3. *Conceptual skills* (or learning to formulate ideas and plans while on the job as an administrator).
4. *Technical skills* (or acquiring the various skills and techniques needed to cope with the various organizational details and problems that arise).
5. *Conjoined skills* (or developing the various managerial skills in some combination or proportion to achieve both immediate objectives and long-range goals). (Zeigler & Bowie, 2007)

This plan enables the teacher and the students to move selectively from theory to practice within each of the five subdivisions or categories shown above. The method for working toward the achievement of the specific competencies or skills is as follows:

(1) through the provision of statements describing the objectives of the modules used to develop the competencies,
(2) to offer "knowledge statements" introducing the trainee to the theoretic bases of the competencies and their roles and functions in the management process, and
(3) by recommending selected laboratory exercises for achieving a degree of success (at least!) based on involvement in a variety of problem-solving experiences.

After the student comprehends the problem to be met or solved, a questioning process determines:

(1) what needs to be known,
(2) where this information may be obtained,
(3) how to organize the actual learning experience,
(4) what the probable result will be, and
(5) how to evaluate the level of competency attainment (where such is possible).

The teaching and learning process employed by the instructor is designed to include a variety of laboratory experiences. In addition to standard lecture and discussion techniques it is assumed that the instructor will include other learning devices available such as:

(1) the case method,
(2) role-playing,
(3) independent study,

(4) interaction with a personal computer,
(5) elementary theory formulation,
(6) response to questionnaires and self-testing devices,
(7) individual projects,
(8) small discussion groups, etc.

When there is time available, the instructor may wish to introduce action or applied research-based on independent investigation (e.g., descriptive research, game theory, debates, internship experiences, panels, forums).

Basically a three-step learning process is recommended. It should involve:

(1) understanding of the objective of the learning experience module,
(2) reading and comprehension of a "knowledge statement" or "lecturette" about the particular competency involved, and
(3) skill learning or competency achievement through analysis and practice.

As the process proceeds, the instructor should:

(1) assess initial student status,
(2) introduce selected experiences to strengthen areas of weakness, and
(3) evaluate competency attainment.

Based on literature analysis and responses from knowledgeable colleagues, the authors decided to offer a lengthy, but incomplete listing of competencies and skills from the five areas selected. Primary competencies were selected from each of the five areas and were considered to be a practical number to include. They were categorized according to:

(1) understandings developed,
(2) skills acquired,
(3) assessments carried out,
(4) plans devised,
(5) experiments undertaken,
(6) evaluations made,
(7) instruments employed, etc.

What then, specifically, are these desirable management competencies or skills that were deemed most important at this point?

1. The Manager's Personal Competencies/Skills (selected from a list including 22 additional competencies/skills)

    a. Determine one's personal philosophy of life and/or religion

    b. Establish priorities in personal values clarification

    c. Develop a personal mission statement

    d. Develop a plan that (tentatively) maps out one's future (i.e., goal-setting in relation to maturity)

    e. Conduct a personal analysis to assist in the development of an individual time-management plan (i.e., planning a work schedule for the week, month, year, etc.)

2. The Manager's Interpersonal Competencies/Skills (selected from a list including 24 additional competencies/skills)

    f. Develop an understanding of self (i.e., self-concept) as required for successful interpersonal competency

    g. Assess interpersonal communication skills (e.g., empathetic listening and responding)

    h. Execute an interpersonal style inventory

    i. Evaluate interpersonal management skills (e.g., selling ideas)

    j. Learn about one's leadership attributes and performance; assess present leadership style

3. The Manager's Conceptual Competencies/Skills (selected from a list including 23 additional competencies/skills)

    k. Understand the development of twentieth century management thought, theory, and process

    l. Analyze the general (external) and immediate (internal) environments

    m. Develop an understanding of that phase of the management process generally known as **PLANNING**

    n. Develop an understanding of that phase of the management process generally known as **ORGANIZING.**

    o. Develop an understanding of that phase of the management process generally known as **STAFFING**

    p. Develop an understanding of that phase of the management process known as

DIRECTING

q. Develop an understanding of that phase of the management process known as **CONTROLLING**

r. Develop an understanding of how to implement a systems approach to the overall management process

4. The Manager's Technical Competencies/Skills (selected from a list including 36 additional competencies/skills)

    s. Learn how to use the meeting as an effective tool for the work group.

    t. Learn about team-building (i.e., developing an understanding of how work groups are formed and maintained.

    u. Execute an in-basket analysis as the manager approaches a day on the job

    v. Understand legal liability in relation to sport management

    Note: The above technical competencies/skills were selected from a total of competencies/skills.

5. The Manager's Conjoined Competencies/Skills (selected from a list including a total of 18 competencies/skills)

    w. Develop an outline of a policies and procedures manual for a special event (e.g., a sports tournament).

    x. Develop an approach to decision-making in relation to one's personal and professional philosophy (including ethical decision-making where applicable).

    y. Carry out a strategic market-planning assessment for a sport and/or physical activity-based program.

    z. Understand how to manage for change.

Successful Student Should Demonstrate Achievement in Representative Number of Competencies/Skills

Obviously there is insufficient time in any one undergraduate course in *any* of the proposed areas in the professional curriculum for physical activity education. However, whatever the situation may be, including the length and extent of the course experience (i.e., quarter, term, or semester), the successful student should demonstrate achievement and/or completion of at least a *representative sampling* of the competencies/skills deemed necessary in each of the eight areas (e.g., functional effects of physical activity, socio-cultural foundations of developmental physical activity) for eventual awarding of the baccalaureate degree.

Since a "competency-development approach" has not been used fully previously in the field except possibly to a limited extent in selected courses, some problems may arise regarding what shape or form the completed "laboratory reports" should assume in the various courses included in the curriculum. Each instructor will necessarily have to experiment with the laboratory phase of the course in question. Recommendations for time involvement and other expectations for actual student involvement in written reports and analyses will be needed. The instructor, based on ongoing experience and student evaluation, has to decide how much time will be allotted to lectures and how much laboratory experience will be offered. In addition to the occasional quiz, the instructor and/or a teaching assistant will have a set of exercises to correct with each "laboratory report" submitted. Also, there would normally be some sort of a "knowledge final" based on the course material included. It would probably be best for both the instructor and student to hand in each set of laboratory experiences by specified dates throughout the semester.

Concluding Statement

In this analysis the investigator argued that physical education, as a field of endeavor within educational institutions, has gradually but steadily declined in the second half of the twentieth century. The question was asked rhetorically whether physical education per se can ever achieve the aims and objectives envisioned by its leaders in the first half of the twentieth century. Indeed, can the field of physical education ever hope to become vital to the provision of healthful, developmental physical activity for all of the country's population whether these people are students or members of the general public?

This question was answered in the affirmative—i.e., that the field could become a full-fledged profession if the present field of physical education and educational sport (or sport and physical education as called within NASPE) were to make a number of changes in its present modus operandi. These recommended changes are as follows:

1. That the *profession* be called physical activity education,
2. That the *discipline* be called developmental physical activity,
3. That professional practitioners be known as *physical activity educators*,

4. That physical activity educators adopt a broadly based, consensual model for the body of knowledge and the competencies/skills required for their professional endeavors,

5. That *professional literacy* for the practitioner be defined as the expert knowledge and competency desired for the physical activity educator,

> (Note: Such professional literacy is over and above the concept of *cultural literacy* prescribed by Hirsch for all Americans.)

6. That the physical activity educator should steadily become known more as *a specialist in human physical activity in exercise, sport, and related physical activity,*

7. That physical activity educators should promote and develop their own their own profession of *physical activity education* and their own *discipline* of developmental physical activity. (The intent here is that use of terms and names identified primarily with other disciplines and professions should be avoided to the greatest possible extent [e.g., physiology of exercise instead of physical activity science, sociology of sport instead of socio-cultural aspects of physical activity].)

8. That physical activity educators should become experts in their own *self-described* profession, (This means a departure from the present "jack-of-all-trades, master-of- none" image now held. A thoroughgoing competency– development approach should be instituted in all professional preparation programs for physical activity educators prior to the awarding of the baccalaureate degree.)

9. That the profession, employing a systems approach, needs to develop an evolving online inventory of scientific findings about developmental physical activity that is categorized and arranged as ordered generalizations for daily use by the professional practitioner,

10. *That to accomplish the ultimate professional goal, involvement with competitive sport as a coach should be separated from the duties of the physical activity educator in the educational environment,* and

11. That the professional efforts of the physical activity educator should be extended to serve the public on a lifelong basis in society at large, (This would involve licensing and/or certification for such public professional practice.)

Such a halcyon state, one that is still possible in the foreseeable future, could be achieved if the established professional association and those responsible for professional preparation in colleges and universities become ready for such a development. The challenge is to guide qualified and motivated professional students to full literacy in a discipline called developmental physical activity, while at the same time preparing them professionally to a high standard in physical activity education. If this were to become the norm, and these graduates were imbued with a life purpose to provide people of all ages and conditions with purposeful, developmental physical activity, physical activity educators could indeed create a nation of healthy, vigorous people that would set an example for the world.

References

Adelman, M. (1971). A bibliography of master's and doctoral studies related to the history of sport and athletics in the United States (1930-1967). In E. F. Zeigler, M.L. Howell, & M. Trekell (Eds. & Aus.), *Research in the history, philosophy,and international aspects of physical education and sport: Bibliographies and techniques* (pp. 131-161). Champaign, IL: Stipes.

Berelson, B., & Steiner, G.A. (1964). *Human behavior.* NY: Harcourt, Brace, Jovanovich.

ENCARTA World English Dictionary. (1999). NY: St. Martin's Press.

Hirsch, E. D., Jr., Kett, J, F., & Trefil, J. (1991). *The dictionary of cultural literacy.* Boston: Houghton Mifflin.

Katz, R. L. (Sept.-Oct,, 1974). Skills of an effective administrator. *Harvard Business Review,* 51, 5:90-102.

Newell, K.M. (Dec, 1990). Physical education in higher education: Chaos out of order. *Quest,* 42, 1:227-242.

Siedentop, D. (Dec. 1880). Commentary: The world according to Newell. *Quest, 42, 1:315-322.*

Snyder, R. A., & Scott, H. A. (1954). *Professional preparation in health, physical education, and recreation.* NY: McGraw-Hill.

Zeigler, E. F. (1962). A history of undergraduate professional preparation for physical education in the United States (1861-1961). In E. F. Zeigler (Ed.) *A history of physical education and sport in the United States and Canada* (pp. 225-253). Champaign, IL: Stipes. (This was originally published in 1962 as a background chapter in a national conference of professional preparation sponsored by the AAHPER, Washington, DC.)

Zeigler, E. F. (1982). *Physical education and sport: An introduction.* Philadelphia: Lea & Febiger.

Zeigler, E. F. (1990). *Sport and physical education: Past, present, future.* Champaign, IL: Stipes.

Zeigler, E. F. & Bowie, G. W. (1995). *Management competency development in sport and physical education.* Champaign, IL: Stipes.

Zeigler, E. F. (1997). From one image to a sharper one. *The Physical Educator,* 54, 1: 1-6.

Selection #6
Finding a Life Purpose
in Sport Management Education

Introduction

During the 20th century, competitive sport somehow became one of the important social institutions in the world. Social institutions are created and nurtured within society to further the positive development of the people living within that culture. Take democracy as a type of political institution that is being promoted in the Western world. In the realm of economics, capitalism--with certain reservations--is also regarded as an important social institution. This means that where democracy, capitalism, and sport are encouraged to function, it is intended that each singly will bring about more "good" than "bad."

However, in each case, we are finding this assumption being challenged. In North America, the percentage of people voting in elections has decreased steadily, while at the same time the gap between the rich and the poor is steadily increasing. What does this mean as we move into the 21st century? Will the present brand of "combined" democratic capitalism improve so that we can claim with certainty that it is producing more "good" than "bad"?

At the same time, the development of social institution of competitive sport in the United States, for example, has reached the point where a claim that it does more good than harm can be challenged. But the world seemingly has no awareness of this contention and permits its expansion without question. "Sport is good for people, and more involvement with sport is better" seems to be the conventional wisdom. In the meantime, the large majority of the population is getting inadequate involvement in physical activity at the same time as these same people are being expected to pay increasing amounts of money to watch skilled others play games. It has even been stated recently that the coming generation will be the first to die before their parents die. I am forced to ask "What *are* we promoting, and why *are* we doing it?" I simply do not have a complete answer to these questions based on scientific evidence at this time.

Why is this so? It is because we need to develop a theory of sport that would permit us to assess whether sport is fulfilling its presumed function of promoting good in a society. Sport philosophy as a discipline should be fundamental in any assessment of the findings of sport arts and sciences. At present it has not developed sufficiently to fulfill that function in the world."

The former president of Columbia University, Nicholas Murray Butler, is purported to have said: "There are three kinds of people in the world today: (1) those who make things happen, (2) a larger number who watch things happen, and (3) the vast majority who never even know that anything is going on!" Our fundamental task in sport management education is to discover, motivate, and develop a number of young people who will make things happen in the field in the 21st century. If these people can then find a life purpose in this work, as professional practitioners or social-science scholars, they will be in a position to serve society efficiently, effectively, and--most importantly!--throughout their entire lives. (However, I must state at the outset--with all due respect--that I find it difficult to believe that a great many of those who have enrolled in sport management programs all over North America in recent years really knew that they were getting into.)

It is still accurate to state that there has been relatively little evidence that sport managers or administrators, wherever they may be functioning, are generally concerned with the theoretical aspects of management. Admittedly it appears to have been similar to the emphases indicated in educational administration research at the time where the topics investigated also shied away, or at least investigators were just beginning to understand the need for, theoretical investigation. See, for example, *An analysis of doctoral research problems in school administration* by H.A. Taylor, a doctoral study completed at Stanford University in 1954. The problems most investigated related to finance; business affairs; planning, maintenance, and operation of the school plant; and teacher personnel, all topics that Gross identified as specific rather than general administrative processes where motivating, communicating, etc. are involved. However, it is also important to understand that most educational administration professors' understanding of administrative theory and the meaning of terms had most definitely matured by the late 1960s (see Penny, 1968, pp. 107, 121). The situation was just the opposite with the practical or technical aspects of the broader aspects of management in the public sector in the 1950s (Trethaway, 1953, p. 458 et ff.).

There is also still a paradoxical situation in physical education and athletics at the college or university when one is imprudent enough to discuss such a thing as "management theory." The practitioners don't believe such theory will help them on the job, and the scientist has yet to be convinced of the scientific quality of any such investigation. The above notwithstanding, and despite the inadequacies in professional preparation for management in physical education and athletics administration that existed for decades, it must be confessed that courses in the organization and administration of physical education and athletics have been offered in our field since 1890 (Zeigler, 1951)!

By 1927 they were typically included in professional curricula throughout the United States (Elliott). Since that time there has been a proliferation of similar courses relating to administration and supervision at both the undergraduate and graduate levels. In addition, literally thousands of master's theses and doctoral dissertations have been deposited on the shelves of our libraries. Most of these studies involve the descriptive method of research, or some technique thereof, and there is unquestionably a body of knowledge of sorts about practice of an administrative nature. Relatively speaking, however, there is still a paucity of research in management theory. What we have is an endless stream of articles, theses, dissertations, monographs, and texts on administration or management as a subject-matter area, but what it all adds up to is anybody's guess.

However, during the 1980s, a steady advancement was made in management science in both business and educational administration. Yet, it was still apparent that little had been done similarly to develop management competencies and skills in sport and physical education management programs. Our field was simply not ready to take a progressive step forward. We believe this to be true because the books I published, for example, promoting the case method approach to the teaching of human relations and management (1959), as well as management competency development in sport and physical education (1983), were premature. Undaunted, we now are reasonably secure in the knowledge that some progress in understanding the complexity of professional management training has been made since then.

And so, looking ahead in this first quarter of the 21st century, I can state again that more attention should undoubtedly be devoted to management theory as well as practice--not to mention the skills required to be an effective and efficient manager--if professionals in the field hope to have a worthwhile profession. I believe that a significant minority of our colleagues is now aware of this deficiency, and I trust that those involved with management training will continue to implement positive changes. I believe further that social trends and the job market is forcing professionals in the field to develop sufficiently strong attitudes (psychologically speaking) to bring about this much needed change.

Status of Management Thought, Theory, and Practice in Physical Education and Educational Sport

What can be said at the present about the status of the development of management thought, theory, and practice in physical education and sport? If those working in the area are searching for academic respectability, and this appears to be the case, management theory in this field must somehow steadily and increasingly strive for a sound theoretical basis. The fact is that, even though organization and administration have a long history in our professional preparation programs, investigation into these topics has not achieved the recognition that has been accorded to research in, for example, sport and physical education history. Thompson (in Halpin, 1958, pp. 29-33) explained how we could improve this situation. First, the terms and concepts used must be clear, and they must be related to systematic theory. Second, the theory that we are able to develop should be "generalizable" (and therefore abstract). Third, the research endeavor should be as value-free as possible; if we want to introduce values, they should be treated as variables in the investigative methodology. Fourth, such scholarly endeavor will undoubtedly be based on the social (and primarily the behavioral) sciences. Finally, fifth, correlations are interesting and also significant, but adequate theory should, in the final analysis, clarify processes that will produce quality performance.

The Sport and Physical Activity Manager Defined

Defined traditionally, we might say that the sport and physical activity manager is one who plans, organizes, staffs, leads (or directs), and controls (i.e., monitors and evaluates) progress toward pre-determined goals within programs of developmental physical activity for people of all ages, be they in normal, accelerated, or special populations." In 1983, Zeigler & Bowie defined management more precisely as involving "the execution of managerial acts, including conceptual, technical, human, and conjoined skills, while combining varying degrees of planning, organizing, staff, directing, and controlling within the management process to assist an organization to achieve its goals." Applied to our field, the above description of the management process would apply to any organization that somehow, somewhere in North America is offering at least some aspect of developmental physical activity in sport, exercise, dance, and play to some degree to one or more sectors of the population.

It will not be discussed here at length, but it should be understood that competitive sport in educational institutions, for example, has faced differing marketing environments in each of the past three decades (i.e., the 1960s, 1970s, and 1980s). In the 1960s there was a great need for additional revenue sources as operating costs skyrocketed. This need continued in the 1970s and was further exacerbated by changing social and economic influences (e.g., social values, slower economic growth). In the 1980s a need existed more than ever for sport programs to develop individual strategic marketing plans with concurrent evaluation schedules to serve as control mechanisms (Zeigler and Campbell, 1984).

A Slowly Growing Awareness of the Managerial Revolution

Even after efforts by a number of us over the past three or four decades to upgrade management theory and practice applied to our field--that is within educational circles in physical education and athletics at least--the new manager or administrator is typically still not truly aware of the managerial revolution that has occurred within this time period. (If he or she is aware of it, the difficult and laborious aspects of the management process are usually turned over to someone with training in business practice.) This is undoubtedly considerably less true for people who assume managerial posts in recreation and other public, semi-public and private agencies where developmental physical activity is a considerable part of the organization's program. But even those in these other groups, if they have only had one course in administration or management within one of our departments as part of their background preparation, these young men and women have only a vague understanding of the many aspects and ramifications of the position being undertaken. What's even worse is the fact that even after the individual is on the job, such a person is still not cognizant of the unbelievable complexity of the position! They learn to do what they do by trial and error! The typical approach is to work overtime to get control of the new responsibility and to meet the seemingly endless demands of higher administration, faculty, staff, and students (or the public as consumers or whatever).

Quite soon one gets the feeling that a treadmill is in operation and that the angle is getting sharper, thereby creating a situation where one must trot at a brisk pace simply not to fall off the back end! It's an uneasy feeling because the pressure is there constantly; some people end up with duodenal spasms and an ulcer. Work tends to pile up in enormous quantities when one is absent from the office for just a few short days. Then, too, all the while there is the feeling that he or she is merely doing what is practical and expedient at the moment. The pattern of operation does indeed become one of trial and error, and it seems impossible to take time out for extended future planning. Finally, because of the many, increasing, and persistent demands that are made upon his or her office, the administrator reasons that more help is needed--both administrative and secretarial. No matter whether budgetary pressures increase, and so-called management in decline becomes a perennial syndrome, there will probably continue to be an increase in positions of this type now and in the foreseeable future. It's the simple truth that "assistants need assistants of their own!" What is the answer to this dilemma? VanderZwaag (1984) offered a concise prescription for the prevailing malady: "What is needed is an integrated sport management program that proceeds from a systematic approach to management."

Time Is Running Out on Us

We really don't have much choice at the present other than to make all possible efforts to place professional preparation for administrative leadership within our field on an increasingly academically sound basis. At present the need for vastly improved leadership comes at us from a number of different directions. We simply do not have enough fine leaders in any field--and our field is no exception to this statement. If we don't have good leadership, an organization or enterprise soon begins to falter and even to stumble. Our field needs fine people who will take charge in the behaviorally oriented work environment of today's world. We have all heard that management involves the accomplishment of an objective through the enlistment of others to work closely with management. However, as Zoffer (1985) states: "But I would add to that the need to achieve a certain excellence--accomplishing goals efficiently, cost-effectively and imaginatively, while respecting the lives and welfare of the broader community." Interestingly, there is no doubt but that sport and physical education has achieved greater recognition within educational circles on this continent than in any other geographical area of the world. (It should be mentioned that recent developments in Japan, Europe, and Australia are encouraging for sport management.) Such achievement is an accomplished fact, but we now have to continue in the direction of upgrading professional preparation for administrative or managerial leadership so that the profession of sport and physical education will consolidate those gains made and--like the successful basketball team--continue to "move strongly down court on balance toward the goal" (Rothermel, 1966).

Those of us who have been functioning in physical education and sport for many years often take solace in statements like, "But we are still a young field; give us time!" There may be a grain of truth here, but let's not forget that the evidence at hand points to the offering of a course in the organization and administration of physical education and athletics as far back as 1890 (Zeigler, 1951, p. 28), and by 1927 such courses were typically included in professional curricula throughout the country (Elliott, 1927, p. 46). Typically such courses were based on what might be called a "principles approach." For example, the author (EFZ) took courses at Columbia Teachers College in the 1940s that stressed the principles of physical education and sport administration according to such notable early leaders in physical education administration there as William L. Hughes, Clifford L. Brownell, Harry M. Scott, and Patricia Hagman. The authority for such principles usually emanated from the experiences of these professors themselves and, of course, their earlier teachers.

Today, courses—entire programs often (!)--are offered at the undergraduate, master's and doctoral levels in physical education/kinesiology, and the subject matter of administration or management, broadly or narrowly defined, is included to such an extent that a disinterested observer would suspect the presence of a vast storehouse of under girding knowledge. This is hardly true, although the situation has improved enormously since the description immediately above. This, incidentally, is the same approach that this investigator followed until about the mid-1950s when he began to question the source and validity of all of these principles he had been taught--and which principles he was presumably still using both in teaching the administration course and in practice with his associates as a chairperson. (See Zeigler, 1959.)

It is true, as stated above, that administration has been an area of limited scholarly investigation in physical education and athletics since the early days of the twentieth century. Early studies were often carried out by the administrators themselves and concerned such topics as departmental organization, staffing, and facilities. As master's programs developed in the early years of the century, and then were followed by the first doctoral programs in the 1920s, the number of topics subsumed under the administration area broadened. Soon theses and dissertations became a basic sources of research. Cureton (1949, pp. 21-59) carried out a survey of completed research for the years 1930 through 1946 and listed 420 doctoral dissertations in all sub-areas of the field in his report. Also, whenever there were such general reviews of physical education research as in, for example, the Encyclopedia of Educational Research, research about administration was typically included as a sub-topic (e.g., Esslinger, 1941, pp. 801-814; Esslinger, 1950, pp. 820-835; Rarick, 1960, pp. 973-975; and Montoye & Cunningham, 1969, 963-973). Typical headings and sub-headings were organization and administration, physical education status, administrative practices, policies and procedures, facilities, etc.

Analysis of Research Reports (Trethaway)

Trethaway (1953) completed a doctoral study tracing early physical education research in which he examined the files of the National Research Committee, an ongoing committee project that was the predecessor of the present AAHPERD Research Council. In total, he collected the titles of 3083 research reports based on research reports of varying quality in physical education competitive athletics, and school recreation between 1895 and 1940. Then he developed a sampling of 789 abstracts from the total and summarized what he found to have been the major developments in each of the three areas.

Interestingly, there have been more studies completed in this area within physical education and athletics, as it was typically designated then, than in any other (with the possible exception of studies about the functional effects of physical activity or the physiological aspects of exercise and sport). This vast number of master's theses and doctoral dissertations may be found on the shelves of our libraries and/or electronic retrieval systems (e.g., CD/ROMs). The large majority of these investigations was carried out using descriptive method research, or a technique thereof, and there does exist undoubtedly a certain body of knowledge about the various aspects of administrative practice relating to our field.

Interestingly, Zeigler (1959, p. 51)), noting the overly heavy dependence on this type of research being carried out, made an effort to introduce the Harvard case method technique of research (also a descriptive research technique) to the field in the late 1950s. At that time he called for research that would contribute more significantly to administrative thought and practice. Beeman (1960), then intramural and recreational sports director at Michigan State University, completed the first doctoral dissertation of this type.

Daniels and McCristal Organize the Big Ten Body-of-Knowledge Project

After Arthur Daniels of Indiana University, working with King McCristal of the University of Illinois and others, effected the actual formation of the Big Ten Body-of-Knowledge Project, Zeigler & McCristal (1967) traced the history of this highly significant undertaking for the future of physical education. This "sub disciplinary approach" to the development of scientific knowledge about developmental physical activity in exercise, sport, and related expressive movement, upon the encouragement of McCristal and Zeigler included administrative theory as one of the sub disciplinary areas. At that time the availability of pure research relative to administrative theory was very poor, however. So, Zeigler encouraged Spaeth in the mid-1960s to make an assessment of its status when pressure for the field to take a "disciplinary approach" came to the fore because of Arthur Conant's criticism of administration courses in physical education. Spaeth's conclusion (1967, p. 145) was that "there is an almost total lack of theoretical orientation in the design of research and interpretation of findings in the sample of of administrative research . . . reviewed in this investigation."

> (Note: The use of the word "theoretical" means "existing only in theory, not practical; thus, a statement of a truth to be demonstrated" [*Random House Dictionary, The*, 1987, p. 1967]. "A theory is essentially a set of assumptions from which a set of empirical laws [principles] may be derived" [Griffiths, 1959, p. 28]. The matter at hand, therefore, was to assess the availability of, and possibility that, hypothetical statements may be shown to be true about the most effective means of administering programs of sport and physical activity.)

An Assessment in the Mid-1960s (Spaeth)

Spaeth (1967) recommended strongly that we must strive in future research to examine management as a process or group of processes rather than as an area of content (such as the "nuts and bolts" approach, or the "this is how you organize a round-robin tournament" explanation). The execution of studies related to the various technical concerns of managing physical education and education is, of course, highly important to the practitioner, but we must also investigate the more fundamental, broader processes of management that might be designated as decision-making, communicating, activating, planning, evaluating, etc. as they relate to our field (see Figure 1 below). For the period under consideration in this monograph, it was decided that this taxonomy proposed by Gross would be followed basically..

Spaeth's analysis of the relationship of administrative theory to administrative research prior to 1967 (as paraphrased from Spaeth, 1975, Chap. 3 and her 1967 thesis) revealed an almost total lack of a theoretical orientation both in the design of the research itself and in the interpretation of the findings in the sampling that she conducted. She discovered that completed research could be classified according to task areas grouped under two major headings: program aspects (including curriculum development and evaluation and relating students to the program) and technical-managerial aspects (including personnel administration, finance and business management, facilities and equipment, and public relations).

She found further that the program aspects in order of frequency studied were: intercollegiate athletic programs for men, college physical education programs, interscholastic athletics for boys, intramural programs in colleges, elementary school physical education programs, intercollegiate athletics for women, interscholastic programs for girls, and intramural programs in public schools.

Insofar as investigation about the technical-managerial aspects of physical education and athletics in order of frequency studied were: personnel (including, in order of frequency, characteristics of men and women faculty members; job analysis of administrators, supervisors, and directors; characteristics, qualifications, and attitudes of administrators; job analysis of faculty, teachers, and coaches; department chairmen at the college and university level; administrative or leadership behavior; and selection of faculty); facilities and equipment; finance, insurance, and liability; and public relations.

It was interesting to note further that certain of the topics listed above were studied more intensively in some decades than others. Much of the research referred to fell within what might be called the traditional framework of task areas and very little to what can be called the administrative processes. Further examination of the literature within sport and physical education in the mid-1960s by Spaeth (Zeigler & Spaeth, 1975) had indicated also that the field was still almost completely unaware of the development of administrative theory and research that was taking place in other fields.

Field Is Alerted to Need for More Interdisciplinary Work (Penny)

Penny (1968, reported in 1975, p. 74) found significant differences between the two groups (i.e., professors of educational administration and professors of physical education and athletics) in their understanding of the meanings of significant concepts in administrative theory. This clearly indicated that professors in physical education and sport needed more interdisciplinary work. Hunter (1971) found the same result when he investigated athletic administrators. The need for improved ordinary language and more sophisticated professional language terms was apparent then and has become even more urgent today. Fortunately, there is now a reasonable degree of consensus on the meanings of the significant concepts that appear in the developing body-of-knowledge relative to management theory and practice within public administration, business administration, and management science. This statement applies generally also to specialists in administrative theory within professional education (i.e., they attach similar meanings to specific, significant concepts associated with the subject matter).

A Plea For A Broader Approach to the Teaching of Administration Courses in Physical Education and Sport (Paton)

Similarly, Paton (in Zeigler and Spaeth, 1975, p. 14) suggested a significantly broader approach to the teaching of administration courses in sport and physical education. This approach should be characterized by an emphasis in which the area of content specifically related to sport and physical education would depend increasingly on a body of knowledge developed through management research and theory in our field. Further, educational institutions provide the setting within which many sport and physical education programs are managed. Thus, current efforts to develop management theory and research about the broad administrative process mentioned above within the educational setting are still directly relevant to our field. The fact that management/administration is practiced in a specific setting has tended to obscure the fundamental similarities of the managerial process. The study of administration as administration should eventually also provide a sounder theoretical base for understanding the management process. Finally, and last but not least, underlying all management theory and research are the social sciences (and still more specifically, the behavioral sciences). Concepts and theories related to the behavior of people in organizations have much to offer to an understanding of administration or management.

Baker and Collins Continue Bibliographic Work Begun by Zeigler and Spaeth

Zeigler and Spaeth (1973) made an effort to compile the research that had been completed by offering a selected bibliography of approximately 250 studies related to the administration of physical education and athletics that had been carried out during the 45-year period from 1927 to 1972. Then, Baker and Collins (1983), after discussions with Zeigler, carried out their project involving a retrieval system extending from 1971 to 1982. They assessed the 7,855 thesis and dissertation reports that had been indexed and abstracted in Completed Research in Health, Physical Education and Recreation between 1971 and 1981 (Volumes 13-23). (Studies related specifically to the administration of intramurals and recreational sports were excluded.) General descriptors, based on a modified framework of the conceptual structure employed originally by Spaeth (1967), were devised by the investigators. They added "legal considerations" as a heading in the area of "technical administrative concerns, but excluded the category of "curriculum development" (Baker and Collins, 1983, p. xiii). This change was made since King and Baker (1982) had already carried out a bibliographic compilation of curriculum studies based on completed thesis investigations. (See Fig. 1).

Interestingly, Baker and Collins reported that approximately ten per cent of completed thesis research in all of physical education could be related to administration or management. In fact, as noted earlier, the number of completed theses in the administration or management area are exceeded only slightly by those that are "exercise physiological" in nature. For the ten-year period under consideration, they found a total of 758 studies (9.8% of all theses completed). Finally, the contents of the 758 studies were analyzed to determine a scheme of sub–groupings within each general category. As we look to the future, of course, the next step is to understand where all of these findings from these studies are, as well as what they contribute to the development of ordered generalizations or principles about management theory and practice in sport and physical education.

In an effort to establish this sub professional aspect of the field's under girding discipline on a sounder footing, the Stipes Publishing Co. decided to add two additional monographs to the Stipes Monograph Series on Sport and Physical Education Management. The first is the present monograph that, in addition to this historical essay, includes the earlier Zeigler/Spaeth bibliography (1973) with the addition of brief annotations to each item provided through the combined efforts of Thomas Sinclair and Zeigler, respectively. The Baker/Collins publication then extends the research retrieval from 1971 to 1982. Their listing came primarily from Completed Research for those years and indicates where a particular study may be found within these volumes (not the institution where the thesis was completed). Two interesting questions for future bibliographers to consider are (1) whether master's theses (where carried out) should be included, and (2) whether the original Zeigler/Spaeth "taxonomy," as modified by Baker/Collins, should be further adapted to the 1990s decade.

The above notwithstanding, and despite positive efforts by a steadily increasing number of scholars largely within the North American Society for Sport Management since its beginning in the mid-1980s, general awareness of the theoretic literature--or any significant contribution to it--has only increased slowly in the past thirty years since Spaeth's analysis. This seeming (evident?) lack of awareness and concern is troubling since the field has recently begun to appreciate that people should be prepared more carefully and thoroughly for the "assumption of the managerial risk." For example, since opportunities to specialize in streams or areas of concentration within physical education training programs have begun, the sport management specialization now appears to have been the most popular program of the 1980s. Further, its growth is continuing on into the 1990s. One is forced to speculate about the intellectual level of these programs when the majority of professors and instructors have typically been such reluctant, unproductive scholars.

The late University of Michigan researcher, Paul Hunsicker, suggested an aphorism to the effect that "No master's thesis or doctoral dissertation ever startled the academic world." Unfortunately, this insightful comment could well be an apt description of the status of research in management theory and practice in sport and physical education. All together, however, one might argue that completed physical education and sport management theses have made at least some contribution to our understanding of administrative practice in the area. However, contributions to management theory still have not really made much of a dent in the bulk of the many problems and conundrums facing the professional practitioner.

The Situation in the Mid-1990s

In the mid-1990s, we really didn't have much choice other than to make all possible efforts to place professional preparation for administrative leadership within our field on a more academically sound basis. This question of leadership came toward us from a number of different directions these days. We simply don't seem to have enough fine leaders in any field--and our field is no exception to this statement. If we don't have good leadership, any organization or enterprise soon begins to falter and even to stumble. Our field needs fine people who will take charge in the behaviorally oriented work environment of today's world. We've all heard that management involves the accomplishment of an objective through the enlistment of others to work closely with you. However, as Zoffer (1985) stated: "But I would add to that the need to achieve a certain excellence--accomplishing goals efficiently, cost-effectively and imaginatively, while respecting the lives and welfare of the broader community."

There is no doubt but that physical education and (educational) sport has up to this time achieved greater recognition within educational circles on this continent than in any other geographical area of the western world. Such achievement is an accomplished fact, but we now have to continue in the direction of upgrading professional preparation for administrative or managerial leadership so that the field of physical activity education will consolidate those gains made and--like the successful basketball team--continue to "move strongly down court toward the goal on balance" (Rothermel, 1966).

Up to this point, in addition to some introductory and background material, it has been argued essentially (a) that the world is changing and becoming increasingly complex with each passing day fostering a steadily growing development in management thought, theory, and practice, a development that has had obvious implications for the field of sport and physical education; (b) that sport and physical education needs managers who function effectively and efficiently on the basis of tenable management theory to organize and administer its far-flung programs; and (c) that we have not advanced very far in preparing our people to manage from both a theoretical and practical standpoint, an inadequacy that I believe we should correct as soon as possible by promoting sound theoretical knowledge and by implementing management competency development programs of high quality that include well-planned laboratory experiences.

Let us assume that we can agree on the need for improving the quality of sport and physical activity management in the relatively near future. This need is not peculiar to our profession, however, since we are hearing pleas from all over North America about a growing need for a higher quality in managerial performance than may have been present in the past. To meet the challenge to North American industry and business, for example, we were exhorted a generation ago to consider "Theory Z" as wisdom coming from our Japanese colleagues (Ouchi, 1982)--actually a debatable assumption as it has turned out. Also, there has been a spate of books with the world "excellence" in the title. For example, in a 1980s book entitled *Creating Excellence* (Hickman and Silva, 1984), we were presented with a list of "new age skills" that management executives should cultivate: (a) creative insight: asking the right questions; (b) sensitivity: doing unto others; (c) vision: creating the future; (d) versatility: anticipating change; (e) focus: implementing change; and (f) patience: living in the long term (pp. 99-246). After acquiring these skills, you begin to "walk on water!"

The Present Need: An "Action-Theory Marriage!"

What has been stated above provides some substantiation for the gradual emergence of management science--indeed, a need for an "action-theory marriage!" Many say that management thought is too practical, while others avow that it is usually too theoretical. This may seem to be true, but I believe it can be said more accurately that really practical administrative thought will simply have to be based on far more tenable knowledge and theory than is yet available. Scholarly investigation on this topic should be carried out to the greatest possible extent on the "observable facts of real-life administration" (Gross, 1964). A manager on the job is typically confronted with a real-life situation to resolve. To resolve the problem effectively and efficiently, something better than trial and error is needed in our increasingly complex social environment. That "something" should be the most tenable theory available. In other words, a research strategy is needed that is characterized by a "theory-research balance" based on the results of sound theoretical and applied investigation.

Even though I have been emphasizing that the manager is being faced with a relatively fast-moving social system, a condition from which managers of sport and physical education cannot (and probably should not wish to) escape, change for us has somehow not occurred as rapidly as in certain other segments of society. However, managers in our field must now recognize the fact that they too are being put on notice about the fluid nature of their environments. Managers simply must take advantage of every opportunity to prepare themselves to keep ahead (or at least abreast) of their associates intellectually. This is necessary because they must be ready to meet change head-on and make the alterations and modifications necessary so that growth (if desired and/or desirable) and survival will be ensured (the ecological approach, if you will).

Don't Forget the Carry-Over Constants and/or Generalizations

The above momentary digression is not meant to imply for an instant that there are not a great many constants and/or generalizations that carry over from yesterday to today and thence to tomorrow which help to maintain the structure and vitality of sport and physical education. This means, for example, that much of what is known about human nature today will be identical or quite similar tomorrow. It forewarns the manager that he or she shouldn't throw the baby out with the bath water just because many changes seem to be taking place. The great problem seems to be the urgent need to both strengthen and focus the body of knowledge available to the management profession so that the literally astounding development in the area of technology is reasonably approximated by the understanding and knowledge available about effective and efficient administrative behavior. While such a balance is being established, the tried-and-true constants or "principles" from the past should be used daily and only discarded or modified when there is ample evidence (scientific or normative) available to warrant any change.

116

Hence, the manager, in addition to relying on the wisdom of the past, should make it a habit over the years to increase his or her theoretical and practical knowledge. I believe that the field still has an opportunity to relate significantly to the developing social science of management. However, we can't dally much longer! I say this with a full understanding that so many professionals in our field are only dimly aware of the scientific development that has occurred in management science. Second, the vast enterprise that is sport and physical education for its very survival as a recognizable entity simply must relate more effectively to the urgent need for qualified sport and physical activity managers. The North American Society for Sport Management, inaugurated in the mid-1980s is making a significant contribution to this development. Additionally, such development should continue to be carried out in full cooperation with the National Association for Sport and Physical Education within the AAHPERD and the PHE Canada.

Concluding Statement

At this point Peter Drucker's advice (1993, Chap. 12) about the idea of "The Educated Person" in Post-Capitalist Society seems like a good way to begin to close this essay. He states that a great transformation has been taking place in the world in regard to (a) a move from capitalism to a knowledge society, (b) a trend from nation-states to mega–states, and (c) a shift from a market economy based on traditional market institutions to a market that organizes economic activity around information and knowledge (Chap. 10). In this "new world," Drucker claims that the technological revolution will gradually "engulf" our schools as we all rethink the role of the school and the way it functions. The direct challenge to our society, therefore, is the way that we use the new technology in what he calls post-capitalist society--i.e., the knowledge society (Chap. 11, 197). If we have the wisdom to shift rapidly and fully to a knowledge society that puts the person in the center of the process, we will be able to remain in the forefront of progress.

This post-capitalist society needs "a leadership group, which can focus local, particular, separate traditions onto a common and shared commitment to values, a common concept of excellence, and on mutual respect" (p. 212). However, what is required, Drucker insists, is a new and different kind of educated person than the Deconstructionists, the radical feminists, the anti-Westerners, and the Humanists want (p. 212). What is needed, he maintains, is an educated person who has the knowledge and the commitment to cope with the present situation, as well as being prepared for "life in a global world" (p. 214). Leaders in this society under transformation will use sound organizational theory as a tool enabling them to use their specialized knowledge wisely. Gross's earlier prediction about the need for an action-theory marriage will indeed come to pass (1964, pp. 844-856).

Finally, keeping the basic need for leaders ("educated persons," according to Drucker) firmly in mind, the author should state his personal and continuing interest in a leadership spectrum (or perhaps a continuum) in which, as one moves from left to right (i.e., from anarchy to dictatorship), the manager gradually exercises greater authority and the staff members have lesser areas of freedom. (He has also employed this same continuum to the teaching act in a way similar to the approach of the late Muska Mosston; see Zeigler, 1964, pp. 258-261.) Through long experience he has developed a distinct aversion to one-person, arbitrary, authoritative decisions--especially in educational settings--although he wouldn't like to work in such a setting at any time anywhere else either.

Of course, it is appreciated that in certain lines of work, such as the military or fire-fighting, there typically isn't sufficient time to have discussion and then to take a vote before action is taken. Nevertheless, staff members should be involved in the decision-making process to the greatest possible extent--if they are willing to make serious efforts to be well informed on the matter at hand. Further, once a decision is made democratically by informed members of the group, the organization can and should demand loyal support from all members of the group. (The assumption here is that opportunities will be provided subsequently for people to be convinced in democratic fashion at a not-too-distant future date that a contravening decision should be made.)

In this changing (internal and external) organizational environment that we have been discussing, the interpersonal skills of the leader(s) need continuing examination and study. Certainly the leader must "know himself or herself" and know those with whom direct or indirect association is established. The executive needs to establish an open climate. By this is meant that (a) associates can collect information about a problem accurately, (b) bring these data back to the decision-making group, and then (c) take part in the planning and execution of future actions (Bennis & Slater, 1968).

The concept of 'leadership,' however, has been an elusive one down through the years. For a long time what was called "trait theory" was in vogue--that is, there was concern about the prospective manager's personal characteristics, ones that presumably made him or her a fine leader. In the 1940s, however, trait theory declined because investigations along this line produced no clear-cut results. Thus, even though this approach had, and still has, some descriptive value, it has been supplanted to a large degree by so-called "situational theory." With this approach it is argued (a) that there are situational factors that can be delineated in a finite way and (b) that they vary according to a number of other factors (Filley, House, & Kerr, 1976). Some of these factors, for example, are (a) the leader's age and experience, (b) the size of the group led, (c) the cultural expectations of subordinates, (d) the time required and allowed for decision-making). Chelladurai (1985), in his discussion of leadership, refers to charismatic leadership and organizational leadership, the latter being "just one of the functions of a manager who is placed in charge of a group and its activities, and is, in turn, guided by superiors and organizational factors" (p. 139).

Even though it has been emphasized that the manager is now faced with a relatively fast-moving social system, a condition from which managers of sport and physical activity cannot (and probably should not wish to) escape, somehow change for us is occurring less rapidly than in certain other segments of society. However, managers must recognize the fact that they have been put on notice about the fluid nature of their particular environments as well. Managers simply must avail themselves of every opportunity to prepare themselves to keep ahead (or at least abreast) of their associates intellectually. This is the major reason why the present data base of completed research available should be continually updated and amplified. This is absolutely necessary because managerial leaders must be ready to meet change head-on. They have to understand when and how to make necessary alterations and modifications so that effective and efficient growth (if desired and/or desirable) and long-term survival will be ensured.

References & Bibliography

Andrews, K. R. (Ed.), *Human relations and administration* (pp. 94-111).
Cambridge, MA: Harvard University Press.

Argyris, C. (1957). *Personality and organization* NY: Harper & Bros.

Baker, J. A. W. & Collins, M .S. (1983). *Research on administration of physical education and athletics 1971-1982: A retrieval system.* Reseda, CA: Mojave.

Barnard, C. I. (1938*). The functions of the executive.* Cambridge, MA: Harvard Univ. Press.

Bedeian, A. G. (1985). Management, historical development of. In L. R. Bittel, & Ramsey, J. E. (Eds.), *Handbook for professional managers* (pp. 491-496). NY: McGraw-Hill.

Bennis, W. & Slater, P. E. (1968). *The temporary society.* New York: Harper & Row.

Bittel, L. R. & Ramsey, J. E. (1985). *Handbook for professional managers.* NY: McGraw-Hill.

Chelladurai, P. (1985). *Sport management.* London, Canada: Sport Dynamics.

Cureton, T. K. (March 1949). Doctorate theses reported by graduate departments of health, physical education and recreation 1930-1946, inclusively. *Research Quarterly*, 20, 21-59.

Drucker, P. F. (1954*). The practice of management.* New York: Harper & Row.

Drucker, P. F. (1993). *Post-capitalist society.* NY: HarperBusiness.

Elliott, R. (1927*). The organization of professional training in physical education in state universities.* New York: Columbia Teachers College.
Encyclopedia of Educational Research, The. (1969). (4th Ed.). NY: Macmillan.

Esslinger, A. A. (1941). Physical education. In *Encyclopedia of Educational Research* (pp. 801-814). NY: Macmillan.

Esslinger, A. A. (1950) Physical education. In *Encyclopedia of Educational Research* (2nd Ed.) (820-835) NY: Macmillan..

Fayol, H.(1949). *General and industrial management.* NY: Pitman.

Filley, A. C., House, R. J. & Kerr, S. (1976). *Managerial process and Organizational behavior.* (2nd Ed.). Glenview, IL: Scott, Foresman.

George, C. S., Jr. (1972). *The history of management thought.* (2nd Ed.). Englewood Cliffs, NJ: Prentice-Hall.

Goodwin, M. (1986). When the cash register is the scoreboard. *The New York Times,* June 8, 27-28.

Gordon, P. J. (Spring 1966). Transcend the current debate on administrative theory. *Hospital Administration*, 11(2), 6-23.

Gross, B. M. (1964). *The managing of organizations.* New York: The Free Press of Glencoe (Macmillan).

Halpin, A. W. (1958). The development of theory in educational administration. In A.W. Halpin (Ed.), *Administrative theory in education.* New York: Macmillan.

Hickman, C. R. & Silva, M. A. (1984). *Creating excellence.* New York: New American Library.

Hodgetts, R. M. (1979). *Management: Theory, process and practice.* (2nd Ed.). Philadelphia: Saunders.

Hower, R. M. (Sept.-Oct. 1953). Final lecture, advanced management program In Katz, R. L. (1974), Skills of an effective administrator. *Harvard Business Review,* 52, 90-112.

Hunter, J. (1971). *An analysis of meanings attached to selected concepts by administrators of the Big Ten Conference and the Central Intercollegiate Athletic Association.* Master's thesis, University of Illinois, C-U.

King, H. A. & Baker, J. A. W. (1982). Conceptualization and bibliography of research in teaching physical education based on theses and dissertations. *Journal of Teaching Physical Education,* 2(1), 63-102.

Koontz, H. (December 1961). The management theory jungle. *Journal of the Academy of Management,* 4(3), 174-188.

Koontz, H. (1985). Management theory, science, and approaches. In L. R. Bittel, & Ramsey, J. E., *Handbook for professional managers* (pp. 506-518). NY: McGraw-Hill.

Luthans, F. & Stewart, T. I. (1977). A general contingency theory of management. *Academy of Management Review,* 182, 190.

McCleary, L. E. & McIntyre, K. (March 1972). Competency development and The methodology of college teaching: A model and proposal. *The Bulletin (NASSP),* 56, 53-59.

McCleary, L. E. (1973). Competency-based educational administration and application to related fields. In *Proceedings of the Conference on Administrative Competence.* Tempe, AZ: Bureau of Educational Research, Arizona State University, 26-38.

Mintzberg, H. (1973). *The nature of managerial work.* NY: Harper & Row.

Montoye, H. & Cunningham, D. (1969). Physical education. In *Encyclopedia of Educational Research* (4th Ed.) (pp. 963-973). NY: Macmillan.

Odiorne, G. S. (1965). *Management by objectives.* New York: Pitman.

Ouchi, W. G. (1981). *Theory Z.* Reading, MA: Addison-Wesley.

Paris, R. (1975). A selected listing of doctoral dissertations in administrative theory and practice related to physical education and sport 1971 to 1978. In *Administrative theory and practice in physical education and athletics* (Appendix). (E.F. Zeigler & M.J. Spaeth, Eds.). Englewood Cliffs, NJ: Prentice-Hall.

Parsons, T. (1958) Some ingredients of a general theory of formal organization. In Halpin, A.W. (Ed.), *Administrative theory in education* (p. 44). New York: Macmillan.

Penny, W. J. (1968). *An analysis of meanings attached to selected concepts in administrative theory.* Doctoral dissertation, University of Illinois, C-U.

Rarick, G. L. (1960). Physical education. In *Encyclopedia of Educational Research* (3rd Ed.) (973-95). NY: Macmillan.

Rosenberg, J. M. (1978). *Dictionary of business and management.* NY: John Wiley.

Rothermel, B. L. (1966). Conversation with the author, Oct. 3.

Snyder, R. A. & Scott, H .A. (1954). *Professional preparation in health, physical education, and recreation*. New York: McGraw-Hill.

Spaeth, M. J. (1967). *An analysis of administrative research in physical education in relation to a research paradigm*. Doctoral dissertation, University of Illinois, C-U.

Tesconi, C. A., Jr. & Morris, V. C. (1972). *The anti-man culture*. Urbana, IL: University of Illinois Press.

Thompson, J. D. (1958). Modern approaches to theory in administration. In Halpin, A.W., *Administrative theory in education*. New York: Macmillan.

Tillett, A. D., Kempner, T., & Wills, G. (1970). *Management thinkers*. Baltimore: Penguin.

Toffler, A. (1970). *Future shock*. New York: Random House.

Toffler, A. (1980). *The third wave*. New York: William Morrow.

VanderZwaag, H. J. (1984). *Sport management in schools and colleges*. NY: John Wiley.

Wren, D. A. (1979). *The evolution of management thouyght*. (2nd Ed.). NY: Wiley.

Zeigler, E .F. (1951). *A history of professional preparation for physical education in the United States, 1861-1948*. Eugene, OR: Microfiche Publications, University of Oregon.

Zeigler, E .F. (1959). *Administration of physical education and athletics: The case method approach*. Englewood Cliffs, NJ: Prentice-Hall.

Zeigler, E. F. & McCristal, K .J. (December 1967). A history of the Big Ten Body-of-Knowledge Project. *Quest*, 9, 28-41.

Zeigler, E. F. (1972). A model for optimum professional development in a field called "X." In *Proceedings of the First Canadian Symposium on the Philosophy of Sport and Physical Activity*. Ottawa, Canada: Sport Canada Directorate, pp. 16-28.

Zeigler, E. F. & Spaeth, M. J. (1973). A selected bibliography of completed research on administrative theory and practice in physical education and athletics. In *Proceedings of the Big Ten Symposium on Administrative Theory and Practice*, Ann Arbor, MI, pp. 143-153.

Zeigler, E. F., Spaeth, M. J. & Paton, G. A. (1975). Theory and research in the administration of physical education. In Zeigler, E.F. & Spaeth, M.J., *Administrative theory and practice in physical education and athletics*. Englewood Cliffs, NJ: Prentice-Hall.

Zeigler, E. F. & Spaeth, M. J. (Eds.). (1975). *Administrative theory and practice in physical education and athletics*. Englewood Cliffs, NJ: Prentice-Hall.

Zeigler, E. F. & Campbell, J. (1984). *Strategic market planning: An aid to the evaluation of an athletic/recreation program*. Champaign, IL: Stipes.

Zeigler, E .F. & Bowie, G. W. (2007). *Management competency development in sport and physical education*. Victoria, BC, Canada: Trafford.

Zoffer, H. J. (1985). Training managers to take charge. In Business (Section 3, 2), *The New York Times*, Oct. 20.

Selection #7
Balancing Life's Conflicting Aspects:
A Challenge for the
Sport & Physical Activity Administrator

(Author's Note: This background essay is intended to be synoptic in nature. It represents an evolving version of many of the ideas, opinions, and recommendations expressed by the author about management theory and practice as applied to physical education and sport in a variety of publications over a period of approximately 60years. Prior to a collaborative effort with Gary Bowie (Lethbridge) designed to introduce a management competency development approach to professional preparation in physical education and educational sport, the author had collaborated earlier, also, with Marcia Spaeth (retired from SUNY, Cortland) and Garth Paton and Terry Haggerty (now both at New Brunswick, but earlier at Western Ontario). Some of this material (i.e., that related to proposed areas of administrative research and that related to the professional preparation program) had been researched by Professor Spaeth and Professor Paton, respectively and appeared in Zeigler and Spaeth [1975]). Analysis has shown that there are now well over 200 names to describe the educational units in which we function at the college and university level. Fortunately, the "name situation" has been quite a bit better at the elementary and secondary levels of the education system. In the mid-1990s, the author found that the term "physical education and sport" was the term most used in the world today (Zeigler, 1994, p. 50). Since the mid-1980s, the term "kinesiology" has made significant progress at the university level in North America. (My personal position is that "physical activity education" would be an appropriate name for our professional endeavors, but I personally believe, also, that "developmental physical activity" would be an excellent accompanying title for our disciplinary component at the university level. See Zeigler, 2003a and 2003b.)The world marches on. We simply can't allow ourselves to spend too much time and effort on the question of what the field should be called. Nevertheless, it is extremely important to us ultimately because it defines what we do. So I would urge you to keep this subject firmly in mind as you strive to move the field ahead in the 21st century.)

In this essay I hope to bring this dilemma down to the personal level in an effort to get you, the reader, to figure out--unless you are absolutely certain where you stand on the matter already–whether or where you are going in the years ahead in a field that is so uncertain as well. Nevertheless, translating the disciplinary theory of "kinesiology" into generalizations about professional practice in physical activity education is fundamentally important to our society. The lives of people of all ages and conditions can be affected positively if this aim is carried out efficiently and effectively. Our task in the field today is to discover a host of young Canadians who will "make things happen" so that the field of developmental physical activity will prosper and thereby fulfill the potential for humankind that it inherently offers.

The purpose of this analysis was to develop a means whereby a sport and physical activity administrator (e.g., of physical education and educational sport1) might better comprehend the need to balance life's "conflicting aspects."2 These conflicting aspects are typically the broadening of one's professional vision while simultaneously seeking to maintain perspective as to his or her chosen aims and objectives in life. It was decided to employ a systems analysis approach to help explain what can be called "human and natural (or physical) ecologic interaction." The main problem of the study was first divided into five sub-problems (phrased as questions) for subsequent investigation:

1. Why should a physical activity administrator understand the various ramifications of ecology for humankind?

2. How can systems analysis coordinated with "human and natural ecologic interaction" apply to the *organizational* task? of such an administrator?

3. How can systems analysis coordinated with human and natural ecological interaction apply to the *personal* development of this administrator?

4. How can the two approaches be merged to achieve both *successful professional* life and a *fulfilling personal* life?

5. What may be reasonably concluded from this discussion?

Problem #1:
Why Should A Physical Activity Administrator Understand the Ramifications of Ecology for Humankind?

124

For this analysis, ecology was defined as "the field of study that treats the relationships and interactions of human beings and other living organisms with each other and with their natural (or physical) environment" (Hawley, 1986, p. 2). Ecology, which is much more than so-called "environmentalism," is about truly understanding relationships with and/or interactions between humans and other organisms within the environment. This involvement has no doubt been with humankind over the centuries. In addition, the apparent continuing lack of understanding and full appreciation of it by leaders, not to mention almost all others, has still not been overcome. Further, the steadily increasing size of the world's population and the accompanying vast societal development has exacerbated the problem even further.

To put the matter more simply, the basic underlying issue of dwindling supply and increasing demand has never been brought home sufficiently to the world's leadership, much less to the majority of the people. And, in the relatively few cases where it has, urgent *present* need has almost invariably thrust the need for preparation to meet impending *future* disasters aside. In fact, that appears to be exactly what is happening at this very time.

Despite the ever-increasing importance of this subject to humankind, somehow the vital importance of the subject of ecology as a *fundamental social institution* such as economics, politics, etc. did not begin to receive serious attention by at least a segment of society until the early 1960s.

Today, however, selected countries and certain groups within these countries are striving to come to grips with the need to face up to the headlong collision looming between ecology and economics as conflicting social forces. For example, Epstein (1997) reported that "five years after 10,000 diplomats from 178 countries pledged to clean up the world at the United Nations-sponsored Rio Earth Summit, the first formal assessment of that pledge begins today" (March 13). At the same session, Maurice Strong, the 1992 conference chair, stated that "the process of deterioration has continued…"

Since 1970, many educators have gradually come to understand that the problem of ecology was here to stay. Zeigler (1989; 2003), for example, designated it as a persistent problem faced by the field of sport and physical education in the same way as he had identified the five other basic social forces (or influences) of values, politics, nationalism, economics, and religion back in 1964. No longer, as it had almost always been possible in the past, could people simply move elsewhere to locate another abundant supply of game to hunt, water to drink, or mineral resources to exploit when on-site resources are depleted. Today, as this problem is gradually being recognized globally with seemingly little response, the time is past due for the profession of physical education and sport to also pay special attention to this social force in the various aspects of its work.

More specifically, there are several very important reasons right now for the field to show ever-greater awareness of *human ecologic interaction* with its many ramifications for humankind. First, the promotion and subsequent development of such an awareness could soon result in the field's general acceptance of an overall human and natural (physical) ecologic orientation that could be designed to underlie all of its professional efforts. Such awareness and subsequent orientation would call the profession's attention to the fact that our basic concern as part-time and full-time administrators should be with the *total* life cycle of people considered both individually and collectively.

Second, the graduates of professional education programs, who subsequently serve as administrators or managers in organizations of all types functioning in culturally influenced environments, need to be so prepared they will understand and then commit themselves to the application of an overall ecological approach in their work. In this context this means that they, as professional managers serving as administrators, have a basic responsibility to develop and strengthen their particular institution or organization in which they serve so that it will have an ongoing capability *to adapt successfully to the changing (natural and cultural) environment in which it is located.*

They need to keep in mind that fundamental changes in society are continually taking place, and that they are accordingly influencing professionals in their administrative endeavor positively, negatively, or possibly not at all. This means that, at the practitioner's level, they should be (must be?) ever ready to meet such change (or lack of it) directly and adapt to it successfully if and when it occurs. For example, there appears to be an ever-present need to understand "cutback management" (or "management in decline," as it is often called. This, and other approaches are often called on in today's rapidly shifting environment. Another very important understanding that can serve all administrators well is a reasonably basic comprehension of change process itself, a development that is ever present and requires the ongoing attention of the administrator.

Problem No. 2:
How Can Systems Analysis,
Coordinated with Human and Natural Ecologic Interaction,
Apply to the *Organizational* Task of the Administrator??

The scope of the systems function in management today has gone far beyond the dreams of the "scientific management" pioneers such as Taylor, the Gilbreths, and Henri Fayol. Today the sport management profession should be fully aware of the potentialities of an ongoing systems analysis approach. Such an approach should be *coordinated with* the best type of overall human and natural (physical) ecologic interaction as the profession seeks to serve the public professionally through the medium of sport and physical activity. Concurrently, in this analysis of the *professional* function (i.e., organizational "task") of the manager, the same systems-approach concept can be merged with overall human ecologic interaction as applied to the sport manager's *personal* development.

The first consideration here is with the intricacies of a systems approach that give attention to *how* this can be done most efficiently. The assumption behind a systems approach to human and natural ecologic interaction is that the physical activity-delivery organization and its administrator(s)--and the people functioning within it as associates--should all understand the importance and ramifications of a complete ecological approach and be committed to its implementation in all aspects of their work. If this were understood fully, they would then strive to serve their clients and constituents in ways that help the organization grow and develop. (At this point there will not be an explanation of *why* the administrator should strive for *general* aims in an ever-changing human and natural environment, or *what* specific objectives might be subsumed under these long range aims.)

With such an approach to management, the managerial team and key associated personnel would seek to develop, employ, and maintain power and influence that lead to the achievement of planned (immediate) objectives en route to long-range aims or goals. In doing so, they should involve many people within the organization in one way or another in assisting with the implementation of the well-recognized, fundamental processes of planning, organizing, staffing, directing, and controlling the operation of the organization (Mackenzie, 1969, pp. 80-87). Throughout this series of experiences it is imperative that good human relations be employed by all through the use of effective and efficient communication techniques. The successful implementation of these various processes is extremely complex, of course. This is why a top-flight managerial team is becoming increasingly necessary to move a complex organization ahead.

The major responsibilities of physical activity administrators (in physical education and sport), presuming they live up a code of ethics, should include:

> (1) the professional's obligations to
>   provide services to all in society who
>   want and need them;
>
> (2) the professional's specific obligations
>   to his/her students/clients as
>   individuals;
>
> (3) the professional's responsibilities to
>   his/her employers/employing
>   organization;
>
> (4) the professional's obligations to his
>   colleagues/peers and to the
>   profession; and
>
> (5) the professional's responsibility to
>   overall society itself (as recommended

Figure 1
A Systems Model for Managerial Effectiveness
in a Professional Training Program in Physical Activity Education

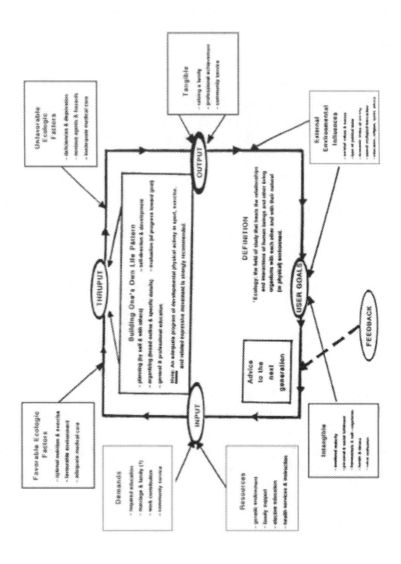

by Bayles in (Zeigler, 1992, pp. 13-14).

All of these obligations should be deliberately included in a code of ethics along with a procedure for disciplinary action to guarantee the enforcement of these responsibilities. (The latter procedure rarely been enforced in any profession to date--with notable exceptions [e.g., medicine, law, psychology]. Several professions have at least made some effort to discipline those colleagues who are reported as having acted unprofessionally and unethically. If a professional acts *illegally* within a given legal jurisdiction, it can, of course, be expected that the political jurisdiction itself will judge the severity of such action and make an appropriate decision. Such a decision will subsequently give guidance to a professional society's committee on ethics as to any disciplinary action it should take.)

To meet these professional obligations, the physical activity administrator will be involved both professionally and personally in an ongoing struggle for recognition and accompanying status as he/she fulfills (1) those important obligations that relate to his/her *professional* life, as well as (2) those obligations that are required for optimum *personal* development. Moving on, it will now be considered first how a schematic, systems-analysis model could assist the manager to comprehend fully the scope and intent of these obligations and/or responsibilities in both "realms" of his or her existence.

A Schematic Model for the Administrative Process That Embodies a Systems Approach

A generation ago a schematic model for the management process was developed (the elements of the set, so to speak) that arranged the elements of a systems approach logically within a behavioral science perspective (Milstein and Belasco, 1973). The concern was with *input, thruput,* and *output,* and it was stressed that these three aspects must be strongly interrelated because any systems outputs "that result from transforming the human and material resources within the educational system must be at least minimally acceptable to environmental groups and organizations" (p. 81). If the outputs are not acceptable, the external groups and organizations will quite simply let it be known in short order that the "lifeline" of human and material resources will be sharply cut or eliminated.

A schematic model of such a systems model is offered here, in this case a systems model for managerial effectiveness with a professional training program for physical activity administrators. Here the goal or output for the purpose of this discussion is related to the education of people for various careers relating to our field. It is a substantive adaptation of the material available in both Milstein and Belasco (1973) and George (1972). (See Figure 1 above.)

Figure 2

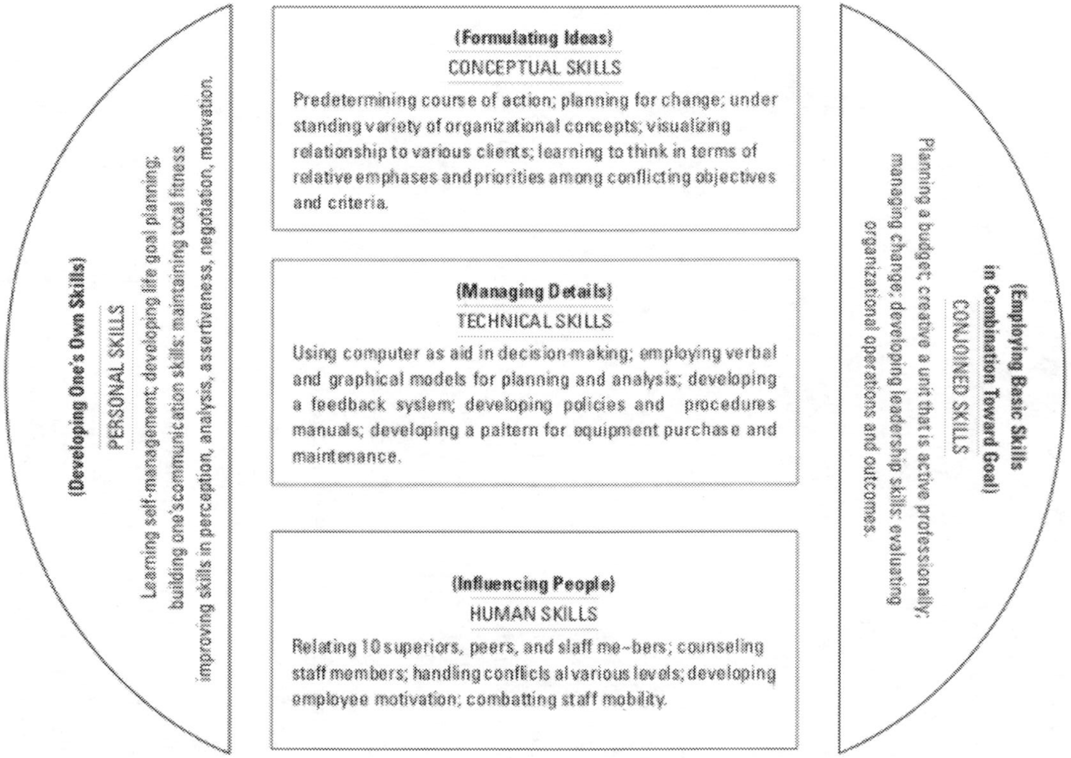

(Employing Basic Skills
in Combination Toward Goal)

CONJOINED SKILLS

Planning a budget; creative a unit that is active professionally;
managing change; developing leadership skills: evaluating
organizational operations and outcomes.

(Formulating Ideas)
CONCEPTUAL SKILLS

Predetermining course of action; planning for change; under
standing variety of organizational concepts; visualizing
relationship to various clients; learning to think in terms of
relative emphases and priorities among conflicting objectives
and criteria.

(Managing Details)
TECHNICAL SKILLS

Using computer as aid in decision-making; employing verbal
and graphical models for planning and analysis; developing
a feedback system; developing policies and procedures
manuals; developing a pattern for equipment purchase and
maintenance.

(Influencing People)
HUMAN SKILLS

Relating 10 superiors, peers, and staff me=bers; counseling
staff members; handing conflicts al various levels; developing
employee motivation; combatting staff mobility.

(Developing One's Own Skills)

PERSONAL SKILLS

Learning self-management; developing life goal planning;
building one'scommunication skills; maintaining total fitness
improving skills in perception, analysis, negotiation, motivation.

The names of three of the categories were taken from Katz, M. L: Skills of an effective administrator Harvard Business Review 52 % 90-102, 1974

Management Development and Process (The knowledge and skills obtained through a competency-based approach).

One definition of administration states that it involves the execution of managerial acts by a competent person, including the application of personal, interpersonal, conceptual, technical, and conjoined skills, while combining varying degrees of planning, organizing, staffing, directing (i.e., leading), and controlling (i.e., evaluation) within the management process to assist an organization to achieve its goals effectively and efficiently (Zeigler and Bowie, 1995, p. 115).

Further, the assumption is that such managerial acts will be directed toward individual and group goals within both the internal and external environments of an organization. In this example (Fig. 1), those directing the professional preparation program within a college or university perceive certain societal demands and/or needs (e.g., a societal demand for various types of physical activity administrators). Depending on the specific circumstance, the university and its alumni and supporters respond by making available (initially or potentially) (1) material and human resources such as available capital, (2) some level of achievement in sport competition and fitness promotion, and (3) a management program staff of good, bad, or indifferent stature. All of this initial development is, of course, ultimately part of the total administrative process itself. After the initial input stage has been started, we are really describing functions that occur within the larger management process that is typically characterized by such terms as planning, organizing, staffing, directing, and controlling (Mackenzie, 1969). For the administrator to execute these functions adequately, he or she should have acquired the necessary knowledge, competencies and skills (adapted from Katz, 1974, with advice from William Penny).

Thinking of the total administrative or managerial process in this example of a system analysis model for maximum effectiveness, keep in mind that there can be three categories of parameters and/or variables that influence the entire undertaking, as follows: (1) environmental *non controllable* parameters (constraints *or* opportunities), (2) internal *controllable* variables, and (3) *partially controllable* variables (that may be external and/or internal). It is important that physical activity administrators understand how strong these variables (influences) may be and accordingly be ever ready to factor their impact into the overall administrative process. Too often it appears that when such a non controllable or partially controllable parameter looms suddenly on the horizon, "internal panic" results because administrators--and thus their organizations, of course--have not planned ahead and typically are *in no way* ready for its appearance.

The environmental *non–controllable* parameters should be viewed as external influences that must be considered seriously. They are such persistent historical problems as (1) the influence of the society's values and norms; (2) the influence of politics (the type of political state and the "stance" of the party or person in power); (3) the influence of nationalism (or whatever powerful "chauvinistic" influence might develop); (4) the influence of the prevailing economic situation (including depressions, tax increases, inflation, etc.); (5) the influence of prevailing religious groups (including boycotts, conflicting events); (6)

the influence of ecology (as discussed above in this paper); and (7) the influence of competition (from other attractions, etc.).

To understand the concept of "administrative effectiveness" generally, as diagrammed in the model (Figure 1), it is necessary to consider specifically the relationship of managerial acts (ACTS) and the external and internal environments (Ee and Ei, respectively) of the organization to the eventual accomplishment of *at least a certain percentage* of the organization's goals (pGg) as well as *at least a certain percentage* of the (total of) individual's goals (pGi) realized.

In other words, an effective administrator would be a person who strives successfully to accomplish the organization's goals to the greatest possible extent, while at the same time giving adequate or ample consideration to what percentage of the goals held by individual employees is achieved. At this point, then, the concept of managerial effectiveness (Me) is added to our ongoing equation as that percentage (p) of the organization's and the (total of) individuals' goals that are realized.

> (Note: Initially, the percentage of an individual's goals achieved would be a collective percentage; however, where individual goal achievement exists with a differentiated reward system and a varying pay scale exists, the effectiveness of any one person could be evaluated as well.)

Thus

$$Me = (pGg) + (pGi)$$

Similarly, if we accept that managerial acts (Aplanning, Aorganizing, Astaffing, etc.) are a function of a percentage (% of the attainment of) of Gg and Gi, then

$$M = F (<pGg + (pGi>)$$

Further, if G (Gg + Gi) is known, it follows that Gi) is a function of it.

> (**Note**: For those interested, a much more detailed analysis of this mathematical model seeking to explain the administrative process is available in Zeigler and Bowie, 1995, pp. 115-120.)

Problem #3:
How Can Systems Analysis,
Coordinated with Human and Natural Ecologic Interaction,
Apply to the *Personal* Development of the Administrator?

But what of *the individual* who is involved professionally in the managerial task itself--i.e., the first-level, second-level, etc. administrator? Adoption of this approach mandates that this person should have regular opportunities for *both*

Figure 3

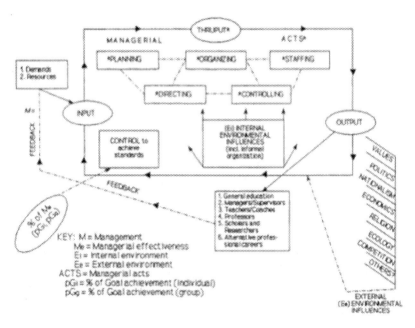

A System Analysis Model for Managerial Effectiveness
in a Professional Preparation Program for
Development Physical Activity Administrators

personal and professional growth. This can be accomplished by implementing a similar plan for the administrator, also, one that outlines a system analysis of the administrator's own human ecologic interaction as he or she strives *to achieve a life purpose in this profession* while concurrently serving the organization's clientele and the larger community.

If this is to be carried out successfully, such a plan should also be based on a model that includes (1) *input* factors such as demands and resources; (2) *thruput* factors such as planning, evaluation, general & professional education, and evaluation; (3) tangible *output* factors such as (possibly) raising a family, professional achievement, and community service, and (4) intangible *user goals'* factors such as emotional maturity, personal and social fulfillment, homeostasis and self-regulation, health & fitness, and personal & social value realization.

Basically, the discussion at this point outlines how physical activity administrators can use a systems analysis approach to achieve optimal health (so-called wellness) for an effective personal and professional life within a reasonably balanced lifestyle. The idea of achieving optimal health within one's lifestyle has been equated with, and compressed in recent years by many to, the concept of "wellness":

> Wellness can be described as a lifestyle designed to reach
> one's highest potential for wholeness and wellbeing.
> Wellness has to do with a zest for living, feeling good
> about oneself, having goals and purposes for life . . . This
> concept is far more than freedom from symptoms of
> illness and basic health maintenance, but reaches beyond
> to an optimal level of well-being (*ERIC Digest* 3, 1986).

These thoughts and ideas are really not new, but they have been placed in a more modern perspective here. Many years ago Jesse Feiring Williams defined positive health as "the ability to live best and serve most." The wellness movement has similarly recommended a balanced lifestyle. It has encouraged people to assume more responsibility for their health and to view health in the same light as Williams did earlier--that is, in a positive light in which the person's "wellness" involved all aspects of a unified organism.

In this light, at the input stage the physical education and sport administrator will typically acquire a better understanding of the *demands* (e.g., required education) made upon him or her, as well as an understanding of the *resources* (e.g., genetic endowment) necessary for a satisfactory response. (See the left section of Figure 3.)

Next, at what is called the thruput stage, the manager will appreciate more fully what steps should be taken as the individual plans, organizes, and carries out life plans. At this stage these steps should be carried out optimally through self-direction with evaluation at several strategic points along the way. (See the middle section toward the top of Figure 3.)

While all of this is taking place, there are a number of external, natural and social environmental influences impinging upon the manager's development (e.g., changing societal values, declining economic status; see bottom right of Figure 3.) An administrator may have control over some of these influences, but others are often beyond control. These include both favorable and unfavorable ecologic factors. (See top right and left of Figure 3.) In the final analysis, the administrator must make a number of crucial decisions throughout life. Such decisions may be made before the fact, so to speak, while others are made as best possible in response to natural and social factors that may often be completely or partially beyond the manager's ability to control them.

In the third or output stage of an administrator's life viewed through a system analysis perspective, the manager will be asked to consider what she or he wants both her/his extrinsic, measurable and her/his intrinsic, non-measurable life goals to be. The administrator will need also to seek some sort of relationship between these measurable goals and what may be called intrinsic (i.e., typically less measurable life goals).

(**Note**: See "tangible" output at right
of Figure 3 and "intangible" output
stated as "user goals" at the bottom
left of Figure 3.)

In the first case, the tangible output, this refers to the person's achievement in his or her chosen career or occupation, as well as family life (however defined) and community service. In the second instance, he or she will need to assess the matter of achievement of personal and social fulfillment through the possible self-realization of those values that are felt to be most important.

(**Note:** A more detailed outline of this
analysis of a desirable life cycle is
offered below in the Appendix.)

Finally, toward the end of this system loop, provision should be made for feedback resulting in advice to the next generation. This lifelong process for the individual is typically influenced by (1) such *external environmental influences* as (e.g.) the economic status of the society; (2) such favorable ecologic factors as (e.g.) adequate medical care; and (3) such unfavorable ecologic factors as (e.g.) the presence of noxious agents & hazards.

Problem No. 4:
How Can the Two Approaches Be Merged
to Achieve Both Successful *Professional* Lives and
Personally Fulfilling Lives?

Turning attention away from self-management (i.e., the personal life pattern of the individual physical activity administrator) and back to the overall organizational administrative task itself, it becomes apparent that these two managerial techniques can be merged successfully. Whether these techniques will be in any particular organization involved with the administration of sport and physical activity depends on the overall administrative philosophy prevailing. On the surface an ecological orientation merged with a systems analysis approach to management would almost necessarily result in an "organizational management climate" that is eclectic in nature.

An "eclectic" administrative style may be needed because of the increasing number of situations today where a managerial team is responsible for the direction in which the organization is heading. This means that it may include, where possible and when desirable, any or all aspects of the traditional, behavioral, or decision-making patterns of administrative behavior. Thus administrators may find themselves functioning with an amalgam of traditional principles, cooperative behavioralist ideas, and decisionalist competitive strategies (Gibson, Ivancevich, and Donnelly, 1997, pp. 433-439).

Problem No. 5:
What May Be Concluded from this Discussion?

In the twenty-first century, such an "amalgamated" approach to professional *and* personal management behavior as discussed here may indeed become both necessary and desirable. This would be true so long as the original formulation of aims and objectives has occurred democratically. And, as it has happened, in Western culture people have been increasingly involved in the decision-making process in all aspects of life. As a result, an organization that fails to prepare its people adequately (i.e., both theoretically and emotionally) for the introduction of change could well find its seemingly realizable goals to be thwarted--or at least temporarily blocked--by (1) human conflicts, (2) natural or cultural barriers within the general (external), or (3) changing interpersonal and/or situational circumstances within the immediate (internal) environment (Mikalachki, A., Zeigler, E.F., & Leyshon, G.A., 1988, pp. 1-17).

In respect to the organization itself and its achievement of predetermined group and individual goals, it should be borne in mind that such organizational "growth" does not necessarily mean growth in size. This is especially important where an "ecological-oriented" business strategy has been adopted on the basis of an overall philosophical stance. It does mean that the adaptive behavior of those involved in the administrative task who (1) subscribe to an "ecological orientation" philosophically and (2) employ a systems approach functionally should be in a strong position to help the organization to remain viable, to be stronger, to remain competitive, and to be increasingly more effective and efficient in the accomplishment of its long range aims and immediately realizable objectives.

Finally, similar problems or obstacles of varying nature and intensity may arise within the broader general (external) environment. Of course, the hope is that such situations would serve as challenges to physical activity administrators and their teams. The response to problems or obstacles should be heuristic in nature in the sense that a particular management team would be prepared to react to the prevailing demands and needs by adapting or possible adjusting means, behavior, and even ends at some point along the line. Developmental physical activity administrators should proceed only on the basis that the future belongs to those who manage effectively and efficiently in the pursuit of planned organizational goals.

Note

1. Actually, the term "developmental physical activity" is recommended now for consideration as a disciplinary name for the field. It seems appropriate for the field, but may be too long to ever be accepted. What the field is all about, however, is really *developmental* physical activity in exercise, sport, and related expressive activities, but it would take a large office door to hold all of those words together on it! In this instance it was meant to cover those men and women who will be serving--to a greater or lesser extent--as *administrators* in physical (activity)

education, intramurals & physical recreation, or inter-institutional athletics (or some combination thereof).

References

Bayles, M.D. (1981). *Professional Ethics*. Belmont, CA: Wadsworth.

Epstein, J. (1997). Rio Summit's promises still unfulfilled. *The Globe and Mail* (Toronto), March 13, A12.

George, C.S. (1972). *The history of management thought (2nd Ed.)*. Englewood Cliffs, NJ: Prentice-Hall.

Gibson, J.I., Ivancevich, J.M., & Donnelly, J.H., Jr. (1997). *Organizations (9th Ed.)*. Chicago, IL: Irwin.

Hawley, A.H. (1986). *Human ecology: A theoretical essay*. Chicago: Univ. of Chicago Press.

Katz, R.L. (Sept.-Oct. 1974). Skills of an effective administrator. *Harvard Business Review*, **51**, 5:90-112.

Mackenzie, R.A. (1969). The management process in 3-D. *Harvard Education Review*, **47**: 80-87.

Mikalachki, A,, Zeigler, E.F., & Leyshon, G.A. (1988). *Change process in sport and physical education management*. Champaign, IL: Stipes.

Milstein, M.M. & Belasco, J.A. (1973). *Educational administration and the behavioral sciences: A systems perspective*. Boston: Allyn.

Prevention (July 1988). High health in the middle years. **40**: 7: 35-36, 38-47, 100, 105-107, 110.

Zeigler, E.F. (1964). *Philosophical foundations for physical, health, and recreation education*. Englewood Cliffs, NJ: Prentice-Hall.

Zeigler, E.F. (1989). *An introduction to sport and physical philosophy*. Carmel, IN: Benchmark Press.

Zeigler, E.F. (1992). *Professional ethics for sport managers*. Champaign, IL: Stipes.

Zeigler, E. F. (2003). Socio-Cultural Foundations of Physical Education and Educational Sport. Aachen, Germany: Meyer and Meyer.

Zeigler, E.F. & Bowie, G.W. (2007) *Management competency development in sport and physical education*. Victoria, BC: Trafford.

APPENDIX

EMPLOYING THE INGREDIENTS OF A SYSTEMS ANALYSIS APPROACH, COORDINATED WITH HUMAN AND NATURAL ECOLOGIC INTERACTION, IN A QUEST FOR OPTIMAL HEALTH AND EFFECTIVE LIVING

INPUT Stage A: What *Demands* Are Made on a Person
in Today's World?

1. Early Family Membership
2. Education
3. Marriage & Family
4. Work Contribution
5. Community Service

INPUT Stage B: What *Resources* Are Typically Provided?

1. Early Family Support
2. Educational Opportunities
3. External Social Influences
4. Employment Opportunities
5. Health & Community Services

THRUPUT Stage A: What *Steps* Should Be Taken in Developing
One's Own Life As Fully As Possible?

1. Planning for the Long Haul Ahead
2. Organizing the Required Factors & Details
3. Implementing Life Stages Through Self-Direction
4. Evaluation of Progress Made in Goal Achievement
5. Modifying or Redirecting One's Developmental Pattern
6. Planning for Retirement

THRUPUT Stage B: What *External Environmental Factors*
Might Be Encountered?

1. Favorable Ecologic Factors:

a. Good Heredity; No Disabling Disease
b. Healthy Environment; No Debilitating Factors
c. Safe Living; No Careless Risk
d. Optimal Nutrition, Exercise, & Rest
e. Challenges; Satisfying Work & Recreation
f. Commitment to High Values

g. Competent Medical & Dental Care
h. Homeostasis & Self-Regulation; Emotional Maturity
i. Personal & Social Fulfillment; Freedom & Privacy

2. Unfavorable Ecologic Factors

a. Poor Heredity; Disabling Disease
b. Unhealthy Environment; Noxious Agents & Hazards
c. Unsafe Living; Careless Risk
d. Inadequate Nutrition, Exercise, & Rest
e. Little Challenge; Unrewarding Work & Recreation
f. Lack of Commitment to High Values
g. Inadequate Medical & Dental Care
h. Deprivation; Excesses; Immaturity
i. Low Level of Achievement & Personal Fulfillment;
   Restraints & Overcrowding

3. Improved Health in the Middle Years (40-49)

a. Assessment of nutritional intake
(including reasonable coffee intake, compensating
for "metabolic slowdown"; watch amounts of alcohol,
desserts, and fat consumed; pare diet down &
exercise)

b. Body conditioning
(work with weights; stretch; watch for "middle-age
spread"; strive for consistency, not intensity;
exercise will burn off fat)

c. Circulo-respiratory conditioning
(regular, moderate exercise within "threshold zone"
will keep heart healthy--serves to lower high blood
pressure and blood cholesterol)

d. Contraception
(continue birth-control methods for one year post-
menstrually; barrier contraceptives still recommended
for middle years; check new methods available carefully; consider clip sterilization)

e. Good sex
(sexual interest peaks for women in late 30's or
early 40's; males better lovers at this stage;
communication of feelings; stay healthy; maintain
strength of PC and/or vaginal muscles; vaginal
lubricants; remain active sexually; women may

consider HRT.

f. Healthy relationships
(beware of burnout and boredom; involvement in shared
tasks and interests; cultivation of friends)

g. Job transition
(change positions only for the right reasons; be more
concerned about fulfilling needs and interests than
before building size of bank account or stock
holdings; your age is biggest asset; experience
brings ability to solve practical problems)

h. Brainpower
(stay mentally active and even work for improvement;
try not to act your age; limit TV viewing time;
strive to be productive creatively; boost memory
power and pay attention.

(Note: This section above is based on "High Health
in the Middle Years, *Prevention,* July 1988).

OUTPUT Stage A: Tangible (Extrinsic) Life Accomplishments

1. A Family Raised Successfully
2. Achievement in Chosen Career
3. Record of Community Service
4. Plan Developed for Successful Retirement

OUTPUT Stage B: Intangible (Intrinsic) Life Accomplishments

1. Personal & Social Fulfillment
   through Value Realization
2. System Feedback: Advice to the Next Generation

THE OVERALL GOAL: Optimal Health, Effective Living,
                  and Personal & Social Fulfillment

Selection #8
Sport Management Must Show Social Concern As It Develops Tenable Theory

An epoch in civilization approaches closure when many of the fundamental convictions of its advocates are challenged by a substantive minority of the populace. It can be argued that indeed the world is moving into a new epoch as the proponents of postmodernism have been affirming over recent decades. Within such a milieu there are indications that the sport management profession is going to have great difficulty crossing this chasm, this so-called, postmodern divide (Zeigler, 2003, p. 93).

Sport, along with all other social institutions (e.g., religion, politics, economics) is confronted with the need to demonstrate its value and its responsibility in providing a true public service. Sport managers should understand what sport's *true* status is, and how and why such standing occurred. Difficult decisions, often ethical in nature, will have to be made in the years ahead as the members of the sport management societies worldwide strive to continue the development of this profession/discipline.

Professional sport managers should decide to what extent they wish to live up to the broad ideals of the programs being promoted by public, semipublic, or private agencies for all types of people of all ages. Those involved with professional preparation and scholarly endeavor urgently need a theory and a disciplinary model to place professional preparation for administrative or managerial leadership within the field on a gradually improving, sound academic basis. Practitioners need an online service that provides them with scholarly applied findings as they seek to serve in the behaviorally oriented environment of today's world.

Nevertheless, regardless of the concerns I have expressed above, there is no question but that sport has become recognized as one of humankind's fundamental social institutions. However, I believe that there are now strong indications that sport's presumed overall recreational, educational, and entertainment role in the "adventure of civilization" is not being fulfilled adequately. Municipal recreation programs, private sport clubs, and school sport programs are "doing the best that they can" often with limited funding. At the same time the commercialized sport establishment gets almost all of the media attention and is prospering as never before. Thus, an intelligent, concerned citizen can reasonably ask, "What evidence do we have that sport as a social institution is really making a positive contribution to society?" I find myself forced to ask this question: "Is commercially organized sport actually "talking a much better game than it plays." Where or what is sport management's tenable theory? Recalling the well-known fairy tale. I find that I must declare--not that "the king doesn't have any clothes on"–but that "The king should prove (to society) that he is sufficiently clothed to justify our continuing support."

The sport industry is obviously "charging ahead" driven by capitalistic economic theory that overemphasizes ever-increasing gate receipts with an accompanying corollary of winning fueled somehow by related violence. One of the "principal principles" of physical education espoused in the early 1950s by Dr. Arthur Steinhaus (George Williams College) was that "sport was made for man, not man for sport"(1952). This principle of his credo is being countermanded day by day, week by week at all levels around the world. Interestingly, but disturbingly however, a societal majority seems to lend support to this surge in the popularity of professionalized competitive sport. The athletes--those happy people on the way to the bank who welcome being used as commodities as their bank accounts prosper--typically don't understand what is happening. They don't even recognize this as a problem. Neither do many (most?) aspiring sport management students in professional programs.

Everything considered, I am therefore forced to ask, "What are we helping to promote--we who have associated ourselves with sport management--and exactly why are we doing it?" I fear that we are simply going along with the seemingly inevitable tide. In the process we have become pawns to the prevailing sport establishment by "riding the wrong horse." Our present responsibility--to the extent that we are educators and scholars--should be to devote our efforts to provide sport management with tenable theory. This tenable theory should relate to sport and physical activity involvement for all people of all ages in society be they normal, accelerated, or special in status.

Governmental agencies sponsoring "amateur" sport competition should be able to state in their relationship to sport that: if "such-and-such" is done with reasonable efficiency and effectiveness through the sponsorship of sporting activities, then "such-and-such" will (in all probability) result. Personnel in these same agencies are striving to do just this, but not necessarily in an acceptable way consonant with overall societal values. Instead of working assiduously for a "from-the-ground-up" development of young athletes in the hope that they would achieve relatively superior status eventually, they are proceeding in what might be called a fast-track approach. By that I mean that governments are focusing primarily on the recruitment and development of potentially elite athletes who somehow come to their attention, athletes whom they hope will bring fame and glory to their country. So, again, I ask, where is the evidence that organized sport's goal is based on tenable theory consonant with societal values that claim to promote the welfare of all?

I am heartened, however, by a number of publications in the *Journal of Sport Management* that discuss future directions in research. Frisby's E. F. Zeigler Lecture (2005) , in referring to "The Good, The Bad, and The Ugly" strikes just the right note in her conclusion by urging a broadened outlook for sport management. Next Costa's study (2005) using Delphi technique provided excellent discussion based on the opinions of leaders in the field as to future directions. Concern was expressed about the ability to achieve the goals outlined (e.g., additional cross-discipline research) within our own discipline. Then, the entire "Expanding Horizons" issue offered interesting insights and approaches about research for consideration (2005). Finally, Chalip's analysis in his 2005 EFZ Lecture titled "Toward a distinctive sport management discipline," points us toward the achievement of "distinctive relevance" for our field. (This idea of a distinctive approach for a sport-management model strikes a resounding chord with me. Below I will seek to add a bit to the profession's consideration of this problem.)

Fortunately, also, there is a growing minority within the populace that supports a more humanistic position that accepts the steadily mounting evidence that all people--not just elite athletes striving for personal fulfillment and fame-- need to be active in physical recreational activities throughout their entire lives. This leads me to inquire as to what role the professional sport management societies worldwide should play in the guidance of its members toward this end. Hopefully these men and women, serving as qualified professionals seeking the achievement of their society's most desirable values, will increasingly be in a position to assist sport and related physical activity to serve all people in our world society in the best possible way.

Before such a dream can become a reality, however, we need to dig deeply in our respective "cultural psyches" to begin to understand how society got itself in the presently questionable situation. Until at least the majority of people in our world's culture understand what has happened, what should be done, and what can be done, there is little hope for improvement in what I believe to be an increasingly untenable situation.

In retrospect, the 18th century in the Western world witnessed revolutionary thought that had caused it now to be known as the Age of Reason (or "enlightenment"). This outlook was based on ideals of truth, freedom, and reason for all humans. In the United States, however, the Enlightenment vision of Thomas Jefferson that promised political and social liberation was somehow "turned upside down." What happened in American life in the 19th century was that "progress" came to mean "technocratic progress." This was not the anticipated social progress for all people that was to be influenced by the inculcation of such values as justice, freedom, and self-fulfillment. These vital goals of a democratic political system were simply subjugated to the more immediate instrumental values. As Leo Marx explains, this technological advancement "became the fulcrum of the dominant American world view" (1990, p. 5).

In the realm of physical (activity) education there was a "battle of the systems" of exercise and gymnastics that took place in the final quarter of the 20th century. However, it was the burgeoning interest in sport that permitted sport to infiltrate in the program of school physical education as sport skills. This type of experience was expanded in (what was termed) extracurricular activity with team sports for the more highly skilled boys and girls. Earlier physical education programs, where available, as well as programs in wartime eras, undoubtedly stressed the concept of education "of the physical" more than the "roll-out-the-ball" approach so evident in physical education in subsequent decades. There was also the concept of "education through the physical" was also promoted to a degree by the educational progressivists influenced by Deweyan pragmatism. Typically this broader emphasis waned during periods of war and international unrest.

Careful historical analysis of this situation has led me to believe that the steady development of the social institution of competitive sport in the United States over the past 150 years has reached a crossroads (Zeigler, 2005, Chaps. XI , XII). If a claim can reasonably be made that organized sports may be doing as much harm as it does good can be made, I am forced to ask, "Where is the sport management theory needed to refute such a proposition?" In the United States especially, and in much of the remainder of the world, there is seemingly little awareness that such a negative contention about organized sport can be made. The developing world permits without question the commercialization that has brought about sport's expansion and current gargantuan status. The conventional wisdom seems to be that "highly organized sport is good for people and our country. The more involvement an individual can have with sport, either actively or passively, the better he or she will be."

In the meantime, however, the vast majority of the population is getting inadequate involvement in regular, physical activity designed to help them live healthy, active, fulfilling lives. Many of these same people now possess--what Herbert Spencer in the mid-nineteenth century--called "seared physical consciences" He argued that in increasingly urbanized society there is inadequate physical activity education in the schools (1949). These same people simply don't know or appreciate what vigorous physical health "feels like." At the same time throughout their lives they are constantly being encouraged to pay increasing amounts of money to watch "skilled others" play games. (The resultant inactivity has created a crisis situation that will be discussed in some detail below.)

Hard Questions About Present Social Institutions

Social institutions are created and nurtured within a society ostensibly to further the positive development of the people living within that culture. Take democracy, for example, as a type of political institution that is currently being promoted vigorously by the United States throughout the entire world. (Such worldwide change will take time!) Within this form of social development, democracy has "struck up a deep relationship with economics and has found an eager bedfellow with whom to associate"--i.e., the institution of capitalism. Economics, of course, is another vital social institution upon which a society depends fundamentally. As world civilization developed, a great many of the world's countries have promoted with almost messianic zeal such social institutions as democracy, capitalism, and --now!--an increasing involvement with competitive sport. The "theory" is that the addition of highly competitive sport to this mix will bring about more "good" than "bad" for the countries involved. But has it? Disturbing questions have now begun to arise in various quarters.

What does this mean as we move along in the 21st century? Think of the example being set in North America, for example. Is there reasonable hope that the present brand of "combined" democratic capitalism that uses up the world's environmental resources inordinately will somehow improve the world situation in the long run? Can we truly claim with any degree of certainty that this "mix" of democracy and capitalism (with its subsequent inclusion of big-time sport) is producing more "good" than "bad"? (Admittedly, we do need to delineate between "what's 'good'" and "what's 'bad'" more carefully) There is no escaping the fact that the gap economically between the rich and the poor is steadily increasing. This means that "the American dream for all" is beginning to look like a desert mirage. Will the historical "Enlightenment Ideal" remain as an unfulfilled dream forever?

One of the results of the increasing development of the social institution of competitive sport is the creation of sport management societies in the respective regions and countries where such expansion has occurred. At the same time the question may be asked whether this development has reached a point where a claim can be made that highly competitive sport as a social phenomenon may be doing more harm than good in society. It is not that competitive sport does not have the potential for good that is being questioned here. (The world seems to have accepted this as fact!) It's the way that it is being carried out that is the problem. The world community does not really know whether this contention is true or not. Yet sport's expansion is permitted and encouraged almost without question in all quarters. "Sport is good for people, and more involvement with sport of almost any type--extreme sport, professional wrestling--is better" seems to be the conventional wisdom. Witness, also, the millions of dollars that are being parceled out of tax revenues for the several Olympic enterprises perennially. So long as it's thought that "a buck's to be made," also, permit even Evander Holyfield to box professionally in what's called a sport until he won't be able to remember his own name!

In the meantime, the large majority of the population in the developed world is getting inadequate involvement in physical activity, with obesity increasing unduly at all ages and levels. This is a highly significant problem that is increasing daily. Conversely there is rampant starvation in the underdeveloped world where most people, including children, must labor inordinately just to survive. At the same time the public in the technologically developed world is being expected to pay increasing amounts of money to watch "skilled others," either on television or "in the flesh," play types of games and sports increasing in complexity and danger almost exponentially. At the same time, "The National Institutes of Health estimates that Americans will take five years off the average life span," reports Randolph in "The Big, Fat American Kid Crisis" (*The New York Times*, 2006). The eventual outcome of what is happening today can be encapsulated in the grim predictions that the bulk of children and youth in the coming generation of the developed world may be the first to die before their parents because of obesity, less physical activity, and related health problems.

Resultantly, I am forced to ask "What really are we promoting, and do we know why are we doing it?" I do not have a complete answer to these questions, of course. But I do believe this strongly: we need to develop a theory of sport that will permit us to assess whether what we call "competitive sport" is fulfilling its presumed function of promoting good in a society. To do this. we will need to establish connections and relationships with a variety of disciplines in the academic world. Some that come to mind immediately are sport sociology, sport history, sport psychology, sport philosophy, sport economics, as well as selected other fields where research findings could well have application to sport and related physical activity. Some of these fields are anthropology, social geography, and political science--all academic fields that could well be helpful in any assessment of the findings of sport management.

I want to emphasize, also, that the field of sport management must keep a healthy balance between the theoretical and the practical in its ongoing scholarship and research. To do otherwise would be courting the same fate that befell the former Philosophic Society for the Study of Sport (now the IAPS). I'm sad to report that sport philosophy "went disciplinary" in the late 1960s and has never descended from that lofty perch. As the third president, my warning on this point in 1975 was to no avail (Zeigler, 1976). Today the International Association for Sport Philosophy has very few members and "they speak to no one," relatively speaking, except each other. This is an outcome that the field sport management will need to guard against assiduously. (Nevertheless, the disciplinary aspects of sport management should be pursued diligently, but there must be an accompanying pragmatic emphasis on applied research that is regularly and consistently downloaded to the "real world" where sport in its many forms takes place daily.)
.

Sport should be conducted in its various settings now and in the future, both generally and specifically, in a manner that will encourage its proper professional, educational and recreational uses, as well as its semiprofessional and professional concerns To guarantee such a state of affairs, sport must be challenged on an ongoing basis by people at all levels in a variety of ways. If this were to be the case, sport might possibly regain and retain those aspects that can contribute significant value to individual and social living.

In making these assertions, I must first define my terms accurately so that you are fully aware of what I am seeking to critique here. This is necessary because the term "sport," based on both everyday usage and dictionary definition, still exhibits radical ambiguity. Such indecision undoubtedly adds to the present confusion. So, when the word "sport" is used here, it will refer--unless indicated otherwise--to "competitive physical activity, an individual or group competitive activity involving physical exertion or skill, governed by rules, and sometimes engaged in professionally" (*Encarta World English Dictionary*, 1999, p. 1730).

Analyzing Sport's Role in Society

In this process of critiquing competitive sport, I believe further that society should strive to keep sport's drawbacks and/or excesses in check to the greatest possible extent. In recent decades we have witnessed the rise of sport throughout the land to the status of a fundamentalist religion. For example, we find sport being called upon to serve as a redeemer of wayward youth, but--as it is occurring elsewhere--it is also becoming a destroyer of certain fundamental values of individual and social life.

Wilcox (1991), for example, in his empirical analysis, challenged "the widely held notion that sport can fulfill an important role in the development of national character." He stated: "the assumption that sport is conducive to the development of positive human values, or the 'building of character,' should be viewed more as a belief rather than as a fact." He concluded that his study did "provide some evidence to support a relationship between participation in sport and the ranking of human values" (pp. 3, 17, 18, respectively).

Assuming Wilcox's view has reasonable validity, those involved in any way in the institution of sport--if they all together may be considered a collectivity--should contribute a quantity of redeeming social value to our North American culture, not to mention the overall world culture (i.e., a quantity of good leading to improved societal well-being). On the basis of this argument, the following questions are postulated initially for possible subsequent response by concerned agencies and individuals (e.g., federal governments, state and provincial officials, philosophers in the discipline and related professions):

> (1) Can, does, or should a great (i.e., leading) nation
> produce great sport?
>
> (2) With the world being threatened environmentally in a
> variety of ways, should we now be considering an "ecology"
> of sport in which the beneficial and disadvantageous aspects
> of a particular sporting activity are studied through the
> endeavors of scholars in other disciplines as well?
>
> (3) If it is indeed the case that the guardian of the
> "functional satisfaction" resulting from sport is (a) the sports
> person, (b) the spectator, (c) the businessperson who gains
> monetarily, (d) the sport manager, and, in some instances,
> (e) educational administrators and their respective
> governing boards, then who in society should be in a
> position to be the most knowledgeable about the immediate
> objectives and long range aims of sport and related physical
> activity?

(4) If the answer to question No.3 immediately above is that this person should be the trained sport and physical activity management professor, is it too much of a leap to also expect that person's professional association (!) to work to achieve consensus about what sport and closely related physical activity should accomplish? Further, should the professional association have some responsibility as the guardian (or at least the assessor) of whether the aforementioned aims and objectives are being approximated to a greater or lesser degree?

Answering these questions is a truly complex matter. First, as I have stated above, sport and related physical activity have become an extremely powerful social force in society. Secondly, if we grant that sport now has significant power in all world cultures--a power indeed that appears to be growing--we should also recognize that any such social force affecting society can be dangerous if perverted (e.g., through an excess of nationalism or commercialism). With this in mind, I am arguing further that sport has somehow achieved such status as a powerful societal institution without an adequately defined underlying theory. Somehow, most of countries seem to be proceeding generally on a typically unstated assumption that "sport is a good thing for society to encourage, and more sport is even better!" And yet, as explained above, the term "sport" still exhibits radical ambiguity based on both everyday usage and dictionary definition. This obviously adds even more to the present problem and accompanying confusion.)

Delving into this matter more seriously, we may be surprised--or perhaps not. We may well learn that sport is contributing significantly in the development of what are regarded as the *social* values--that is, the values of teamwork, loyalty, self-sacrifice, and perseverance consonant with prevailing corporate capitalism in democracy and in other political systems as well. Conversely, however, we may also discover that there is now a great deal of evidence that sport may be developing an ideal that opposes the fundamental moral virtues of honesty, fairness, and responsibility in the innumerable competitive experiences provided (Lumpkin, Stoll, and Beller, 1999).

Significant to this discussion are the results of investigations carried out by Hahm, Stoll, Beller, Rudd, and others in recent years. The Hahm-Beller Choice Inventory (HBVCI) has now been administered to athletes at different levels in a variety of venues. It demonstrates conclusively that athletes will not support what is considered "the moral ideal" in competition. As Stoll and Beller (1998) see it, for example, an athlete with moral character demonstrates the moral character traits of honesty, fair play, respect, and responsibility whether an official is present to enforce the rules or not. This finding was further substantiated by Priest, Krause, and Beach (1999) who reported that they found changes over a four-year period in a college athlete's ethical value choices were consistent with other investigations. They showed decreases in "sportsmanship orientation" and an increase in "professional" attitudes associated with sport.

On the other hand, even though dictionaries define social character similarly, sport practitioners, including participants, coaches, parents, and officials, have come to believe that character is defined properly by such values as self-sacrifice, teamwork, loyalty, and perseverance. The common expression in competitive sport is: "He/she showed character"--meaning "He/she 'hung in there' to the bitter end!" [or whatever]. Rudd (1999) confirmed that coaches explained character as "work ethic and commitment." This coincides with what sport sociologists have found. Sage (1998. p. 614) explained: "Mottoes and slogans such as 'sports builds character' must be seen in the light of their ideological issues" In other words, competitive sport is structured by the nature of the society in which it occurs. This would appear to mean that over-commercialization, drug-taking, cheating, bribe-taking by officials, violence, etc. at all levels of sport are simply reflections of the culture in which we live. Where does that leave us today as we consider sport's presumed relationship with moral character development?

This discussion about whether sport's presumed educational and recreational roles have justification in fact could go on indefinitely. So many negative incidents have occurred that one hardly knows where to turn to avoid further negative examples. On the one hand we read the almost unbelievably high standards stated in the Code of Conduct developed by the Coaches Council of the National Association for Sport and Physical Education (2001). Conversely we learn that today athletes' concern for the presence of moral values in sport declines over the course of a university career (Priest, Krause, and Beach, 1999).

With this as a backdrop, we learn further that Americans, for example, are increasingly facing the cost and consequences of sedentary living (Booth & Chakravarthy, 2002). Additionally, Malina (2001) tells us that there is a need to track people's involvement in physical activity and sport across their life spans. Finally, Corbin and Pangrazi (2001) explain that we haven't yet been able to devise and accept a uniform definition of wellness for all people. The one thought that emerges from these various assessments is as follows: We give every evidence of wanting our "sport spectaculars" for the few much more than we want all people of all ages and all conditions to have meaningful sport and exercise involvement throughout their lives.

Sport Management Theory and Practice

Defined traditionally, we might say that the sport manager is one who plans, organizes, staffs, leads (or directs), and controls (i.e., monitors and evaluates) progress toward predetermined goals within programs of sport for people of all ages, be they in normal, accelerated, or special populations. To place the current topic in historical perspective (i.e., the beginning of investigation about the management [or administration] of sport and physical activity in educational institutions largely), master's and doctoral degrees about the subject within departments and schools of education in the United States were completed initially at Columbia Teachers College and New York University starting in the mid-1920s. Individually, there were many well-intended, seemingly worthwhile studies completed. However, it was impossible to say what these--literally--thousands of investigations "added up to" 35 years later at the beginning of the 1960s decade was really not known.

In the 1960s, however, research and scholarship in administrative theory and practice related to physical education and athletic administration began to receive attention in several quarters. Through the efforts of King McCristal (dean) and the author (University of Illinois, U-C), we were able to get this area included as one of six subject-matter areas in the Big Ten Body-of-Knowledge Project. In the fall of 1972, a symposium was held on the subject at The University of Michigan, Ann Arbor. In a volume published in 1975, the results of 20 doctoral dissertations carried out at Illinois were published (Zeigler and Spaeth, 1975). However, financial and other constraints in higher education of the 1970s slowed this development down considerably.

Then the rise of a so-called disciplinary approach to the field of physical education, plus the perennial claim of the "educational essentialist" that it is only the hard sciences that provide the basic knowledge, resulted in the introduction of the term kinesiology to supplement (or even supplant!) that of physical education at the university level. This tended to severely downgrade the importance of administrative theory and practice programs within the field, while job opportunities for professors related to biomechanics, exercise physiology, and motor learning increased. Concurrently, however, burgeoning interest in commercialized, highly competitive sport within higher education and in the public sector created a need for the establishment and development of college and university curricula in sport management. So the essence of what was often being eliminated in one program appeared to be springing up in a new curriculum stream--sport management. It was at this point on February 24, 1986 that a small group of us witnessed the successful creation of the now-successful North American Society for Sport Management.

Most of those behind the establishment of NASSM actually envisioned an association with a broad emphasis leading to the promotion of sport and physical activity for all people of all ages. However, interest in highly organized, elite sport seems to have engulfed conference presentations in the various aspects of competitive sport management. Sport management has rapidly become a mushrooming field in its own right that increasingly has its own curriculum independent of former physical education and athletics administration courses in educational institutions. Concurrently, the "eager scientists" in kinesiology, who conceptually relegated administrative theory and practice for physical education and athletics to the dustbin insofar as its place in their disciplinary curriculum is concerned, are presumably now quite happy and relieved in those sites where such separation has actually occurred.

Intramural and recreational sport is actually doing quite well at the college and university level, but is almost nonexistent at the high-school level and lower.

Finally, the near demise of physical activity programs "for the many"--required within education at all levels within education prior to 1950--does not even appear on the radar screen of the large majority of professional preparation personnel in universities. Yet, because of the decline of required physical education, it has become starkly apparent that the health and physical fitness of the populace needs a strong shot in the arm to again establish a firm foothold in public consciousness. (It doesn't seem that the "War on Terrorism" will bring this change. Do we need another world war to accomplish this?) This is true even though--almost daily--reports of scientific studies tell us of the beneficial effects of regular physical activity on the human organism in so many different ways.

In such a developing world environment, then, what is the mission of a field called sport management, still a fledgling profession but one that is rapidly catching on all over the world? Frankly, I believe strongly that our profession needs to understand (define?) its mission much better than appears to be the case at present. Exactly what is its fundamental purpose in society? Further, how does the mission of sport management globally relate to the mission of the various professional associations composed primarily of men and women involved in the professional education of future sport managers? (Keep in mind that the typical professional sport promoters worldwide presently live in "another world"!)

Unfortunately, as I see it, the outlooks or aims of those people who today promote sport competition professionally, and that of those who believe they are promoting such competition educationally, appear to be getting closer all the time. I am referring here to the people involved, for example, in the National Basketball Association or the National Collegiate Athletic Association in the United States, respectively. Granted that the people in both of these associations are operating on the assumption that the provision of highly competitive sport opportunities in society is a good thing. Also, they appear to believe that promoting ever more opportunity for the masses to observe such activity is worthwhile. The fact that the cultivation of a "fan club" for professional sport also provides exorbitant income for the "accelerated few" athletes and a dubious future for the vast majority of athletes who don't "make it" appears to be of little concern. This is unfortunate for that "vast majority" because their educational background has typically been stunted by excessive involvement in competitive sport while enrolled at universities.

Frankly, I believe this assumption of "goodness " for society has become a dubious premise or principle upon which most of these promoters and/or educational administrators are operating. I maintain that this is so unless they can provide accompanying evidence to substantiate to society that the continuation and enlargement of the present trend to increasing commercialization in sport is contributing positively to society as a social institution. To repeat, all social institutions must have an underlying theory to justify their continuing existence. The basic question, I submit, is simply this: In this evolving situation, what kind of "good"--philosophically speaking--can we claim is currently being made by competitive sport?

To one who has followed and written extensively about this development down through the 20th century from both a historical and a philosophical standpoint, I can only report (sadly!) that the excesses and corruption of competitive sport have increased steadily decade by decade. And, even more sadly, the seemingly jaded public (as fans) does not seem to realize--or seems to accept--that sport's status as a desirable social institution is being lowered steadily with each passing year. (I won't even get into the question of the taking of one or more of 400-500 drugs to enhance performance that the sport establishment is facing today.) Competitive sport is forced to stay within the law, but its typically laudable creed espoused so freely requires an enforceable code of ethics in the present--not as a dream for the future.

Concurrently, the low status perennially accorded to physical education--except in times of war when referred to as "physical fitness"--continues. This is true even though ongoing research in kinesiology and physical education--and the field's related disciplines--is steadily making the case for regular, developmental physical activity as an essential, if not a vital, social institution to be employed for the benefit of all. Nevertheless the term "sport," and what it connotes to the average mind, largely overrides the need for the provision of necessary funding of developmental physical activity as a social institution. I firmly believe that provision for the managing and promoting developmental physical activity in sport, exercise, and physical recreation for people of all ages, be they part of accelerated, normal, or special populations, should at least be an auxiliary part of our mission in sport management. Yet we find that our professional associations and disciplinary societies relayed to "physical activity" are steadily and increasingly becoming more disjointed as they grow farther apart. Other professions and disciplines are "filling in" where we should be "producing" (e.g., recreation, medicine).

You can see where I am heading with this analysis. I believe it is now incumbent upon the field of sport management (i.e., these professional organizations worldwide) to investigate and subsequently understand precisely what effect sport, however defined and with all of its ramifications, is having on society. Is it more good than bad? Who knows? The professional and semiprofessional sport managers can't answer this basic question. (Many probably wouldn't want to know anyhow if it meant a possible shifting of emphasis in their offerings.) Therefore I urge the world's various professional sport management associations to take a hard look at what appears to be a steadily growing problem. They need to determine (1) what effect sport is having on society; (2) if there is a problem with the present development, and to what extent the professional associations (e.g., in North America) may unwittingly be part of the problem; and (3) in what ways professional sport management associations can ensure that sport as a whole, and more specifically its many programs at all levels, are moving in the

Table 1
SPORT MANAGEMENT:
SCHOLARLY AND PROFESSIONAL DIMENSIONS

Areas of Scholarly Study & Research	Related Disciplinary Aspects	Professional Aspects
I. BACKGROUND, MEANING & INTERCULTURAL SIGNIFICANCE	-History -Philosophy	−International Relations −Professional Ethics -International & Comparative Aspects
II. SOCIO-CULTURAL & BEHAVIORAL ASPECTS	-Sociology -Economics -Psychology (individ.& social) -Anthropology -Political Science -Geography -Law	-Application of Theory to Practice
III. SPORT MANAGEMENT THEORY	-Management Science -Business Administration	-Application of Theory to Practice (e.g., sport marketing sport finance, facility management, sales)
IV. CURRICULUM THEORY & PROGRAM DEVELOPMENT	-Curriculum Studies	-Application of Theory to Practice

1. *General Education*: universities and colleges typically have a distribution requirement for all students in the humanities, social-science, and natural sciences.
2. *Professional* Core Subjects: an irreducible minimum requirement in the following subjects is required: communication & media relations, economic theory & sport finance, sport marketing, sponsorship & sales, legal aspects, sport governance, sport ethics, the international sport industry, and sport & physical activity internships.
3. *Specialized* Undergraduate Professional Preparation; streaming possibilities may be added in the degree program.
4. *Graduate* Education; three types of specialization are desirable: (1) professional preparation stream; (2) disciplinary stream, (3) practitioner stream)

V. MEASUREMENT & EVALUATION	-Theory about the Measurement Function	-Application of Measurement Theory of Practice

(Note: Reactions and/or recommendations for change or additions to Table 1 would be appreciated at <zeigrog@axion.net>)

right direction? These questions can't be answered satisfactorily without an underlying theory of sport management that meets the needs of all people.

Need for a Theory of Sport Management

Returning to the assertion made earlier, a theory underlying sport management could contribute greatly to the answering of the questions raised immediately above. It would need to be related basically to the social sciences and to certain professions that carry out their own independent research as well (e.g., business administration). It should contain "propositions of fact" that can, at least in principle, be verified empirically. "Propositions of value" are subjective and therefore typically conform to societal values and norms. Therefore, it would not be a philosophy of sport management, although a concerned individual or group might well philosophize about such human activity.

A theory is not a taxonomy, however, although a taxonomy of sport management will necessarily evolve as scientific and scholarly investigation about it is carried out. "A taxonomy may be defined as a classification of data according to their natural relationships, or the principles governing such classifications. . . .In fact, one could probably make a good case to support the contention that any science begins with a taxonomy. . . ." (Griffiths, 1959. p. 17).

A Proposed Taxonomy for Sport Management. Above as Table 1 is included a sample of what a taxonomy of sport management might look like. It includes both scholarly and professional dimensions with three headings defined as (1) areas of scholarly study and research, (2) related disciplinary aspects, and (3) professional aspects. The possibility of "streaming" is mentioned at the undergraduate level. Also, there are three categories of graduate education postulated

By now governmental, educational, and commercial agencies and organizations should be able to argue convincingly that sport is a "relatively homogeneous substance" that can serve at least reasonably well as an indispensable balm or aid to human fulfillment within an individual life (adapted from Barzun [speaking about art], 1974, p. 12). However, the idea of "sport and developmental physical activity for all" on a lifelong basis continues to receive more "lip support" than actual investment based on the monetary input of government toward overall fitness and physical recreational involvement for the general population. Yet the logical argument that--through the process of total psycho-physical involvement--sport provides highly desirable "flow experience" may well be true. The question is "for whom does the bell toll?" (Csikszentmihalyi, 1993, p. 183).

Below you will find "A Model for Sport Management Development (Including a Competency-Based Approach)" (see Figure 1 below) This model is an

Figure 2

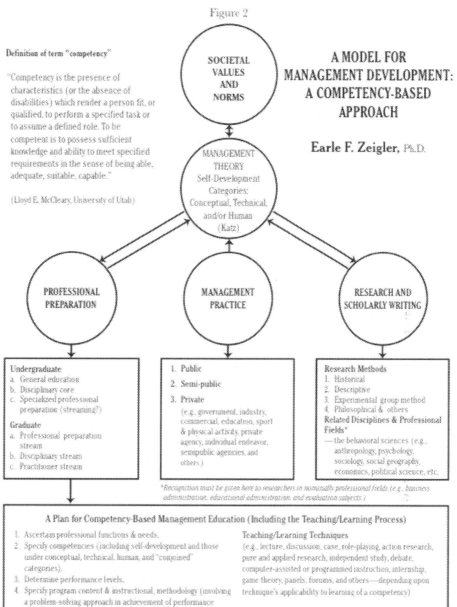

Definition of term "competency"

"Competency is the presence of characteristics (or the absence of disabilities) which render a person fit, or qualified, to perform a specified task or to assume a defined role. To be competent is to possess sufficient knowledge and ability to meet specified requirements in the sense of being able, adequate, suitable, capable."

(Lloyd E. McCleary, University of Utah)

SOCIETAL VALUES AND NORMS

A MODEL FOR MANAGEMENT DEVELOPMENT: A COMPETENCY-BASED APPROACH

Earle F. Zeigler, Ph.D.

MANAGEMENT THEORY
Self-Development Categories:
Conceptual, Technical, and/or Human
(Katz)

PROFESSIONAL PREPARATION

MANAGEMENT PRACTICE

RESEARCH AND SCHOLARLY WRITING

Undergraduate
a. General education
b. Disciplinary core
c. Specialized professional preparation (streaming?)

Graduate
a. Professional preparation stream
b. Disciplinary stream
c. Practitioner stream

1. Public
2. Semi-public
3. Private
   (e.g., government, industry, commercial, education, sport & physical activity, private agency, individual endeavor, semipublic agencies, and others.)

Research Methods
1. Historical
2. Descriptive
3. Experimental group method
4. Philosophical & others

Related Disciplines & Professional Fields*
---- the behavioral sciences (e.g., anthropology, psychology, sociology, social geography, economics, political science, etc.

*Recognition must be given here to researchers in nominally professional fields (e.g., business administration, educational administration, and evaluation subjects.)

A Plan for Competency-Based Management Education (Including the Teaching/Learning Process)

1. Ascertain professional functions & needs.
2. Specify competences (including self-development and those under conceptual, technical, human, and "conjoined" categories).
3. Determine performance levels.
4. Specify program content & instructional, methodology (involving a problem-solving approach in achievement of performance levels: what needs to be known; where obtained; organization of the learning experience; probable results, and others.
5. Identify and evaluate competency attainment.
6. Validate process periodically.

Teaching/Learning Techniques
(e.g., lecture, discussion, case, role-playing, action research, pure and applied research, independent study, debate, computer-assisted or programmed instruction, internship, game theory, panels, forums, and others——depending upon technique's applicability to learning of a competency)

(Adapted from McCleary & McIntyre 1973)

(Note: As it happens, these elements also describe the basic
elements of any profession [as I had suggested in the early 1970s
for the field of management itself]; see Zeigler, 1972).
Subsequently I incorporated the idea of competency and skill-
acquisition into the model based on the recommendation by
Lloyd McCleary, formerly of the University of Illinois, C-U. I
subsequently realized that this entire model configuration fits very
well into a description of the ongoing status of the sport-
management profession.

effort to resolve the relationship between what has been called the disciplinary
aspects and those aspects that have been designated as "professional" in nature. I
have included five elements as the fundamental ones in a model that portrays the
basic elements of the developing sport management profession.

The inclusion of "Societal Values & Norms" as an overarching entity in
the model is based on the sociologic theory that the value system (i.e., the values
and the norms) of a culture will be realized eventually within the society--if all
goes well! Values represent the highest echelon of the social system level of the
entire general action system. These values may be categorized into such "entities"
as artistic values, educational values, social values, sport values, etc. Of course, all
types or categories of values must be values held by personalities. The social values
of a particular social system are those values that are conceived of as
representative of the ideal general character that is desired by those who
ultimately hold the power in the system being described. The most important
social values in North America, for example, have been (1) the rule of law, (2) the
socio-structural facilitation of individual achievement, and (3) the equality of
opportunity (Johnson, 1994).

Norms--not to be confused with values--are the shared, sanctioned rules
which govern the second level of the social structure. The average person finds it
difficult to separate in his or her mind the concepts of values and norms. Keeping
in mind the examples of values offered immediately above, some examples of
norms are (1) the institution of private property, (2) private enterprise, (3) the
monogamous, conjugal family, and (4) the separation of church and state.

Put simply, this means that decisions regarding the development of a
profession are based on the prevailing values and norms over and above any
scientific and/or scholarly evidence that may become available to strengthen
existing theory. Fundamentally, there is a hierarchy of control and conditioning
that operates within the culture that exerts pressure downward affecting all aspects
of the society. (Keep in mind that this pressure may be exerted upward as well.)

Moving downward from the top of Figure 1, the second phase of the
model is called "Sport Management Theory." This is the systematic arrangement
of proven facts or knowledge about a professional field (or discipline in the case of
a subject-matter). From such theory we can also derive assumptions and testable
hypotheses that should soon amplify as a result on ongoing scholarship, research,

and experience. In the process scholars and researchers will also clarify a developing (and presumably) coherent group of general and specific propositions arranged as ordered generalizations) that can be used as principles of explanation for the phenomena that have been observed. Obviously, any profession must have a sound under girding body of knowledge if it hopes to survive with its professional status fully recognized in society. Unfortunately. at present there is no such inventory of scholarly and research findings about sport management theory readily available for those involved in sport management practice, professional preparation, and research and scholarly writing contributing to disciplinary development.

Moving downward once again, the model now expands both downward and to the right and left so that there is a total of three circles. In a sense these three circles would typically "feed" or "draw" knowledge and information from the middle circle above designated as "Sport Management Theory." Note that there are arrows going backward and forward in all directions to explain necessary "reciprocity" among these entities. These arrows show the complexity of the evolving subject.

The circle on the left is designated as "Professional Preparation." It includes the planned program designed to educate the professional practitioner, the teacher of practitioners, and--arguably--the scholar and/or researcher about the subject of professional preparation. The undergraduate program would presumably include (1) general education, (2) a disciplinary core, and (3) specialized professional preparation (conceivably with streaming possibilities). The graduate program could conceivably contain three distinct streams: (1) a professional-preparation stream; (2) a disciplinary stream. and (3) a practitioner stream.

The second of the three circles alongside each other in the upper half of the model is titled "Sport Management Practice." This would include those professional practitioners with degree programs involving general education, a sport management disciplinary-base, and specialized knowledge about the theory and practice of sport management in the range of public, semipublic, and private agencies and programs involved with varying types of sport and physical activity programs.

The third of the three circles (on the right) has been given the title of "Research and Scholarly Writing." Such research knowledge and scholarly writing is developed on an ongoing basis employing existing research methods and techniques to gather knowledge (i.e. propositions of fact) about the subject of sport management at all levels and under all conditions). Such research and scholarly writing is typically carried out by university professors and qualified professionals wherever employed. Obviously, there has been great--continuing!--help in the past provided by scholars and researchers in related disciplines and professional fields (e.g., the behavioral sciences and business administration).

The Next Step for the Sport Management Profession

Now that we have had a look at where sport management has been, and where it is currently, where should it go from here? The obvious answer would appear to be to build on--i.e., add scholarly sport management literature--to the available inventory of completed research on physical education and athletics management that has been made ready for entry into both departmental and personal data banks and/or retrieval systems by the efforts of scholarly people in the field since the mid-1920s. This historical literature has been delineated and recorded for sport and physical education management.

As it exists, it can be stored in such a way that an ongoing data base can be originated, maintained, and developed. To this should be added as soon as possible the results of investigations reported in the Journal of Sport Management and similar publications worldwide (e.g., the International Journal of Sport Management). This is the bare minimum that should be carried out by someone or some group on behalf of . If completed, when professors or graduate students contemplate further research, they could at least determine what research has already been carried out on the particular topic at hand being considered for further research.

Despite the fact that this embryonic inventory of completed research is now available for easy storage and retrieval in a data base, what we have been able to accomplish with this data represents merely a "scratching of the surface." So much more needs to be done by our scholars in sport and related physical activity. At present dedicated practitioners have been overwhelmed by periodical literature, monographs, and books from our field, from the allied professions, and from the related disciplines. Much of this information is interesting and valuable. However, it is so often not geared to the interests of professionals who are fulfilling many duties and responsibilities in the various positions they hold. Also, there is undoubtedly much overlapping material emanating also from the allied professions (notably recreation and park administration). Further, much of the available material--when a person by intent or chance happens to discover it--may be unintelligible, partially understandable, or not available in its essence and in a condensed form to the professional in sport management. Thus, one can only conjecture in what form such information will (or unfortunately won't) be conveyed to the many legislative or advisory boards on whose behalf we are carrying out our endeavor.

To make matters worse, because of provinciality and assorted communication barriers, our field is missing out on important findings now becoming available in Dutch, German, Japanese, Chinese, Italian, and the Scandinavian languages. Further, in addition to the above reason, because of a plethora of rules, regulations, and stipulations, people may not be receiving information about substantive reports of various government agencies at all levels. Such reports should become part of personal and departmental retrieval systems of those carrying out scholarly work in sub disciplinary and sub professional areas of investigation.

Interestingly, Joo and Jackson (2002) analyzed scholarly literature that had appeared in the *Journal of Sport Management* since its inception in 1987. Their analysis of 242 articles published showed that, although Trevor Slack's study in 1996 revealed that 65% of the published articles involved the delivery of either physical education or athletics programs, the emphases in research had shifted in the 1990s to marketing studies. More recently, however, there was a move to the area of organizational behavior. The results of research published in the *Journal of Sport Management*, as well as in the more recent *International Journal of Sport Management* should be entered into our bibliography and inventory as soon as possible. These findings should be correlated with studies reported as part of Zeigler's (1995) and Baker's (1983 and 1995) ongoing thesis and dissertation project with Collins and Zarriello, respectively. (Note: Contact author at <zeigrog@axion.net> to have bibliographic data from 1925-1972 downloaded.)

It is true that bibliographies of scholarly publications are occasionally made available. Further, printouts of bibliographies on specific concepts or uniterms can sometimes be purchased commercially. However, a bibliography is just that--a bibliography. Such a listing is typically not annotated to any degree, and one can hardly recall the last time a thorough bibliographical *commentary* on a topic related to sport management has been published.

The Most Important Point: The Need for an Ongoing Inventory. Still further--and this is really the most important point--it can be argued that the profession simply does not know where it stands in regard to the steadily developing body of knowledge in the many sub disciplinary and sub professional aspects of sport management (e.g., sport ethics, sport law, sport economics, sport marketing). Our profession--any profession for that matter!--needs such information as an inventory to form the basis--the theory, intellectual "underpinning," evidence, body of knowledge--for an evolving professional (practitioner's) handbook. In our case it would immediately become an essential component of every person's professional practice in the field of sport management. Nowhere does our professionals (and scholars, also) have such a steadily evolving "Inventory of Scholarly, Scientific Findings Arranged as Ordered Principles or Generalizations" in their hands (and also online) as an ever-evolving professional handbook to help them in their work daily--be they general manager, ticket manager, marketer, athletic director, head coach, management scholar or researcher, or whatever. Such information is obviously vitally important to the professional practitioner who could make use daily of the essence of this proposed "action-theory marriage." If such an inventory were to be made available, the profession should then carry such an inventory forward on a yearly, 2-, 3-, or 5-year basis of renewal for all practitioners in the profession. This deficiency can--and indeed must--be rectified as we move on into the 21st century.

Formulation of an Inventory of Scientific Findings. This recommendation to develop an inventory of scientific findings about sport management would not be unique to this field. Bernard Berelson and Gary Steiner (1964) postulated such an inventory 42 years ago in what they called the behavioral sciences. In their publication, *Human behavior: An inventory of scientific findings*, the editors and associates reported, integrated, assessed, and classified "the results of several decades of the scientific study of human behavior (p. 3). The basic plan of this formidable undertaking is fundamentally sound; thus, many of their ideas concerning format could be employed in the development of a scientific inventory of findings about sport management. Actually, it could well be carried out in all of the world's existing disciplines and then updated at regular intervals on a worldwide basis in one or more agreed-upon languages. Of course, varying emphases and certain significant differences might be introduced, but the basic approach is still valid. Berelson and Steiner summarized their task as the development of "important statements of proper generality for which there is some good amount of scientific evidence" (p. 5).

How the Inventory Would Be Constructed. The type of inventory recommended would develop through the combined effort of people in the various aspects of sport management and related disciplines and professions. The goal would be to present an inventory of knowledge on the subject of sport management--that is, to assess the present state of knowledge and scholarly thought. Thus, those who prepare this information would be writing as reporters and knowledge-integrators, presenting what they know, and what they think they know, based on the available evidence. Every effort would have to be made to avoid presenting what they hope will be known. Down through the years there appear to have been frequent occasions in many professions where this latter approach has been followed, intentionally or otherwise, where people make declarative statements arguing that such thoughts are indeed based on documented evidence.

In such an inventory, the reader would find series of verified findings, principles and/or generalizations in an ordered 1-2-3-4 arrangement, typically with the citation of sources which generated the information. For example, several general theoretical propositions relative to "organizational behavior" could be considered according to several categories from Berelson and Steiner. The following findings about "The Organization," arranged as ordered generalizations, have been extracted from Berelson & Steiner (1964, pp. 365-373):

> A1   The larger, the more complex, and the more heterogeneous the society, the greater the number of organizations and associations that exist in it.
>
> > A1.1   Organizations tend to call forth organizations: If people organize on one side of an issue, their opponents will organize on the other side.
> > A1.2   There is a tendency for voluntary

associations to become more formal.

A2   There is always a tendency for organizations (of a
        nonprofit character) to turn away, at least partially,
        from their original goals.

   A2.1 Day-to-day decisions of an organization tend
            to be taken as commitments and precedents, often beyond
            the scope for which they were initially intended, and thus
            they come to affect the character of the organization.

In reporting the available material, the language used should be as free as possible from scientific jargon. It should be understandable to the intelligent lay person and, of course, to professional practitioners in the area of sport and physical activity management. This would be difficult, because the findings would range from sport marketing to sport ethics to management competencies in a field that includes many areas of specialization. In any case, what would be presented is currently not available elsewhere in this form. This involves more than delineating by descriptive research technique what might be called "sport management literacy" (see, for example, Zeigler [1994] that presents "physical education and sport foundations" from which certain generalizations as explained above might be drawn). This type of inventory would represent a truly significant contribution to the profession of sport management, as well as the public for whose benefit sport is presumed to serve as a social institution.

To clarify this process further, the reader should understand that it may be necessary to select a particular study for inclusion in the inventory from among similar items available in the sport management literature--and also from among studies carried out in closely related fields (e.g., management science) that have a direct bearing on the major topic at hand The knowledge integrator or synthesizer (i.e. a *qualified* analyst) would be looking primarily for theory, findings, principles, generalizations, and propositions that apply to this field (i.e., the management of sport in its various forms worldwide). After accepting a finding for inclusion, it would be necessary to condense it and similar findings to one distinct principle or generalization. Next, the investigator would organize the material into subheadings that could subsequently be arranged in a logical, coherent, descending manner (e.g., Proposition A1, then A1.1, A1,1a, A1.1b, A1,1c, etc., depending upon the complexity of the proposition at hand). Finally, the resultant material would be reviewed and analyzed in order to eliminate certain technical language that might only confuse the majority of professionals for whom the inventory is primarily intended.

The goal of this project would be an inventory representing a distillation of the literature relating to the management of sport in all its forms, one that would communicate what scholars believe is known about the field to those professionals who are not specialists in the specific sub disciplinary or sub professional area described. This is not to say, of course, that such an inventory could not be helpful to the specialist in his or her own specialty. Further, to some extent there would at first be reliance on secondary summaries of the available literature, but this should be kept to a minimum. However, such reliance would be necessary because of the great bulk and variety of material. Also, the investigators could obtain the benefit of the evaluative judgment of the specialist who may have originally developed a summary or evaluation. Such material would be temporarily helpful in those instances where gaps in the field's own literature still exist (of which there are undoubtedly many).

Then, too, as more evidence is forthcoming, it would provide a base for improved professional operation as the fundamental and specialized management theory grows broader and deeper. Even then, the scholar, as well as the professional user of the generalized theory, would appreciate the necessity of using some qualifying statements in the development of ordered principles or generalizations (e.g., "under certain circumstances"). This inventory could be made available as an evolving professional handbook with the following assumption: that the steadily growing body of scientific findings about the management of developmental physical activity in sport and exercise is needed now by the many professionals in the field--be they managers, supervisors, teachers, coaches, or researchers in public, semipublic, or private agencies.

How This Inventory Would Be Constructed. The type of inventory recommended would develop through the combined effort of people in sport management, its allied professions, and its related disciplines (those that have any direct or tangential interest in the management of sport). The goal would be to present an inventory of knowledge on the subject of the management of sport and related physical activity--that is, to assess the present state of knowledge and scholarly thought. Thus, those who prepare this information would be writing as Reporters and Integrators presenting (1) what they know and (2) what they think they know based on the available evidence. (As mentioned above, every effort would have to be made to avoid presenting what they hope will be known.)

In such an inventory, the reader would find series of verified findings, principles and/or generalizations in an ordered 1-2-3-4 arrangement, typically with the Citation of Sources that generated the information. For example, the following general theoretical propositions relative to human behavior in managerial situations could be considered according to several categories (as adapted from Berelson and Steiner in the area of small-group research). The following theory relating to the athletic director in a university--that is, assumptions or testable hypotheses--might be included in an inventory:

1. That the manner in which the director of athletics leads his/her program is determined more by existing regulations of the educational institution itself, and the expectations of coaches and staff, than the manager's own personality and character traits.
2. That a director of athletics will find it most difficult to shift the department away from established norms.

3. That a director of athletics will receive gradually increasing support from coaches and staff members to the extent that he/she makes it possible for them to realize their personal goals.
4. That a director of athletics who attempts to employ democratic leadership will experience difficulty in reaching his/her own personal goals for the program if there are a significant number of authoritarian personalities in it (adapted from Berelson & Steiner, pp. 341-346).

Concluding Statement

In offering this perspective to the field of sport management, Daniel Wren's cautionary thought was in my mind. In the epilogue of his outstanding *History of Management Theory and Practice* (2005), he stated: "Management is more than an economic activity, however; it is a conceptual task that must mold resources into a proper alignment with the economic, technological, social, and political facets of its environment. We neglect the 'social facets' at our peril!"

It is these very "social facets" of the enterprise that the field of sport management needs to consider more carefully in the twenty-first century. Sport, as all other social institutions, is inevitably being confronted by the need to become truly responsible. Many troubling and difficult decisions, often ethical in nature, will have to be made as the professor of sport management continues the development of this profession/discipline as it seeks to prepare those who will guide sport in the years ahead. The fundamental question facing the profession is: "What *kind* of sport should the profession promote to help shape what sort of world in the 21st century? Professional sport management societies need to decide to what extent they wish to be involved with all types of sport for all types of people of all ages as they take part in healthful sport and physical activity promoted by public, semipublic, or private agencies.

There is no doubt but that the field of sport management made great strides in the closing years of the twentieth century. Nevertheless I believe that the field--both the profession and its related disciplinary effort--must develop underlying management thought, theory, and practice in an ongoing manner to support its professional practitioners. I stress again that practitioners "on the fire line" daily in sport management should be provided with an evolving inventory of ordered generalizations as to the best ways of carrying out their endeavor.

Finally, whatever decisions are made in regard to the future, we must continue to make all possible efforts to place professional preparation for administrative or managerial leadership within our field on a gradually improving, sound academic basis. The question of leadership confronts us from a number of different directions. Our field, and undoubtedly many others, desperately needs a continuing supply of first-class leaders. Any organization or enterprise soon begins to falter and even to stumble if it doesn't have good leadership. We should maintain our efforts to find more fine people who will take charge in the behaviorally oriented, sport management environment of today's world.

References

Baker, J. A. W., & Collins, M. S. (1983). *Research on administration of physical education and athletics 1971-1982*: A retrieval system. Reseda, CA: Mojave.

Baker, J. A. W. & Zarriello, J. (1995). *A bibliography of completed research and scholarly endeavor relating to management in the allied professions (1980-1990 inclusive)*. Champaign, IL: Stipes.

Barzun, Jacques. *The use and abuse of art.* Princeton: Princeton University Press, 1974, pp. 123-150.

Berelson, B., & Steiner, G. A. (1964). *Human behavior; An inventory of scientific findings*. New York: Harcourt, Brace & World.

Booth, F. W., & Chakravarthy, M. V. (2002). Cost and consequences of sedentary living: New battleground for an old enemy. *Research Digest (PCPFS)*, 3(16), 1-8.

Chalip, L. (2006). Toward a distinctive sport management discipline. *Journal of Sport Management*, 20(1), 1-22.

Corbin, C. B. & Pangrazi, R. P. (2001). Toward a uniform definition of wellness: A commentary. *President's Council on Physical Fitness and Sports Research Digest*, 3, 15, 1-8.

Costa, C. A. (2005). The status and future of sport management: A Delphi study. *Journal of Sport Management*, 19(2), 117-143.

Csikszentmihalyi, M. (1993), *The evolving self: A psychology for the third millennium.*   NY: HarperCollins.

Encarta World English Dictionary, The. (1999). NY: St. Martin's Press.

Frisby, W. (2005). The good, the bad, and the ugly. *Journal of Sport Management*, 19(1), 1-12.

Griffiths, D. E. (1959) *Administrative Theory.* NY: Appleton-Century-Crofts.

Hahm, C.H., Beller, J. M., & Stoll, S. K. (1989). *The Hahm-Beller Values Choice Inventory.* Moscow, Idaho: Center for Ethics, The University of Idaho.

Johnson, H. M. (1994). Modern organizations in the Parsonsian theory of action. In A. Farazmand (Ed.), *Modern organizations: Administrative theory in contemporary society* (p. 59). Westport, CT: Praeger.

Joo, J. & Jackson, E. N. (2002). A content analysis of the *Journal of Sport Management::* An analysis of sport management's premier body of knowledge. *Research Quarterly for Exercise and Sport*, 73(1, Suppl.), A111.

Journal of Sport Management. (A special issue of the journal was devoted to The question of sport management research. Dated October, 2005, Vol. 19, No. 4 was titled "Expanding Horizons: Promoting Critical and Innovative Approaches to the Study of Sport Management".)

Kavussanu, M. & Roberts, G. C. (2001). Moral functioning in sport: An achievement goal perspective. *Journal of Sport and Exercise Psychology*, 23, 37-54.

Lumpkin, A., Stoll, S., & Beller, J. M. (1999). *Sport ethics: Applications for fair Play* (2nd ed.). St. Louis, MO: McGraw-Hill.

Malina, R. M.. (2001). Tracking of physical activity across the life span. *Research Digest (PCPFS)*, 3-14, 1-8.

Marx, L. (1990). Does improved technology mean progress? In Teich, A. H.

(Ed.), *Technology and the future*. NY: St. Martin's Press.

National Association for Sport and Physical Education. (2001). The coaches code of conduct. *Strategies*, 15(2), 11.

Priest, R. F., Krause, J. V., & Beach, J. (1999). Four-year changes in college athletes' ethical value choices in sports situations. *Research Quarterly for Exercise and   Sport*, 70(1), 170-178.

Randolph, E. (2006). The big, fat American kid crisis…And 20 things we should do about it. *The New York Times*.

+++++++++++

(see:http://select.nytimes.com/2006/05/10/opinion/10talkingpoints.html?pagewanted= all).

+++++++++++

Rudd, A., Stoll, S. K., & Beller, J. M. (1999). Measuring moral and social character among a group of Division 1A college athletes, non-athletes, and ROTC military students. *Research Quarterly for Exercise and Sport*, 70 (Suppl. 1), 127.

Sage, G. H. (1998). Sports participation as a builder of character? *The World and I*, 3, 629-641.

Spencer, H. (1949). *Education: intellectual, moral, and physical*. London: Watts.

Steinhaus, A. H. (1952). Principal principles of physical education. In *Proceedings of the College Physical Education Association*. Washington, DC: AAHPER, pp. 5-11.

Stoll, S. K. & Beller, J. M. (1998). *Sport as education: On the edge*. NY:Columbia University Teachers College.

Wilcox, R. C. (1991). Sport and national character: An empirical analysis. *Journal of Comparative Physical Education and Sport.*, XIII(1), 3-27.

Wren, D. A. (2005). *The history of management thought*. NJ: John Wiley & Sons.

Zeigler, E. F. (1972). A model for optimum professional development in a field called "X." In *Proceedings of the First Canadian Symposium on the Philosophy of Sport and Physical Activity*. Ottawa, Canada: Sport Canada Directorate, pp.16-28.

Zeigler, E. F. & Spaeth, M. J. (1975). *Administrative theory and practice in physical education and athletics*. Englewood Cliffs, NJ: Prentice-Hall.

Zeigler, E. F. (1976). In sport, as in all of life, man should be comprehensible to man. *Journal of the Philosophy of Sport*, III, 121-126

Zeigler, E. F. (ed. & au.). (1994). *Physical education and kinesiology in North America:Professional and scholarly foundations*. Champaign, IL: Stipes.

Zeigler, E. F. (1995). *A selected, annotated bibliography of completed research on management theory and practice in physical education and athletics to 1972 (including a background essay)*. Champaign, IL: Stipes.

Zeigler, E. F. (2003). Sport's plight in the postmodern world: Implications for The sport management profession," *International Journal of Sport Management*, 4(2), 93- 109.

Zeigler. E. F. (2005). *History and status of American physical education and educational sport*. Victoria, BC: Trafford

Selection #9
In a Technological Age, Commercialized Sport Is Threatening Sport's Potential Value to Humankind!

Humankind's struggle to "make a go of it" in the 20th century starkly outlined what now confronts humanity in the 21st century. Living together peacefully, of course, is an ever-present challenge of the highest magnitude. The great historian, Toynbee, reminded us that civilizations died when they simply did not confront challenges successfully. Climate change, for example, is rapidly developing into such a challenge, as are the ongoing clashes of unwavering religions.

There is another challenge, however, that the world's populace does not seem to recognize has developed over the course of the twentieth century. I am referring to human involvement with sport characterized increasingly by overemphasis, commercialism, and violence as it "progresses professionally, technologically, and commercially." This now appears to have reached the point that it may be having a negative influence on society overall, as well as on the quality and quantity of sport and physical activity programs of children and youth.

Sporting Patterns Forged by Environmental Forces

How did this happen? Phyllis Hill, in her insightful study (1965), titled *A Cultural History of Sport in Illinois*, 1673-1820 concluded that:

> American cultural practices, including sport, have been forged by environmental forces, rather than by Anglo-Saxon tradition unless one claims change and innovation as distinctly Anglo-Saxon traits. Following this line of thought, the English philosophy of sport, of amateurism, of gentlemanly conduct, and of sport for sport's sake is inoperable in a culture where sport is closely tied to personal achievement and success, and where work ethics and sport ethics are so close as to be virtually indistinguishable (1965).

Hill explained further that, even though we complain about professionalism and the related conduct of athletes, we must remember that "halcyon amateurism" was never regarded as a value. In addition, American institutions became less and less tied to British tradition as the settlers moved west. Thus, she stressed that:

> The solution to American sporting problems does not lie in English tradition. Rather, sport in America is a cultural phenomenon, and its problems must be studied and resolved in the American tradition (1975).

166

Whatever the situation may be, sport has emerged as a universal social institution that was presumably designed originally to serve humankind by helping people to cope with an ever more complex societal life characterized by conflict and turmoil. As Hill stated, "Its problems must be studied and resolved in the American tradition." The question remains: How well is society or world culture accomplishing this purpose today? As I assess the situation today, the way the situation, this proclivity to extreme commercialization and "technologizing" of sporting activity, along with its violence and added elements of danger, has become one of the world's major "blind spots". *This activity–presumably designed to serve humankind beneficially–may be doing just the opposite! In a variety of ways, the more complex and commercial it becomes, it is actually introducing beliefs and practices that influence participants and spectators negatively.*

Conceptualizing the Ritual of Sport

I then sought to conceptualize this more precisely–that is, what the ritual of competitive sport means. I recalled that I had discussed the topic a while back with my good friend, now the late professor Harry M. Johnson, Ph.D., of the University of Illinois, UIUC.

Johnson stressed that sport involvement was fundamentally meant to be connected with the all-important values of human life that, in slightly different forms, are vital for all "valuable' human activities. Among these values are the following:

1. Health itself (of course),
2. The value of trying to make a contribution regardless of actual success--the value of effort itself,
3. The value of actual achievement, including excellence,
4. The value of respect for opponents,
5. The value of cooperation (i.e., one's ability to subordinate the self to the attainment of collective goals),
6. The value of fair play (i.e., respect for the rules of competition, which are universal ideally),
7. The value of orderly procedure for the settling of disputes, and
8. The value of grace in intensively competitive situations--including magnanimity in victory and the ability to accept defeat gracefully–and then try to gain victory the next time.

167

To continue, there can be no doubt but that the celebration of such values as these in competitive sport could have this important ritualistic quality described. We can safely say this because the goals of games and what I call educational sport are presumably not intrinsically important. However, we have increasingly decided that intrinsic importance may be given to them adventitiously—and the absence of such "donation" has become an aberration bordering on social dislocation!

Basically, sport is said to be "pure" when the values are practiced and celebrated for their own sake as (for example) human love and a sense of community are celebrated in quite pure form in various civic ceremonies. Thus, when sport is "pure" in this sense, it presumably renews within the performers and knowledgeable spectators specific commitments to the very values that are being displayed and appreciated in public under relatively strict rules and surveillance that guarantee the noninterference of extraneous, unevenly distributed advantages.

In other words, the "purity" of ritual in both Sport and many civic ceremonies should mean that certain social values are highlighted by being removed and protected from the distracting circumstances of everyday life—handicaps and temptations as well as the inevitable involvement of immediately specific goals.

The Ritual Inherent in Sport Competition Must Not Be Corrupted

Thus, careful analysis of the developing situation should be telling us that we must most careful to see to it that the important ritual inherent in sport competition is not endangered, distorted, and corrupted—as it often is now under the following circumstances:

1. When so much emphasis is placed on winning, achievement of all the other values tends to be lost or negated.
2. When the financial rewards of advanced—level participation make sport predominantly a practical activity (rather than a ritual celebrating values for their own sake).
3. When competitive sport becomes largely entertainment for which the public pays "top dollar" so that team owners and competitors may be adequately compensated.

168

(Note: Such competition increasingly involves the
enjoyment of out-and-out brutality and
even foul play rather than being a deeply serious and
lastingly satisfying kind of activity [such as religious
ritual itself is under the finest type of situation].)

4. When too sharp a separation is made between
   the performers and the spectators (consumers).

(Note: In other words, the game (or religious ritual!)
played or enacted before spectators as consumers
needs to have a relationship to the "real life" activities
of those who look on and/or partake.

5. When there is a loss of perspective, and
   skill of a physical nature and outstanding performance
   are made exclusive or the highest of values, we forget
   that these are largely instrumental in nature.

Hence, in addition to the valuable sport experience itself at the time, it is
what these concurrent values are presumably required for subsequently that is
truly important--that is, achievement off the playing field and enjoyment of a fine
life experience through the medium of the sport contest and all that this could
involve.

Viewed in this way, a disinterested observer can say: "Yes, I do
understand what relationship the right kind of involvement in sport and
tangentially related physical activity has to the fundamental purpose of a society."

The Ritual of Sport *Is* Being Corrupted

However, just what are we permitting to happen at present? The ritual of
sport is being corrupted daily. The following is a list of our "transgressions" that
could be easily expanded:

1. Promoting the idea that "WINNING" is the only thing…
2. Spending infinitely more money on varsity sports for the
    few than that spent on intramural sports for the
    vast majority
3. Offering "athletic scholarships" when there is no
    "financial need".
4. Permitting "trash talk" in competitive sport.
5. Permitting "showboating" by athletes after a successful
    play.
6. Permitting "TV sport universities" to debase education
    by promoting semi-professional sport played by so-called

"scholar-athletes".

7. Permitting professional boxing (with the attendant brain damage!)
8. Featuring professional wrestling on television that is a disgusting sham and travesty of the fine sport of wrestling
9. Permitting "all-out" combat ("Extreme Sport") on television (and now it's offered for women too!).
10. Permitting (promoting?) the development of "high-risk" sport where "life and limb" are increasingly threatened.
11. Promoting the idea that competitive sport is good for young people, but then denying funding for intramural sport for the large majority of students in the schools.
12. Permitting professional boxing as a sport for women too!
13. Encouraging the whole idea of "martial-art" sport–when it's "self-defense" that should be stressed—not aggression!
14. Failing to take action sooner--and more strongly!– against drugs in sport. This abuse will "kill" sport in the long run… (Is this the antidote?)
15. Permitting the type of sport in which studies have shown *fair play, honesty, and sportsmanship actually decline in a university experience* (Stoll et al.).
16. Paying ridiculously high salaries to professional athletes thus creating a "false sense of values" to youth.
17. Permitting the concept of "hero" to be applied to professional athletes, an unworthy of such ascription thus unduly influencing youth as to what's important in life.
18. Overemphasizing the importance of involvement (*and winning!*) in *international* sport competition. (the "Own the podium" mentality)
19. Permitting the expansion of "violent" sports, but not also making appropriate provisions for excellent "sport injury care" for all.
20. Fostering a way of life that encourages "spectatoritis" instead of actual ongoing involvement in healthful physical activity and sport.

The Appropriate Remedies for "Errant" Sport Must Be Instituted

If these conditions are true, it means that we need to assess the evolving situation carefully and then proceed to institute the appropriate remedies. To provide us with an approach that should help to communicate with policy makers at all levels about this ever-increasing problem, consider the five–question approach to the building of effective communication skills recommended by Mark Bowden, a communications specialist (*National Post*, Canada, 2008 11 24, FP3).

Note: These five questions are repeated from the Prologue in this volume.

Question 1: Where are we now?

The answer is that we have in so many instances permitted deviation from the basic, valuable purposes for which sport was originally created. Osterhoudt (2006) tells us that competitive sport has become increasingly devoted to "the production, distribution, and consumption of commodities, power, wealth, fame, and privilege in predominantly medical, military, character enhancement, acculturative, political, commercial, entertainment, and recreational terms, which is to say in *instrumental* terms" (R. G. Osterhoudt in *Sport As a Form of Human Fulfillment*, Victoria, BC, CA: Trafford, 2006)).

Question 2. Why are we here?

The answer is that we are here because society has mistakenly permitted the excess of capitalistic and technological development to influence and adversely sport in the same way that other societal institutions have been influenced by these influences. Sport does indeed seem to be "the opiate of the masses"! Such development and "progress" have also joined forces with ongoing technological advancement confronting society almost irresistibly.

Question 3. Where do we want to be?

The answer is–as mentioned above–that we want to make certain that we create a situation where *"Sport involvement is related to and connected with the all-important values of human life that, in slightly different forms, are vital for all 'valuable' human activities."*

Question 4. How do we get there?

The answer is that we should be most careful to see to it, therefore, that *the important ritual inherent in sport competition* is maintained to the greatest extent possible. As we have seen, it is endangered, distorted, and corrupted by the presence of the following circumstances:

a. When so much emphasis is placed on winning, achievement of all the other values tends to be lost or negated.

b. When the financial rewards of advanced–level participation make sport predominantly a practical activity (rather than a ritual celebrating values for their own sake).

c. When competitive sport becomes largely entertainment for which the public pays "top dollar" so that team owners and competitors may be adequately compensated.

> (Note: Such competition increasingly involves the enjoyment of out-and-out brutality and even foul play rather than being a deeply serious and lastingly satisfying kind of activity.)

d. When too sharp a separation is made between the performers and the spectators (consumers).

> (Note: In other words, the game or context that is played or enacted before spectators or consumers needs to have a relationship to the "real life" activities of those who look on and/or partake.

e. When there is a loss of perspective, and skill of a physical nature and outstanding performance are made exclusive or the highest of values, we forget that these are largely *instrumental* in nature for the achievement of power, wealth, fame, and privilege in predominantly commercial and entertainment enterprises.

Thus, it is what these values are presumably required for subsequently is what's really important--that is, achievement off the playing field and enjoyment of a fine life experience through the medium of the sport contest and all that this could involve.

Question 5. What exactly should we do?

The answer is that we should encourage all professionals active in physical activity education and educational sport to accept *quality* as the first priority of their professional endeavors. Their personal involvement and specialization should include a high level of competency and skill under girded by established knowledge about the highest type of aims and objectives in competitive sport that our field should be promoting. On such a basis, it can be argued that the role of professional task sport coaches and physical activity educators is as important as any in society.

Concluding Statement

The present is no time for indecision, half-hearted commitment, imprecise knowledge, and general unwillingness to debate this position about the highest or ideal form of sport participation with the public at all levels. If we hope to bring the benefits of the "*right* kind" of sport participation to children and youth, we must sharpen our focus and improve the quality of our professional effort. Only in this way will we be able to combat the modification process that capitalistic society and accompanying technology have visited upon us in respect to people's understanding of what constitutes the finest type of competitive sport. In the 21st century, humankind deserves better than the type of sport as a social institution that "somehow" gradually materialized in the 20th century.

Selection #10
The Olympic Games:
A Question of Values

There's a vocal minority who believe the Olympic Games should be abolished. There's another minority, including the Games officials and the athletes, who presumably feel the enterprise is doing just fine. There's a larger minority undoubtedly solidly behind the commercial aspects of the undertaking. They have a good thing going; they liked the Games the way they are developing--the bigger, the better! Finally, there's the vast majority to whom the Olympics are either interesting, somewhat interesting, or a bore. This "vast majority," if the Games weren't there every four years, would probably agree that the world would go on just the same, and some other social phenomenon would take up their leisure time.

The people love a spectacle. The 2000 Olympic Games held in Sydney, Australia were a spectacle, from start to finish. Sydney, Australia evidently wanted worldwide recognition. Without doubt, Sydney got recognition! The world's outstanding athletes wanted the opportunity to demonstrate their excellence. From all reports they had such an occasion to their heart's and ability's content. The International Olympic Committee, along with their counterparts in each of the 200 participating nations, earnestly desired the show to go on; it went on with a bang! Obviously, Sydney spent an enormous amount of money and energy to finance and otherwise support this extravaganza and surrounding competition. The IOC and its affiliates will presumably remain solvent for another four years, while Sydney contemplates its involvement with this enormous event and its aftermath. "Problem, what problem?" most people in the public sector would assuredly ask if they were confronted with such a question..

The Problem

This analysis revolves around the criticisms of the "abolish the Games group." Sir William Rees-Mogg (1988, pp. 7-8), is one of the Olympic Movement's most vituperative opponents. He believes the problem is of enormous magnitude. In fact, he lists fifteen sub–problems in no particular order of importance except for the first criticism that sets the tone for the remainder: "The Olympic Games have become a grotesque jamboree of international hypocrisy. Whatever idealism they once had has been lost. The Games now stand for some of the things which are most rotten and corrupt in the modern world, for prestige, nationalism, publicity, prejudice, bureaucracy, and the exploitation of talent" (p. 7).

It would not be appropriate to enumerate here *in great detail* the remaining 14 problems and issues brought forward by Rees-Mogg. Simply put, however, he states that "The Games have been taken over by a vulgar nationalism, in place of the spirit of internationalism for which they were revived" (p.7). He decries also that, in addition to promoting racial intolerance, "the objectives of many national Olympic programmes is the glorification and self-assertion of totalitarian state regimes," often "vile regimes guilty of many of the crimes which the Olympic Games are supposed to outlaw" (p. 7).

Rees-Mogg decries further "The administration of the Olympic Games [that] is politically influenced and morally bankrupt" (p. 7). Additionally, at this point, he asserts that "the international bureaucracies of several sports have become among the most odious of the world." In this respect he lashes out especially at tennis, chess, cricket, and track and field. Still further, he charges that threats by countries to boycott the Olympics have time and again made it a political arena akin to the United Nations.

The messenger has not completed his message. Rees-Mogg condemns "the worship of professionally abnormal muscular development." He states that it is "a form of idolatry to which ordinary life is often sacrificed" (p. 7). Since 1988, when these words were written, these problems have not been corrected. They have actually worsened (e.g., ever-more drugs to enhance performance, bribery of officials assigned to site selection). The problem of drug ingestion to promote bodily development for enhanced performance has now become legendary. Couple this with over-training begun at early ages in selected sports for both boys and girls, and it can be argued that natural , all-round development has been thwarted for a great many young people, not to mention that only a minute number makes it through to "Olympic glory." More could be said, but the point has been made. Basically, Rees-Mogg has claimed that it has become a world "in which good *values* are taken by dishonest men and put to shameful uses" (p. 8).

Social Forces as Value Determinants

In the present discussion about the Olympic Games, it may be worthwhile to first take a brief look at the "Olympic Games Problem" from the standpoint of the discipline of sociology. This is because in an analysis such as this, the investigator soon realizes the importance of the major social forces (e.g., values, economics, religion) as determinants of the direction a society may take at any given moment. Sociology can indeed help with the question of *values*. For example, Parsons' complex theory of social action can be used to place any theory of social or individual values in perspective. His general action system is composed of four major analytically separable subsystems: (a) *the cultural system*, (b) *the social system*, (c) *the psychological system*, and (d) *the system of the behavioral organism*. The theory explains how these subsystems compose *a hierarchy of societal control and conditioning* (Johnson, 1969, pp. 46-58; Johnson, 1994, pp. 57 et ff.).

The cultural system at the top in the action-theory hierarchy provides the basic structure and its components, in a sense, thereby, programming the complete action system. The social system is next in descending order; it has to be more or less harmoniously related to the *functional* problems of social systems. The same holds for the structure and functional problems of the third level, the psychological system (personality), and the fourth level, the system of the behavioral organism. Further, the subsystem of culture exercises "control" over the social system, and so on up and down the scale. Legitimization is provided to the level below or "pressure to conform" if there is inconsistency. Thus, there is a "strain toward consistency" among the system levels, led and controlled from above downwards.

What is immediately important to keep in mind is that there are *four levels of structure within the social system* itself (e.g., Hong Kong as a social system within Southeast Asia and, more recently, in its developing relationship with Mainland China's culture). Proceeding from the highest to the lowest level, i.e., from the general to the more specific, we again find four levels that are designated as (a) values, (b) norms, (c) the structure of collectivities, and (d) the structure of roles. All of these levels are normative in that the social structure is composed of sanctioned cultural limits within which certain types of behavior are mandatory or acceptable. Keeping in mind for the present discussion that *values are at the top* --the highest level--and that there are many categories of values (scientific, artistic, *sport*, and values for personalities, etc.). These social values--including *sport* values too, of course--are simply assessments of the ideal general character for the social system in question. Finally, the basic point to keep in mind here is that *individual* values about sport will *inevitably* be "conditioned" by the social values prevailing in any given culture. In other words, there will be very strong pressure to conform.

Use of the Term "Value" in Philosophy

Moving from the discipline of sociology to that of philosophy, the investigator will use the term "value" as equivalent to the concepts of "worth" and "goodness." The opposite of these terms (i.e., "evil") will be referred to as "disvalue." It is possible, also, to draw a distinction between two kinds of value; namely, *intrinsic* value and *extrinsic* value. When a human experience has intrinsic value, therefore, it is good or valuable in itself--i.e., an end in itself. An experience that has extrinsic value is one that brings about goodness or value also, but such goodness or value serves *as a means to the achievement of something or some gain in life..*

One of the four major subdivisions of philosophy has been called *axiology* (or the study of values). Until philosophy's so-called "Age of Analysis" became so strongly entrenched in the Western world at least, it was argued typically that the study of values was *the* end result of philosophizing as a process. It was argued that a person should develop a system of values consistent with his/her beliefs in the subdivisions of *metaphysics* (questions about reality), *epistemology* (acquisition of knowledge), and *logic* (exact relating of ideas). Some believed that values existed only because of the interest of the "valuer" *(the interest theory). The existence theory*, conversely, held that values exist independently in the universe, although they are important in a vacuum, so to speak. They could be considered as "essence" added to "existence". A pragmatist (e.g., an experimentalist) views value in a significantly different manner *(the experimentalist theory)*. Here values that yield practical results that have "cash value" bring about the possibility of greater happiness through

176

more effective values in the future. One further theory, *the part-whole theory*, is explained by the idea that effective relating of parts to the whole brings about the highest values (Zeigler, 1989, pp. 29-31).

Domains of Value Under Axiology

The study of ethics under axiology considers morality, conduct, good and evil, and ultimate objectives in life. There are a number of approaches to the problem of whether life, as humans know it, is worthwhile. Some people are eternally hopeful *(optimism)*, while others wonder whether life is worth the struggle *(pessimism)*. In between these two extremes there is the golden mean *(meliorism)* that would have humans facing life boldly while striving constantly to improve one's situation. In the latter instance it is not possible to make final decisions about whether good or evil will prevail in the world.

A second most important question under ethics is what is most important in life for the individual. This is a fundamental question, of course, in this discussion about human values in relation to the Olympic Games. What is the ultimate end of a person's existence? Some would argue that pleasure is the highest good *(hedonism)*. One position or approach under hedonism in modern history is known as *utilitarianism*.. Here society becomes the focus, not the individual. The basic idea is to promote the greatest happiness for the greatest number in the community. Another important way of looking at the *summum bonum* (or highest good) in life is called *perfectionism*. With such an approach the individual is aiming for complete self-realization, and a similar goal is envisioned for society as well.

A logical progression following from an individual's decision about the greatest good in life is the standard of conduct that he or she sets for the "practice of living." A *naturalistic* approach would not have a person do anything that leads to self-destruction; self-preservation is basic. In the late 18th century in Germany, Immanuel Kant, known as an *idealist* , felt that a person should act on only what should be considered a universal law. Similarly, orthodox religion decrees that humans must obey God's wishes that have been decreed with a purpose for all humankind. *Pragmatism*, defined loosely, suggest a trial run in a person's imagination to discover the possible consequences of planned actions.

Continuing with this line of philosophic thought a bit further because of the obvious relationship it has to involvement with the Olympic Games in one way or another (i.e., as participant, official, coach, governing body member, advertiser, governmental official, what have you?), certain interests we develop are apt to guide people's conduct in life. Those who are too self-centered are egotistical *(egoism)*, while those feel their life purpose is to serve others are called altruistic *(altruism)*. Many would argue, however, that Aristotle's concept of the "golden mean" should be deemed best, a desirable aim for a person to fulfill with his or her life span.

There are, of course other areas of value under the axiology subdivision of philosophy over and above ethics that treats moral conduct (e.g., *aesthetics* , that has to do with the "feelings" aspects of a human's conscious life). Further, because there has been a need to define still further values in the life of humans, specialized philosophies of education and religion have developed, for example. This applies further to a sub department of the mother discipline of philosophy that has become known as sport philosophy. In sport philosophy, people would presumably make decisions about the kind, nature, and worth of values that are intrinsic to, say, the involvement of people in sport however defined.

An Assessment of the Problem

The problem, the author believes, is this: opportunities for participation in all competitive sport--not just *Olympic* sport-- moved historically from amateurism to semi-professionalism, and then on to full-blown professionalism. The Olympic Movement, because of a variety of social pressures, followed suit in both ancient times and in the present. When the International Olympic Committee gave that final push to the pendulum and admitted professional athletes to play in the Games, they may have pleased *most* of the spectators and *all* of the advertising and media representatives. But in so doing the floodgates were opened, and the original ideals upon which the Games were reactivated were completely abandoned. This is what caused Sir Rees-Mogg to state that crass commercialism had won the day. This abandonment of any semblance of what was the original Olympic ideal was the "straw that broke the camel's back." This ultimate decision regarding eligibility for participation has been devastating to those people who earnestly believe that money and sport are like oil and water; they simply do not mix! Their response has been to abandon any further interest in, or support for, the entire Olympic Movement.

The question must, therefore be asked: "What should rampant professionalism in competitive sport at the Olympic Games mean to any given country of the 200 nations involved?" This is not a simple question to answer responsibly. In this brief statement, it should be made clear that the professed social values of a country *should* ultimately prevail--and they *will* prevail in the final analysis. However, this ultimate determination will not take place rapidly. The social values of a social system will eventually have a strong influence on the individual values held by most citizens in that country, also. If a country is moving toward the most important twin values of equalitarianism and achievement, for example, what implications does that have for competitive sport in that political entity? The following are some questions to be asked *before* a strong continuing commitment is made to sponsor such involvement through governmental and/or private funding:

1. Can it be shown that involvement in competitive sport at one or the other of the three levels (i.e., amateur, semiprofessional, professional) brings about desirable *social* values (i.e., more value than disvalue)?

2. Can it be shown that involvement in competitive sport at one or the other of the three levels (i.e., amateur, semiprofessional, or professional) brings about desirable *individual* values of both an *intrinsic* and *extrinsic* nature (i.e., creates more value than disvalue)?

3. If the answer to Questions #1 and #2 immediately are both affirmative (i.e., that involvement in competitive sport at any or all of the three levels postulated [i.e., *amateur, semiprofessional, and professional* sport] provides a sufficient amount of social and individual value to warrant such promotion), *can* sufficient funds be made available to support or permit this promotion at any or all of the three levels listed?

4. If funding to support participation in competitive sport at any or all of the three levels (amateur, semi–professional, professional) is *not* available (or such participation is *not* deemed advisable), should priorities--as determined by the will of the people--be established about the importance of each level to the country based on analysis of the potential social *and* individual values that may accrue to the society and its citizens from such competitive sport participation at one or more levels?

Concluding Statement

In this analysis the investigator asks whether a country should be involved with, or continue involvement with, the ongoing Olympic Movement--as well as *all* competitive sport--unless the people in that country first answer some basic questions. These questions ask to what extent such involvement can be related to the social and individual values that the country holds as important for all of its citizens. Initially, study will be needed to determine whether sport competition at either or all of the three levels (i.e., amateur, semi-professional, and professional) does indeed provide positive social and individual value (i.e., more value than disvalue) in the country concerned. Then careful assessment--through the efforts of qualified social scientists and philosophers--should be made of the populace's opinions and basic beliefs about such involvement. If participation in competitive sport at each of the three levels can make this claim to being a social institution that provides positive value to the country, these efforts should be supported to the extent possible--including the sending of a team to future Olympic Games. If sufficient funding for the support of *all* three levels of participation is *not* available, from either governmental or private sources, *the expressed will of the people should be established to determine what priorities will be invoked.*

References

Johnson, H.M. (1969). The relevance of the theory of action to historians. *Social Science Quarterlty 21*(2), 46-58.

Johnson, H.M. (1994). Modern organizations in the Parsonsian theory of action. In A. Farazmond, *Modern organizations: Administrative theory in contemporary society*, pp. 57 et ff. Westport, CT: Praeger.

Rees-Mogg, W. (1988). The decline of the Olympics into physical and moral squalor.*Coaching Focus, 8 (1988)*, 7.

Zeigler, E.F. (1989). *Sport and physical education philosophy.*. Carmel, IN: Benchmark.

Selection #11
Rebellion in Canadian Interuniversity Sport:
Implications for Financial Aid to All Students

(Preamble: During the years of the "Great Depression" (i.e., the 1930s) after the stock market crash of 1929, the writer worked his way through college in the States. Stepson of a minister, he worked 20-25 hours a week during the school year, and full-time during summers, for the entire four-year experience. In addition, he played several sports, took part in a variety of campus activities, and had a steady girl friend. Somehow, [!] he "survived", but his formal education necessarily suffered. Eventually he became a department head and coached football, swimming, and wrestling at Western in the period from 1949 to 1956. After administrative stints at Michigan and Illinois, he returned to become the first dean of the Faculty of Physical Education in 1971 and semi-retired finally in 1989. He believes strongly that a qualified university student preparing today to contribute to 21st century society should not face the same financial problems.)

Any intelligent observer cannot help wonder about competitive sport's place in society today. Considering the obvious excesses of commercialized sport, we could argue that increasingly they seem to be emulating the level of the Circus Maximus era of ancient Rome. (Those athletes back then often died, however, instead of becoming millionaires...)

The term "sport" has become ubiquitous. Highly commercialized sport is indeed "light years" away from the initial sporting experience of a young girl or boy facing juvenile competition for the first time.

Have you ever wondered, for example, why fans in the Canadian Football League's Toronto, Calgary, or Vancouver teams, get all excited about watching talented, but basically second-level Americans athletes represent their cities' honor in gridiron battle? What motivates these fans? We know what motivates the athletes.

The Role of Sport and Physical Recreation in Canadian University Life

Now direct your attention to the role of competitive sport and physical recreation in Canadian university life. All students should have a fine *intramural* sport and physical recreation program available to them. In addition, in North America, as opposed to the rest of the world, competitive, *extramural* sport programs for men, and then for women as well, developed within the universities themselves during the 20th century.

This development has been good, but disturbing problems have risen along the way. Canada's geography and the ever-present concern about "sleeping with an elephant" (in this case the National Collegiate Athletic Association of the USA) have become problems of immediate concern.

Why Are Some Universities Considering Secession from Canadian Interuniversity Sport?

Thus, the question is being asked today: "Why are the Thunderbirds of the University of British Columbia and the Clan of Simon Fraser University moving to secede from Canadian Interuniversity Sport Both universities are moving to join with Division II of the National Collegiate Athletics Association in the United States?"

Is it just a question of "easier access" to opponents by heading south instead of traveling far across the Canadian terrain? Is it that NCAA Division II status allows student-athletes to receive aid that includes the costs of tuition and fees, room and board, books and supplies, and other expenses related to attendance at the University?

Why should UBC and SFU not move to Division I status in the States? Who wants to be a second-class citizen? The answer to that is simple. Division I in the NCAA amounts to becoming a professional athlete. Division IA is only a short step behind. ?

The approach of Canadian University Sport (CIS) is dull, you see. It does not permit purely athletic scholarships. However, each university seems to have figured out its own unique way of assisting "scholar-athletes" to "some extent or another" This despite the CIS stipulation that financial aid is limited for student-athletes to tuition and fees only.

Consider this information from the discussion guide recently made available to members of the UBC university community in Vancouver:

UBC athletics and recreation is dedicated to attracting the best student-athletes from around the world and considers athletic scholarships as an integral part of this plan.

UBC's Millennium Breakfast is the largest single-day athletic scholarship fundraiser in Canada and has raised in excess of $5 million since 2000. Funds raised through this event go directly into

UBC's Athletic Scholarship Endowment, which ensures that athletes have opportunities to realize their athletic and academic goals in Canada for decades to come.

UBC's Athletic Scholarship Endowment is approximately $9 million. While the Athletic Scholarship Endowment is used to fund athletic scholarships, the UBC varsity teams, as well as the Department as a whole, are funded through student fees (40%) and business operations (60%), which is revenue generated through facility rental, sport camps, sponsorship and fundraising.

Donors to the Athletic Scholarship Endowment are connected to UBC Athletics and Recreation through sport — 90% of donors are former university, national or international athletes and the remaining 10% are connected in some way to a current or former varsity athlete.

UBC is in contact with more than 9,000 athletic alumni who are essential to UBC Athletics and Recreation's campaign to raise $75 million for the Athletic Scholarship Endowment over the next 10 years, which will further enhance UBC's athletic program.

This is impressive, you might say at first glance. However, if you compare it to Division I universities in the U.S.A., it is "chicken-feed". The annual budget for athletics at The Ohio State University is about 121 million dollars. The head football coach at the University of Tennessee earns $2,200,000 annually. That is big business! The athletics department at OSU typically contributes a million dollars to the University's operating budget after paying its own expenses. The university president there "minds his p's and q's" before issuing a directive to the athletics department. It could have *him* fired if he tried to upset their applecart in any way.

It becomes obvious that we are talking about different kinds of sport in different universities. It appears that individual involvement in sport assumes different characteristics as it runs the gamut of a spectrum–from frivolity to play to competition to work!

What Is This Ritual Involving Competitive Sport?

Trying to figure this all out more precisely–that is, what the ritual of competitive sport means–I got together a while back with my good friend, now the late professor Harry M. Johnson, Ph.D., of the University of Illinois. After a series of "fireside chats," we concluded that sport involvement should be connected with the all-important values of human life that, in slightly different forms, are vital for all "valuable' human activities.

Among these values are the following:

      1. Health itself (of course),

      2. The value of trying to make a

contribution regardless of actual
success--the value of effort itself,

3. The value of actual achievement,
including excellence,

4. The value of respect for opponents,

5. The value of cooperation (i.e., one's
ability to subordinate the self to the
attainment of collective goals),

6. The value of fair play (i.e., respect
for the rules of competition,
which are universalistic ideally),

7. The value of orderly procedure for
the settling of disputes, and

8. The value of grace in intensively
competitive situations--including
magnanimity in victory and
the ability to accept defeat
gracefully--and then try to gain
victory the next time.2

To continue, there can be no doubt but that the celebration of such values as these (immediately above) in competitive sport has this important ritualistic quality described. We can safely say this because the goals of games and what is called *educational* sport are presumably not *intrinsically* important. However, we decided that intrinsic importance may be given to them adventitiously--and the absence of such "donation" has become an aberration bordering on social dislocation.

Basically, sport is said to be "pure" when the values are practiced and celebrated for their own sake as (for example) human love and a sense of community are celebrated in quite pure form in various civic ceremonies. Thus, when sport is "pure" in this sense, it presumably renews within the performers and knowledgeable spectators specific commitments to the very values that are being displayed and appreciated in public under relatively strict rules and surveillance that serves to guarantee the noninterference of extraneous, unevenly distributed advantages.

In other words, the "purity" of ritual in both civic ceremonies and sport means that certain social values are highlighted by being removed and protected from the distracting circumstances of everyday life--handicaps and temptations as well as the inevitable involvement of immediately specific goals.

184

The Ritual Inherent in Sport Competition
Must Not Be Corrupted

So, it can be argued successfully through careful analysis that we must be most careful to see to it that the important ritual inherent in sport competition is not endangered, distorted, and corrupted under the following circumstances:

1. When so much emphasis is placed on winning, achievement of all the other values tends to be lost or negated.

2. When the financial rewards of advanced–level participation make sport predominantly a practical activity (rather than a ritual celebrating values for their own sake).

3. When competitive sport becomes largely entertainment for which the public pays "top dollar" so that team owners and competitors may be adequately compensated.

(Note: Such competition increasingly involves the enjoyment of out-and-out brutality and even foul play rather than being a deeply serious and lastingly satisfying kind of activity [such as religious ritual itself is under the finest type of situation].)

4. When too sharp a separation is made between the performers and the spectators (consumers).

(Note: In other words, the game (or religious ritual!) played or enacted before spectators or consumers needs to have a relationship to the "real life" activities of those who look on and/or partake.

5. When there is a loss of perspective, and skill of a physical nature and outstanding performance are made exclusive or the highest of values, we forget that these are largely instrumental in nature.

*Thus, it is what these values are presumably required for **subsequently** is what's really important--that is, achievement off the playing field and enjoyment of a fine life*
experience through the medium of the sport contest and all that this could involve

Viewed in this way, a disinterested observer can say: "Yes, I do see what relationship this has to the fundamental purpose of a university wherever located in Canada?" I can understand how such experience is part of what a university education all about.

Why Are Athletes Being Singled Out
For Special Attention?

However, the question remains as to why athletes only are being singled out for "special attention" financially, when students with other, but equally important talents, are not rewarded in the same fashion.

Young people coming to universities, in addition to their knowledge, competencies, and skills acquired in their prior educational experiences, bring with them quality experiences in other educationally related aspects of life that have been deemed worthwhile traditionally.

These "quality experiences" in educationally related areas include: (1) aesthetic and creative activities, (2) communication activities, (3) social activities, (4) ancillary educational activities, AND (5) sport activities. They are all important. Students with these backgrounds help to create a vital, vibrant university community.

These young men and women come from families with varying financial backgrounds. After gaining admission, and as along as they remain bona fide students, they deserve an opportunity to experience a university education free from ever-present financial worries. In addition, after graduation they should not have to contend with staggering future debt incurred during this period when they are acquiring the background for future employment.

Universities Should Make an Even Greater
Ongoing Commitment to Student Financial Aid

Universities should be commended, of course, for their ongoing commitment to help all academically qualified citizens and permanent residents to achieve their educational goals as free from financial concerns as possible. With Canada's approach to multiculturalism, the need to build on this commitment looms even larger.

At Western, for example, the four methods of financial assistance available include (1) OSAP and other government assistance programs, (2) Bursaries (Admissions and In-Course), (3) Government Assistance Program, and (4) Work Study. The following data is taken from the University's website:

> OSAP provides financial assistance for educational costs and basic living expenses to students in postsecondary education. The amount of OSAP assistance awarded is determined by comparing educational costs (such as tuition fees, books, and basic living expenses) and personal resources (such as parental income, summer and study period income, scholarships and awards, and assets). OSAP applications are available in the spring for the upcoming September study period.

Admission Bursaries: These bursaries are non-repayable, taxable grants awarded on the basis of financial need for entering first-year students. Admission Bursaries generally range in value from $250 to $3,000. To be eligible for bursary assistance, you must be a Canadian citizen or a permanent resident, and you must demonstrate financial need. Further information on how to apply for an Admission Bursary will be provided when Western acknowledges your admission application (we'll send a package to you in the mail).

In-Course Bursaries: Bursary assistance is also available to students after first-year if they continue to have financial need. To be eligible, you must be a Canadian citizen or a permanent resident, and must complete a financial need application that is available each year in August.

Government Assistance Program Student Financial Services also administers other government assistance programs, such as the Part-Time Canada Student Loan Program, Canada Study Grant for High-Need Part-Time Students Program, and the Bursary for Students with Disabilities Program.

Work Study: Over 2,000 on-campus employment opportunities are available each year through Work Study to allow upper-year students to work in flexible environments, gain experience, and contribute financially to their education-related expenses. Students have achieved success working in laboratories, designing Web pages, writing journals, and assisting in the administration of the university. To qualify for the Work Study program, you must be a Canadian citizen or a permanent resident enrolled in at least a 60 per cent course load, and you must have financial need. Online applications are available each year in August.

Now Is the Time for Provincial Governments and Universities to Institute a Level Playing Field for All Canadian Students in Higher Education

Canada should be at the forefront in all aspects of university education. Candidates for admission should be evaluated without the need for financial help arising. Financial aid should be based solely on demonstrated need. The assertion made here is that the full, *demonstrated* financial need of every qualified student admitted should be met. *There should be no need for merit scholarships and athletic scholarships.*

If such a plan were implemented, monetary grants to low-income and middle-income families would increase significantly. In addition, students would find that the amount they must contribute from their own earnings would decrease. In addition to money earned from summer employment, additional funds can be earned *from no more than 10 hours of on- or off-campus employment.* There should be no need to work longer or to take out monetary loans.

Concluding Statement

The writer submits that this proposal is not radical. It is forward looking and should be implemented at the first possible moment. Qualified young people of today should not be burdened with financial problems during the vital university period. They should not have to be looking for dubious athletic scholarships in the States *or in Canada.*

Provincial governments, universities, foundations, alumni, and business should commit at this time to create an ideal situation for **all** qualified people to obtain full benefit from the university experience.

Selection #12
Where Have They Gone?
(or How About a Canadian "Ivy League" Arrangement for Inter-University Sport?)

When I came to Canada in 1949, the football teams in the Canadian Interuniversity Athletic Union were from the University of Toronto, McGill University, Queens University, and The University of Western Ontario. At Western, John Metras was the head coach; (Dr.) Jack Fairs was the backfield coach, and I became the line coach. Happily, due to a combination of circumstances, Western emerged as Canadian champions in both 1949-50 and 1950-51.

How times have changed! As I checked the rankings while writing this piece, none of the football teams from these four universities are listed in the first ten! This tells me that these four universities have maintained their academic standards for student admission and student retention. It tells me, also, that they are not "buying" their athletes in one way or another. (I hasten to add, however, that *all* worthy students *with proven financial need* should be helped.)

Should the present lowly status of the "Big Four" universities vis-à-vis national football standing concern us? It has been reported that Nero fiddled while Rome burned! But then we are not certain he had all of his mental faculties. Here, in this plaintive commentary, I argue we too are "fiddling while some aspects of university competitive sport are catching fire!"

What do I mean by this? I mean basically that several (potentially [?] box-office) university sports are gradually sliding into semi-professionalism. Let me say quickly that I have no quarrel with a young person striving for excellence in competitive sport on a semiprofessional or professional basis. Why should anyone? After all, sport is a legitimate aspect of our culture despite the evident abuses that are prevailing increasingly.

It would help, however, if much of the sham and hypocrisy could be removed from competitive sport. In other fields, the field of music, for example, the problem of amateurism, semi–professionalism, and professionalism has been resolved quite nicely. The person who plays the trumpet in the high school band is an *amateur*. If he or she is good enough to play with some group regularly on weekends for--say--one hundred dollars a night, then we can agree that *semi–professionalism* is being achieved. Who can be critical of this? Finally, this person might eventually choose to become a professional musician or music teacher as a lifetime occupation. At this point the individual really is a *professional* because his or her entire living will come from this source.

Such a graduated scheme was--and is!--viewed for a long time as quite acceptable in our society for musicians, artists, sculptors, actors, and many others-

-but not for athletes! Why are athletes so different when it comes to involvement either within educational circles or on national- and international-level teams? Granted there have been several breakthroughs in isolated instances (e.g., trust funds established by government for downhill skiers, etc.), but this has been accompanied by a lot of smirking and/or grimacing by diehard purists.

However, most unfortunately, cheating and deceit developed gradually and steadily with this semi-professionalism throughout the 20th century for so many young men (and now young women too) in commercialized U.S. university sport. And these athletes are often underprivileged youngsters too, more Black than white. They spend so much time on football, for example, that they rarely earn a baccalaureate degree in the allotted four years. This is why I am so worried that this "U.S. cancer" will continue to spread north of the border.

Further, because of the excessive pressure exerted when semi–professionalism in university sport is permitted, there are now more than four hundred substances that may be ingested as many coaches and athletes seek to bring about improved performance in sport. Anabolic steroids are just the tip of the iceberg! Frankly, I argue daily that we simply should not be increasingly placing our Canadian university athletes, male or female, in such a position that-- because of excessive pressure to win--they are tempted to experiment with potentially harmful drugs.

Generally speaking, Canada has done quite well until now. High school teacher/coaches in Canada can, by and large, take a bow for preserving athletics of an educational nature in their programs for both young men and women. Undoubtedly there has been much support from principals and superintendents too. Now I am worried that Canadian university and college presidents and deans won't continue to show as much sense--that they won't be unduly swayed by wealthy alumni or a federal government that from time to time seem determined to use the universities as training grounds for international elite sport. We need to ask ourselves over and again what "owning the podium" does to all concerned when such a situation prevails.

Our problem now is that there are conflicting forces at work within our federal government and universities that are gradually leading us down the garden path to a Canadian version of the "scholar-athlete" as identified by both the National Collegiate Athletic Association and the National Association for Intercollegiate Athletics in the United States. Many of our Canadian officials argue that we are too intelligent and wise to allow the worst elements of the U.S. system to develop within higher education here. This may be true, but I doubt it. I have been naive at times, but I am not stupid. I have personally seen these forces at work in three major U.S. universities.

I taught and coached in, and also administered departments of physical education in, major universities in the United States (at Yale as an instructor-coach, and at Michigan and Illinois as an administrator). I know firsthand what developed over there. So, when I--having been department head here from 1950-56--had the opportunity to return to Canada as the first dean of the Faculty of Physical Education (now "School of Kinesiology") at Western in the early 1970s, I heaved a great sigh of relief. The symptoms of an incipient ulcer vanished. I was so happy to return to the situation as envisioned at The University of Western Ontario (by Dr. Wes Dunn and committee) in which the new faculty's undergraduate program, graduate program, intercollegiate athletics program, and physical recreation and intramurals program could strive for a concept of "balanced excellence" in a truly educational environment.

But that was then; now, some 35 years later, the situation in higher education has changed markedly in all parts of the country. Western has truly been favored because of the very high quality of its athletic administrators and coaches since the faculty started. Many people (e.g., Dr. Darwin Semotiuk as both football coach and then athletics administrator) contributed to this unique development. However, social forces at work and certain professional concerns within the field, have placed us in a true "crossroads dilemma."

Also, from time to time, student groups clamor to have athletics, interuniversity and recreational, placed under their aegis. Their concern is understandable, but they should appreciate that both Dean Jim Weese, Faculty of Health Sciences, and Director Earl Noble, School of Kinesiology, are dedicated to preserve what they consider to be *educational* and *recreational* sport here at Western. Nevertheless, university administrators and faculty across the land need to be kept on alert to the growing, insidious influence of the media barrage emanating from the States covering the exploits of the majority of universities and colleges where semi–professional athletics prevails.

As matters are "progressing," the best hope for retention of "athletic sanity" for some Canadian universities (e.g., those relating to Ontario interuniversity athletics) would be the establishment of a Canadian "Ivy League." This will leave an assortment of other institutions in the east, west and Quebec, selling their "academic souls" for a mess of pottage in a wide-open Canadian league. Question: Exactly how does the resultant media attention and notoriety of such present endeavor benefit them? Winning football teams may attract attention, but they do not make a great university!

Truly, it is not fair to athletes and coaches when they do so well within the Ontario Universities' Athletic Association to have them advance to national play-downs competing with teams from the other three conferences where athletic scholarships or other financial enticements have been instituted. We want our male and female athletes to continue to do the best that they can within an educational environment. Expanding what I said about football above, semiprofessional sport does not a great university make!

Canada, and Canadian universities especially, should be wiser than their commercialized U.S. counterparts are with their overall sport programs. Our objective should be solely to profit from the benefits that a sound program of developmental physical activity in sport, exercise, and related expressive activities can bring for all people in our country--accelerated, normal, or special.

The situation is not a simple one to resolve. However, we certainly don't want Canada as a nation to ever approximate the former East Germany (DDR) in the realm of competitive sport--that is, a country with a small population, functioning in a political orbit that encourages the winning of a disproportionate number of Olympic medals in order to justify its political system. Actually, we could never accomplish this goal anyhow without a severe perversion of our fundamental principles.

Canada can do *reasonably well* in international sport as well as provide healthful physical activity and physical recreation for all its citizens. Achieving such a balance does seems difficult to accomplish, but it can be done without perverting secondary or higher education. At the university level, we have a sufficient number of problems while we strive to avoid shabbiness because of inadequate support. Permitting an increasing, unhealthy type of "athletic-scholarship mentality" to "creep" into university sport would eventually make us ridiculous and laughable to those who truly understand how it "ought to be." It would also have a deleterious effect at the lower educational levels. It's better to be proud and somewhat poorer financially, yet remain honorable and fair as we promote fine educational and recreational sport for all of our students.

Selection #13
"Rah, Rah, Rah" for Moral Character in University Sport?

Does a university improve its "greatness" by commercializing its competitive sport program? What is *great* sport? Historically, this question has been answered by North American universities in different ways. One response to this query has been the commercialization of university sport with substantive financial aid to superior athletes in various "gate receipt sports." This approach became a steadily increasing phenomenon for many universities throughout the 20th century.

Other universities and colleges did not follow suit, however. They sought to have *great* sports for all students involved, but they also sought to keep athletic programs in perspective with the institutions' overall educational goal. *In the latter case (e.g., The Ivy League), financial aid was provided only to academically qualified students with proven need.* In addition, athletic competency was not singled out to the exclusion of other worthwhile activities in which students participate.

Considering the whole picture today, the result of these different approaches is that now it would take the proverbial Philadelphia lawyer to understand the distinctions in university classification in this regard by the National Collegiate Athletic Association and the National Association for Intercollegiate Athletics. Fortunately, for Canada, it is much simpler to decipher the situation.

Fundamentally, however, before even considering what is occurring in the realm of university and college sport, there is an urgent need to challenge the underlying human values and norms that have determined the direction the United States itself as it heads into the 21st century. These values and norms are the important determinants of choices that are made in education, as well as in other aspects of life. A basic question to be answered initially is: "What type of character do we seek for people?" I asked this question *generally* in *A Way Out of Ethical Confusion* (2004, p. iii) while referring to Commager's 1966 *specific* list of 12 traits–i.e., what he called "common denominators"–that he attributed to Americans at that time.

In this list are many traits, some of which apply directly to the topic of sport's relationship to character. These are:

(1) self-confidence;
(2) materialism;
(3) complacency bordering occasionally on arrogance;
(4) cultivation of the competitive spirit; and
(5) indifference to, and exasperation with, laws,
    rules, and regulations" (p. 7).

I believe personally that the situation had deteriorated during the course of the 20th century. If true, my assessment has significance in a search for an answer to the topic at hand. Should competitive sport develop character? If so, what type of "character" should it develop?

Critiquing Competitive Sport

In this process of critiquing competitive sport, there does appear to be many questions–i.e., possible drawbacks–that should be raised. The reader may agree that society should strive to keep sport's drawbacks in check to the greatest possible extent. This is important because, in recent decades, we have witnessed the rise of sport throughout the United States to the status of a fundamentalist religion. (In Canada, only the sport of hockey is undoubtedly a "fundamental religion" for a significant portion of the population.). In addition, as it is occurring elsewhere, it appears to be becoming *a destroyer of certain fundamental values of individual and social life*. Nevertheless, at times, in other venues sport is at times being called upon to serve as *a redeemer of wayward youth*.

Additionally, the knowledge emanating from onrushing science and technology has concurrently also become *the tempter of many coaches and athletes*. The whole question of drug-taking all around the world to promote superior performance, for example, has reached dangerous levels. This development has added another ethical and legal dimension to the personal and professional conduct of those people who are unduly anxious for recognition and financial gain.

Beliefs such as these have created a vacuum of positive belief for overemphasized sport (i.e., sport as an anti-value) for others like me who wants to view *"educational" and/or recreational competitive sport as a life-enhancer*. It has become difficult to find that approach in interuniversity sport, generally speaking, except in those sports that are not sustained through gate receipts--golf, tennis, gymnastics, soccer, and almost all of women's sport).

To get to the heart of the matter as we proceed with this discussion, it is important to consider the fundamental nature of the society in which such competitive sport is taking place. The grand social theory of Talcott Parsons provides useful direction for us as we seek to understand that is going on.

Parsonsian Theory: The General Action System

Initially, to understand this social theory, a person should appreciate that Parsons' "general action system" (*implying instrumental activism*) is viewed as being composed of four subsystems: (a) cultural system, (b) social system, (c) psychological system, and (d) behavioral-organic system. What this means, viewed from a different perspective, is that *explicit* human behavior is comprised of aspects that are (a) cultural, (b) social, (c) psychological, and (d) organic. These four subsystems together compose *a cybernetic hierarchy of control and conditioning* that operates in both directions (i.e., both up and down). Johnson (1994) explains that an example of a cybernetic system might be a thermostat used with an air-conditioning unit [p. 57] . . . there is an "instrumental activism" occasioned by the "value pattern" of modern societies in which a person's self–esteem depends on the extent a contribution is made in some way to life's advancement.)

The reader might already be aware of the general ideas within social theory that explain primary and secondary control in society. However, this person might not understand specifically that Parsons' contribution (his innovation!) to this theory is the application of cybernetics to what has become known as the four, functional categories (**L-I-G-A**) proceeding from the most controlling level**, L**, to the least controlling, **A**. These terms are used as variables in Parsons' formal paradigm that can be employed systematically to assist in the functional analysis of what Johnson (1994) calls "an indefinite large number of empirical problems" (p. 58). (See Figure 1 below).

The first of the subsystems is "culture," which according to Johnson (1969) "provides the figure in the carpet-the structure and, in a sense, the 'programming' for the action system as a whole" (p. 46). The structure of this type of system is typically geared to the functional problems of that level that arise--and so on down the scale, respectively. Thus, it is the subsystem of culture that legitimates and also influences the level below it (the social system). Typically, there is a definite strain toward consistency. However, the influence works both upward and downward within Parsons' action system, thereby creating a hierarchy of influence or conditioning. Social life being what it has been and is, it is almost inevitable that strain will develop within the system. Johnson explains this as "dissatisfaction with the level of effectiveness on the functioning of the system in which the strain is felt" (p. 47).

Such dissatisfaction may, for example, relate to particular aspects of a social system as follows:

> (1) the level of effectiveness of resource procurement;
> (2) the success of goal attainment;
> (3) the justice or appropriateness of allocation of rewards or
>   facilities; or
> (4) the degree to which units of the system are committed to
>   realizing (or maintaining) the values of the system.

Thus, it is *the hierarchy of control and conditioning* that comes into play when the sources of change (e.g., new religious or scientific ideas) begin to cause strain in the larger social systems, whereas the smaller social systems tend to be "strained" by the change that often develops at the personality or psychological system levels. In addition, it is quite apparent that social systems are often influenced considerably by contact with other social systems.

FIGURE 1

THE FUNCTIONAL PROBLEMS OF SOCIAL SYSTEMS*

	Instrumental	Consummatory
INTERNAL	(L) LATENT PATTERN MAINTENANCE & TENSION MANAGEMENT (Involves Stability & Continuity in Relations Among Units)	(I) INTEGRATION (Involves Success & Satisfaction in Inter- Unit Relationships)
EXTERNAL	(A) ADAPTATION (Involves Stability & Continuity in Relation to External Environment)	(G) GOAL-ATTAINMENT (Involves Success & Satisfaction in Relation to External Environment)

*Adapted from Johnson, H.M. (1994). Modern organizations in the Parsonsian theory of action. In A. Farazmand (Ed.), *Modern organizations: Administrative theory in contemporary society* (p. 59). Westport, CT: Praeger; and Hills, R.J. (1968). *Toward a science of organization* (p. 21). Eugene, OR: Center for Advanced Study of Administration.

Levels of Structure Within the Social System

Just as there were *four subsystems within the total action system* defined by Parsons and others (i.e., cultural system, social system, psychological system, and behavioral-organic system), there also appear to be four levels within that subsystem (immediately above) that has been identified as the social system or structure. These levels, proceeding from "highest" to "lowest," are (1) values, (2) norms, (3) the structure of collectivities, and (4) the structure of roles. Typically the higher levels are more general than the lower ones, with the latter group giving quite specific guidance to those segments or units of the particular system to which they apply. These "units" or "segments" are either collectivities or individuals in their capacity as role occupants.

Values represent the highest echelon of the social system level of the entire general action system. These values may be categorized into such "entities" as artistic values, educational values, social values, sport values, etc. Of course, all types or categories of values must be values of personalities. The social values of a particular social system are those values that are considered representative of the ideal general character that is desired by those who ultimately hold the power in the system being described. The most important social values in North America, for example, have been (1) the rule of law, (2) the socio-structural facilitation of individual achievement, and (3) the equality of opportunity (Johnson, 1969, p. 48).

Norms are the shared, sanctioned rules that govern the second level of the social structure. The average person finds it difficult to separate in his or her mind the concepts of values and norms. Keeping in mind the examples of values offered immediately above, some examples of norms are (1) the institution of private property, (2) private enterprise, (3) the monogamous, conjugal family, and (4) the separation of church and state.

Collectivities are interaction systems that may be distinguished by their goals, their composition, and their size. A collectivity is characterized by conforming acts and by deviant acts, which are both classes of members' action that relates to the structure of the system. Interestingly (and oddly) enough, each collectivity has a structure that consists of four levels also [and not to be discussed here]. In a pluralistic society, one finds an extremely large variety of collectivities that are held together to a varying extent by an overlapping membership constituency. Thus, members of one collectivity can and do exert greater or lesser amounts of influence upon the members of the other collectivities to which they belong.

Roles refer to the behavioral organisms (the actual humans) that interact within each collectivity. Each role has a current normative structure specific to it, even though such a role may be gradually changing. (For example, the role of the sport manager or physical educator/coach could be in a transitory state in that certain second-level norms could be changing. Yet, each specific sport manager (or physical educator/coach) still has definite normative obligations that are possible to delineate more specifically than the more generalized second-level norms, examples of which were offered above.)

A hierarchy of control and conditioning. Finally, it appears that these four levels of social structure themselves also compose *a hierarchy of control and conditioning.* As Johnson (p. 49) explains, the higher levels "legitimate, guide, and control" the lower levels, and pressure of both a direct and indirect nature can be—and generally is—employed when the infraction or violation occurs and is known.

Social Values Influence Sport Values

Keeping in mind for the present discussion that *values are at the top*—the highest level—and that they strongly influence the levels below. In addition, there are many categories of values (scientific, artistic, *sport*, and values for personalities, etc.). These social values—including *sport* values too, of course—are simply assessments of the ideal general character for the social system in question. *Finally, the basic point to keep in mind here is that individual values about sport will inevitably be "conditioned" by the social values prevailing in any given culture. In other words, there will be very strong pressure to conform.*

With the above theory in mind, we can appreciate that, when an athlete or team at any level of sport is considered to have displayed character, the word "character" may well be associated with a host of values such as teamwork, loyalty, self-sacrifice, perseverance, work ethic, and mental toughness. As a specific example, a high school athletic director defined an athlete's character as "a willingness to try no matter what the situation. An attempt to continually improve; a willingness to give all up for the cause; and sacrificing without expectations." In another example, a high school coach asserted: "Character is the belief in self-worth and your own work ethic. . . ." (Rudd *et al.*, 1999).

In professional sport, character has been defined similarly. For instance, players who work hard and don't complain about salaries are praised. Athletes who have the desire and ability to play with injuries are deemed "heroes." In this respect, such athletes "show character." The notion here is that an athlete of character is one who displays values such as teamwork, loyalty, self-sacrifice, perseverance, work ethic, and mental toughness.

Conversely, *sport scholars in the area of character development have defined character with a different set of values.* Sport scholars, including sport philosophers and sport psychologists more commonly define an athlete of character as one who is honest, fair, responsible, respectful, and compassionate (Stoll and Beller, 1998).

It does indeed seem, therefore, that at present there are two distinct definitions of character maintained by two camps. The first camp consists of coaches, administrators, and players who may typically define character with social values such as teamwork, loyalty, self-sacrifice, and perseverance. This could be designated as *"social character."* The second camp consists of sport scholars, and people of earlier generations still alive, who typically define character with moral values such as honesty, fairness, responsibility, compassion, and respect. This is commonly referred to by many of them as *"moral character."* The existence of these two camps, each with their respective definitions of character, suggests that there is confusion and disagreement concerning the definition of character in sport. (Of course, there may be some people "in the middle" who accept an overlapping, possibly conflicting set of values to describe the term "character.")

Resultantly, the differences in the way character is defined may provide strong evidence why many feel there is a lack of sportsmanship in competitive sport today. Similarly, these same people decry the "winning at-all-cost" mentality that seems to prevail in athletics now somewhat generally. Many coaches, athletic administrators, and parents may indeed place such a premium on *social* values such as teamwork, loyalty, self-sacrifice, and work ethic that they forget, or at least downplay, any emphasis on the time-honored *moral* values such as honesty, fairness, responsibility, and respect.

I am simply stating above here what I personally believe to be obvious in sport's development historically. It has become an extremely powerful social force in society. Secondly, if we grant that sport now has significant power in our North American culture—and a power growing all around the world for that matter—we should also recognize that any such social force affecting society can be dangerous if perverted (e.g., nationalism, commercialism). With this in mind, I an arguing further that sport has somehow become this powerful societal institution related to nationalism and commercialism! Yet, sport has somehow also moved to such status is society almost "by osmosis" (i.e., *without an adequately defined underlying theory.*

Somehow, most of society seems to be proceeding generally on a typically unstated stated assumption that "sport is a good thing for society to encourage, and the more sport that is offered, the better it will be!" Yet, over and above the precisely defined addition above, the term "sport" also still exhibits radical ambiguity based on both its everyday usage and additional dictionary definitions. This unwitting (?) confusion obviously adds even more to the present problem and accompanying confusion that prevails in people's minds.

Need for a Theory of Sport

This evident confusion as to "what sport is all about" is disturbing. I believe further that governmental agencies (especially!) sponsoring "amateur" sport competition should be able to state in their relationship to sport that, if such-and-such is done with reasonable efficiency and effectiveness within sporting activities, then such-and-such will (in all probability) result. Governmental personnel are in many cases doing just this, but not necessarily in the manner many of us would like them to become involved. Instead of working assiduously to create a from-the-ground-up development of young athletes in the hope that some might achieve superior status eventually, they are proceeding in what might be called a fast-track approach. By that I mean that governments are focusing directly on the development of elite athletes whom they hope will bring "fame and glory" to their country "tomorrow" (so to speak). In addition, the message that superior athletes receive is: "If you earn a medal, we'll really help you financially." In Canada, this is termed the "Own the Podium" approach.

By now, we should by now be able to argue that sport is a "relatively homogeneous substance" that can serve at least reasonably well as an indispensable balm or aid to human fulfillment within an individual life (Barzun, 1974, p. 12). The idea of "sport and developmental physical activity for all" on a lifelong basis continues to receive more "lip support" than actual investment based on monetary input to promote overall fitness and physical recreational involvement for the general population. Yet, the logical argument that–through the process of total psycho-physical involvement–sport does indeed provide "flow experience" for the individual may well be true. The question is "for whom does the bell toll?" (Csikszentmihalyi, 1993, p. 183).

It is general knowledge that John Dewey urged the educational system to place great emphasis on *direct* involvement (i.e., "We learn by doing"). The assumption has been, also, that sport has a contribution to make to the young person's development. However, Wilcox in his empirical analysis (1991) challenged "the widely held notion that sport can fulfill an important role in the development of national character." He stated that "the assumption that sport is conducive to the development of positive human values, or the 'building of character,' should be viewed more as a belief rather than as a fact." He concluded that his study did "provide some evidence to support a relationship between participation in sport and the ranking of human values" (pp. 3, 17, 18, respectively).

Assuming Wilcox's view has reasonable validity, those people involved in any way in the institution of sport–if they all together may be considered a collectivity–should contribute a quantity of redeeming social value to our North American culture. This value should extend to the overall world culture as well (i.e., a quantity of good leading to improved societal wellbeing). On the basis of this argument, the following questions are postulated initially for possible subsequent response by concerned agencies and individuals (e.g., federal governments, state and provincial officials, philosophers in the discipline and related professions):

> (1) Can, does, or should a great (i.e., leading) nation produce great sport?
>
> (2) With the world being threatened environmentally in a variety of ways, should we now be considering an "ecology" of sport in which the beneficial and disadvantageous aspects of a particular sporting activity are studied through the endeavors of scholars in other disciplines?
>
> (3) If it is indeed the case that the guardian of the "functional satisfaction" resulting from sport is:

(a) the sportsperson,

(b) the spectator,

(c) the businessperson who gains monetarily and, in some instances, and

(d) educational administrators and their respective governing boards, then who in society should be in a position to be the most knowledgeable about the immediate objectives and long range aims of sport?

(4) Additionally, if the answer to question No.3 above is that this person should actually be the trained philosopher of sport and physical activity, is it too much of a leap to also expect that this group of persons should work (a) to achieve consensus about what sport should accomplish and then also should (b) have some responsibility as the guardians (or at least the assessors) of whether those aims and objectives are being approximated to a greater or lesser degree?

Were we to delve into this matter more seriously, we may be surprised--or perhaps not. We may well learn that sport is contributing significantly in the development of what here are regarded as the *social* values--that is, the values of teamwork, loyalty, self-sacrifice, and perseverance. These are the values that are consonant with prevailing corporate capitalism in democracy and in other political systems as well. *Conversely, however, we may also discover that there is now a great deal of evidence that sport may be developing an ideal that opposes the fundamental moral virtues of honesty, fairness, and responsibility in the innumerable competitive experiences provided* (Lumpkin, Stoll, and Beller, 1999).

Significant to this discussion are these results of investigations carried out by Hahm, Stoll, Beller, Rudd, and others in recent years. The Hahm-Beller Choice Inventory (HBVCI) (1989) has now been administered to athletes at different levels in a variety of venues. It demonstrates conclusively that athletes will not support what is considered "the moral ideal" in competition. As Stoll and Beller (1998) explain it, for example, an athlete with moral character demonstrates the moral character traits of honesty, fair play, respect, and responsibility whether an official is present to enforce the rules or not. This finding was substantiated by Priest, Krause, and Beach (1999) who reported that their findings change over a four-year period in a college athlete's ethical value choices were consistent with other investigations. They showed decreases in "sportsmanship orientation" and an increase in "professional" attitudes associated with sport.

On the other hand, even though dictionaries define social character similarly, sport practitioners, including participants, coaches, parents, and officials, have come to believe that character is defined more properly by such values as self-sacrifice, teamwork, loyalty, and perseverance. The common expression in competitive sport is: "He/she showed character"–meaning "He/she 'hung in there' to the bitter end!" [or whatever]. Rudd (1999) confirmed that coaches explained character as "work ethic and commitment."

This finding coincides with what sport sociologists have found. Sage (1998. p. 614) explained that: "Mottoes and slogans such as 'sports builds character' must be seen in the light of their ideological issues" In other words, competitive sport is structured by the nature of the society in which it occurs. This means that over-commercialization, drug-taking, cheating, bribe-taking by officials, violence, etc. at all levels of sport are simply reflections of the culture in which we live. I can only ask: Where does that leave us today as we consider sport's presumed relationship with moral character development?

This discussion about whether sport's presumed educational and recreational roles have justification in fact could go on indefinitely. So many negative incidents have occurred that one hardly knows where to turn to avoid further negative examples. On the one hand, we read the almost unbelievably high standards stated in the various codes of conduct developed by professional associations for public consumption. Conversely, we learn that today athletes' concern for the presence of moral values in sport declines over the course of a university career (Priest, Krause, and Beach, 1999).

With this as a backdrop, we learn further that Americans, for example, are increasingly facing the cost and consequences of sedentary living. There is a need undoubtedly to track people's involvement in physical activity and recreational sport across their life spans. Yet, we haven't been able to devise and accept a uniform definition of wellness for all people. The one thought that emerges from these various assessments is as follows: We give every evidence of wanting our "sport spectaculars" that involve "the few" much more than we want all people of all ages and all conditions to have meaningful sport and exercise involvement throughout their lives.

I am arguing further that sport has somehow achieved such status as a powerful societal institution without an adequately defined underlying theory. Somehow, most of countries seem to be proceeding generally on a typically unstated assumption that "sport is a good thing for society to encourage, and more sport is even better!" Yet, as explained above, the term "sport" still exhibits radical ambiguity based on both everyday usage and dictionary definition. This obviously adds even more to the present problem and accompanying confusion.

Concluding Statement

The evidence is accumulating: Competitive sport is "structured" by the nature of the society in which it occurs. This means that steadily increasing over-commercialization, drug-taking, cheating, bribe-taking by officials, violence, etc. at all levels of sport are simply reflections of the culture in which we live. Where is this taking our society? Is sport's presumed, desirable relationship with moral character becoming history? If so, what can we look forward to in the future?

References

Barzun, J. *The use and abuse of art*. Princeton: Princeton University Press, 1974, pp. 123-150.

Csikszentmihalyi, M. (1993). *The evolving self: A psychology for the third millennium*. NY: HarperCollins.

Hahm, C.H., Beller, J. M., & Stoll, S. K. (1989). *The Hahm-Beller Values Choice Inventory*. Moscow, Idaho: Center for Ethics, The University of Idaho.

Johnson, H. M. (1969). The relevance of the theory of action to historians. *Social Science Quarterly*, No. 2, 46-58.

Johnson, H. M. (1994). Modern organizations in the Parsonsian theory of action. In A. Farazmond (Ed.), *Modern organizations: Administrative theory in contemporary society* (pp. 55-80). Westport, CT: Praeger.

Lumpkin, A., Stoll, S., & Beller, J. M. (1999). *Sport ethics: Applications for fair play* (2nd ed.). St. Louis, MO: McGraw-Hill.

Priest, R. F., Krause, J. V., & Beach, J. (1999). Four-year changes in college athletes' ethical value choices in sports situations. *Research Quarterly for Exercise and Sport*, 70(1), 170-178.

Rudd, A., Stoll, S. K., & Beller, J. M. (1999). Measuring moral and social character among a group of Division 1A college athletes, non-athletes, and ROTC military students. *Research Quarterly for Exercise and Sport*, 70 (Suppl. 1), 127.

Sage, G. H. (1998). Sports participation as a builder of character? *The World and I*, 3, 629-641.

Stoll, S. K. & Beller, J. M. (1998). *Sport as education: On the edge*. NY: Columbia University Teachers College.

Wilcox, R. C. (1991). Sport and national character: An empirical analysis. *Journal of Comparative Physical Education and Sport.*, XIII(1), 3-27.

Zeigler, E. F. (2004). *A way out of ethical confusion*. Victoria, Canada: Trafford.

Selection #14
The "Finest Type" of Sport Competition

Harry M. Johnson, Ph.D.
& Earle F. Zeigler, Ph.D.

This ritual aspect of competitive sport in connected with the all-important values that, in slightly different forms, are vital for all "valuable' human activities. Among these values are the following:

1. Health itself (of course),

2. The value of trying to make a contribution regardless of actual success--the value of effort itself,

3. The value of actual achievement, including excellence,

4. The value of respect for opponents,

5. The value of cooperation (i.e., one's ability to subordinate the self to the attainment of collective goals,

6. The value of fair play (i.e., respect for the rules of competition, which are universalistic ideally),

7. The value of orderly procedure for the settling of disputes, and

8. The value of grace in intensively competitive situations--including magnanimity in victory and the ability to accept defeat gracefully, and then try to gain victory the next time.

Part Three: Looking to the Future in Physical Activity Education and Educational Sport

Selection #15
The Use and Abuse of Sport and Physical Education Philosophy

Note: This was an invited paper requested by Pres. Robert G. Osterhoudt for the annual meeting of the Society in 1994 at The University of Western Ontario, London, ON, Canada. After consideration, only very slight alterations seemed necessary.

With appreciation to Nietzsche and Barzun for the term "use and abuse of" as applied to history and art, respectively, this monograph examines:

(1) from a historical perspective how scholars in the past 100 years, variously related to the profession of physical education and (educational) sport, general philosophy, and educational theory (or philosophy of education) have sought to carry out their function as philosophic analysts of human physical activity in sport, exercise, and related expressive activities;

(2) from a "cultural criticism" perspective the use and abuse of an increasingly important social institution known as sport that functions alongside a concomitant professional movement known worldwide as physical education and sport designed to promote sound health, fitness, and lifetime sports; and

(3) from a philosophical perspective the status of so-called sport philosophy as it looks to its future in the 21st century while struggling in the Philosophic Society for the Study of Sport. In this third part of this paper several recommendations are advanced that may have the potential to raise again the status of our departmental philosophy in the eyes of the physical education/kinesiology profession and the public.

I wish to emphasize that this paper is not intended as an attack, nor is it a defense of sport and concomitant physical activity. It is initially more of an exploration of the advantages and disadvantages of sport and related physical activity for present life. I state boldly first as a given that sport has obviously become an extremely powerful social force in society. If we grant that it now has such power in our culture--a power indeed that appears to be growing steadily-- we can also recognize that any such social force affecting society can be dangerous if perverted (e.g., positive nationalism to blind chauvinism, normal commercialism to excessive commercialism). Accepting the possible (apparent?) truth of these assertions, I believe that, while sport has grown as an important social force, it now also appears to have become a societal institution with an inadequately defined theory. Society, especially television producers, seems to be proceeding generally on the assumption that "sport is good, and more sport is better!"

Within this presently muddled situation in regard to sport's role in society, I feel that most people--including the writer as a sport philosopher hopefully to a significantly lesser degree--are like the proverbial blind person attempting to describe an elephant using the sense of touch only (i.e., here a trunk, there a tusk, next four leathery pillars, etc.). Even though we humans have sight we are akin to a person attempting to assemble a jigsaw puzzle without first seeing the complete picture on the cover of the box. This had led us into developing warped or truncated ideas about the big picture of sport we should be assembling in a presumably forward-looking society. Resultantly, this causes us to ignore concomitant benefits attained from participation in competitive activities.

This "head in the sand" approach is exactly what I wish to condemn. Thus, my primary concern is to state my belief that many of those who call themselves sport philosophers (or sport and physical activity philosophers, or whatever) are presently functioning like the proverbial lemmings marching off the cliff to extinction. Their philosophical approach and endeavor may be sound for what they think they should be doing, but they are suffering from the same malady besetting general philosophy and educational theory or policy (formerly called educational philosophy): they simply aren't "baking bread" in a world where competitive sport--whether it knows it or not--is "starving for educational and ethical nourishment!" Also, at a time when physical education and (educational?) sport in North America really needs guidance, many key sport philosophers have deserted the profession. Further, we aren't even "reproducing ourselves" adequately any more because our status and space in the educational firmanent is declining sharply, and positions simply "ain't out there!" How we came to be in this dilemma; why competitive sport needs educational and ethical nourishment; and what we could do about this are the topics I will discuss.

Historical Review of the Development of Sport and Physical Education Philosophy

In Part 1, therefore, I will initially look backward briefly to refresh ourselves as to how those functioning in what is now called sport and physical activity philosophy have approached their task over the past 100 years. This brief excursion away from the realms of general philosophy and departmental educational policy (i.e., philosophy of education) to what has been happening historically within the field of physical education (or whichever name you like of the more than 150 terms that are in use presently to designate the units in which most of us are employed). To do so I have roughly divided the period of a century more or less into a number of discrete (yet in several cases overlapping) periods--

and will mention at least one example of "philosophizing" from each period--as follows:

(1) a commonsense/rational thought approach;
(2) a normative approach to philosophizing;
(3) a philosophy of education systems/ implications approach;
(4) a theory-building approach;
(5) a phenomenological-existentialistic approach;
(6) a conceptual/language analysis approach; and
(7) an analytic approach to concepts and constructs.

A Common Sense/Rational Thought Approach (late 1880s through early 1920s

Early physical education philosophers, if we may call them that in today's "analytic or post-analytic environment," believed that they had the answers to most of the day's perplexing problems being faced. During the late 1800s and early 1900s, there was typically a combined "common sense and rational thought approach" to this aspect of our field. The report of the Boston Conference on Physical Training included didactic pronouncements by 33 men and women representing what is now known as "the battle of the systems" as propounded by the authorities of the time (Barrows, ed., 1899). Some of the people who philosophized about the importance of "physical training" and their work in it are still recognized today: William G. Anderson, Pierre de Coubertin, Luther Halsey Gulick, Edward Hitchcock, Heinrich Metzner, Nils Posse, and Dudley A. Sargent.

A Normative Approach to Philosophizing (mid-1920s to mid-1950s)

This first period of amateur philosophizing about developmental physical activity in what might be called organized U.S. physical education was followed in the 20th century by what might be identified as a "normative philosophizing approach." Use of this second approach extended roughly from the mid-1920a to the mid-1950s at least--and for some down to the present day. This was the period when all sorts of principles texts appeared, an approach undoubtedly influenced strongly by similar scholarly endeavor emanating from both philosophy itself to a degree, but primarily from schools of education where the great philosophic traditions of Idealism, Realism, and Pragmatism were in vogue. Some influential names from professional education to be mentioned here for the period 1930-1950 might be Mortimer J. Adler, Frederick S. Breed, John S. Brubacher, John Dewey, Herman Harrell Horne, William H. Kilpatrick, and William McGucken (Henry, 1942).

Professors in what was a more unified profession of health, physical education, and recreation caught the flavor of the several philosophic traditions extant, but their analysis was not philosophical in today's scholarly, analytic way. In the late 1940s and early 1950s, here were some "great debates" by such outstanding earlier leaders such as McCloy, Nash, Oberteuffer, and Williams. Additionally, we recall the enunciation of principles during this quite long period by leaders like Clifford L. Brownell, Rosalind Cassidy, Ray Duncan, Arthur Esslinger, Clark Hetherington, William L. Hughes, Mabel Lee, R. Tait McKenzie, Elmer D. Mitchell, N.P. Neilson, Jackson Sharman, Natalie Shepard, Seward C. Staley, Arthur Steinhaus, Agnes Wayman, Thomas D. Wood, and others (names listed alphabetically).

(Editorial Note: Schrag (1994), in his review of Kaminsky <1993>, points out correctly that "prewar philosophers of education in the United States wrote for school teachers and administrators, among others" (p. 365). Beginning in the early 1950s, also, educational philosophers were caught in a situation where more academic respectability was desired, and they wittingly fell into a trap probably set unwittingly by a growing multitude of professors in general philosophy who barely knew such "philosophers of education" were alive. Schrag states further that "When the analysts began work in the late 1950s and 1960s they were writing primarily for each other" <p. 365>. Subsequently, in the late 1960s, I believe that a segment of those professors functioning in physical education and sport philosophy also "wittingly fell into the same sort of trap set for us quite unwittingly" by our colleagues in education-- but initially, of course, by philosophers in the mother discipline. "Credit" for "laying of the bait" for physical education professors should go also to selected, interested professors from general philosophy anxious to "show the light" to physical education professors. Examination of the proceedings of the annual meetings of the Philosophy of Education Society demonstrates with overwhelming conclusiveness that present "educational policy" professors, then known as educational philosophers, hadn't the slightest academic interest in physical education and educational sport.)

A Philosophy of Education Systems (Implications?) Approach (Mid-1950s to Mid-1960s)

In the early to mid-1950s, a few physical educators seemed to "key in" on what might correctly be called the "philosophy of education systems approach" and sought to employ more strictly its so-called "structural analysis or implications technique" for the analysis of different philosophies of physical education.

Between 1954 and 1958, for example, Richard B. Morland carried out his monumental doctoral study at New York University in which he employed this newer approach--to a degree at least--that sought to draw reasonable implications from metaphysical analysis to a specific philosophy of education with resultant inferences for health, physical education, and recreation. A main point of Morland's approach emphasized careful examination of a leader's writings to discover possible recurrent themes that accordingly displayed their basic beliefs as they might relate to the major systems of educational philosophy extant.

Both Davis (1961) and Zeigler (1964) used the so-called Systems/Implications Approach in their texts that exerted considerable influence on professional preparation in the 1960s. Davis's Philosophies fashion physical education (1963), with contributions from Burke, Oberteuffer, Holbrook, and Van Dalen, made a helpful contribution to professionals at the time. Because of criticism within educational philosophy--that it was impossible to draw conclusions without adequate evidence--Zeigler felt constrained to add a step to this technique by gathering available scientific knowledge to lend support to any implications drawn from a specific philosophical position (see note with Zeigler, 1975).

A Theory-Building Approach

A diversion from this "Systems or Implications Approach," with what may be called a "theory-building approach" was begun with some success by Lois Ellfeldt and Eleanor Metheny in the mid-1950s. This was an effort to develop a tentative general theory about the meaning of human movement-kinesthesia. Such movement was defined as "a somatic-sensory experience which can be conceptualized by the human mind" The theory was developed "within the context of the basic assumptions of the philosophy of symbolic transformation as they relate to the nature of the process which enables human being to find meaning in their sensory perceptions" (1958, p. 264). For this purpose, the investigators developed "a vocabulary to refer to these elements in their most general form" (p. 264).

A Phenomenological-Existentialistic Approach

Another interesting approach occurred when Metheny, through her own work and that of a number of her graduate students and others that began in the early 1960s, spearheaded the introduction of a movement that may be called broadly a "Phenomenological-Existentialistic Approach" (or series of techniques) to philosophical endeavor related to sport, exercise, and related human movement (see, for example, Kleinman, 1964; Thomson, 1967; Slusher, 1967; Stone, 1969;). In retrospect, because those espousing existentialism and pheneomenological method in our field seem to have gone "thataway," it seems worthwhile to recall that existentialism, according to Barrett (1959, p. 126), is a philosophy that confronts the human situation in its totality to ask what the basic conditions of human existence are and how man can establish his own meaning out of these conditions. . . . Here philosophy itself--no longer a mere game for technicians or an obsolete discipline superceded by science--becomes a fundamental dimension of human existence. For man is the one animal who not only can, but must ask himself what his life means.

Such an approach quite obviously makes this type of philosophizing potentially vital in the life of the individual because he or she is offered a way of life, of living, if you will. This is in contrast to other leading philosophic positions or approaches in which we are confronted with a depersonalized Nature, a transcendent Deity, or a State seemingly possessing both of these qualities. As Kaplan explained it, "The meaning of life lies in the values which we can find in it, and values are the product of choice" (1961, p. 105). Thus the direction of movement within selected concepts is from existence to choice to freedom!

A Conceptual Analysis & Philosophy of Language

However, just as the systems/implications approach to physical education and sport philosophy and an existentialistic, phenomenological approach were gathering some momentum in the mid-1960s, it became generally apparent that the field of educational philosophy had veered sharply in the direction of the analytic tradition being employed largely in general philosophy in the English-speaking world. One of the first indications of this that deserves mention was the influence of several papers and articles James Keating (1964) in regard to conceptual analysis and sport ethics in the mid-1960s. Immediately after that, other studies exploring aspects of subsequent philosophy of language/analytic approaches or techniques to doing sport philosophy may be noted as well (Paddick, 1967; Spencer-Kraus, 1969; Patrick, 1971; Pearson, 1971; Zeigler, 1974).

> (Note: For those who wish to review sport and physical education literature up to 1970, the monumental study employing what he called "metaphilosophic analysis" was completed by Osterhoudt (1971). This study, which won the Carl Diem Prize in 1972, provides a wealth of material based on Pearson's (1968 "Inquiry Into Inquiry" taxonomy involving construct analysis, system analysis, and concept analysis.)

A Philosophic Analysis Approach to Concepts, Constructs, and Meanings

Finally, the Yale philosopher, Paul Weiss, ushered in what became a strong trend toward "philosophic purism" in this highly interesting decade with the publication of *Sport: A Philosophic Inquiry* (1969), a work that ushered in the significant decade of the 1970s for sport philosophy. A so-called philosophic analysis approach to concepts, constructs, and meanings steadily gained momentum in the field in the 1970s and is still largely in vogue down to the present day. I believe that Sparkes (1991) has defined "analytical philosophy" well as "a wide variety of philosophical movements and tendencies" within the English-speaking world that are dissatisfied with any philosophizing that "attempts to construct large-scale theories of 'reality as a whole,'"and that stress instead "the task of critically elucidating already existing ideas and beliefs" (p. 192).

The organization of the Philosophic Society for the Study of Sport in late 1972, with Paul Weiss as President and Warren Fraleigh as the President-Elect, represented a significant step forward in the development of the sub-disciplinary area. Although this area was not always represented in the many "disciplinary diagrams" being formulated between 1965 and 1975, one nevertheless had the idea that prospective professionals would now increasingly receive significant help both in philosophic self-analysis and analysis of sport and physical education in society.

What did happen is not quite what I had expected--or at least what I had hoped for. I had hoped for a balance between pure and applied sport and physical education philosophy to develop within the profession. Already in 1975, in a presidential address to the PSSS, I stated that sport and physical activity philosophy was "standing at a clear and definite crossroad" (Zeigler, 1976). (Note that already I was not using the term "physical education" in my remarks to the group, because it had become out of vogue and was regarded as a bit unscholarly to do so.) I went on to decry the paucity of material in sport philosophy that related to the subject of man's nature. "Considering the many problems of a highly serious nature extant in sport today," I said, "this paucity of material almost constitutes 'dereliction of duty,' and at the very best may be classified as copying of and fearful, blind allegiance to the mother discipline's presumed correct research technique" (1976, p. 125).

What I was saying--in a polite way--was that many scholars involved with the (then) PSSS needed to communicate more effectively with the profession and with the public by spending a reasonable amount of their time turning out work of an applied nature. Further, it had become obvious to me that the continuing, wholesale adoption of a negative attitude by the large majority of the scholars within the mother discipline of philosophy, and also within educational theory (or policy or philosophy), toward applied endeavor was a most serious mistake for which they would eventually pay in various ways. However, as Barzun (1974, p. 7) explains in referring to the contemporary artist in the mid-1970s on the basis of Daumier's slogan: "One must be of one's own time." Thus, I believe this is the explanation why sport philosophy "went that-a-way" in the early seventies in a plausible, understandable effort to do what was right--so to speak--for the subject-matter of sport philosophy.

In 1982, the Canadian Association for Sport Sciences commissioned a paper on sport and physical activity philosophy for inclusion in The Sport Sciences edited by J.J. Jackson and H.A. Wanger. In this paper, Zeigler (1982) sought to trace the development of the area and to assess its status at that time. Such terms as analytic philosophy, existentialism, normative philosophy, speculative philosophy, systems analysis, construct analysis, concept analysis, and metaphilosophic analysis were defined. An attempt was made to list the "leading contributors" of the time--always a "dangerous" undertaking--because in review one notable omission at least was discovered (the name of rapidly rising Scott Kretchmar). At that time I also paid tribute to the contributions of the eminent Hans Lenk (of the FRG) to sport philosophy, who has since departed from the ranks of (the then) PSSS and sport philosophy for several reasons best left unsaid. Also, I believe it is relevant at this point to mention the "balanced" philosophic endeavors of our Japanese associates, Shinobu Abe and Akio Kataoka.

Now, in 2010, 35 years after I made a plea for a "balanced approach" between pure and applied philosophizing, I am asking parenthetically what all of this "pure" endeavor has indeed added to society as of today. Everything considered, I believe we need a broader, more encompassing orientation for the future. We should now return, armed with improved analytical techniques, to find at least some tentative answers to some of the very basic questions that were being asked as far back as at the end of the 19th century! Of course, the extent to which we can expect or actually get any help from the mother discipline or the departmental discipline known as educational philosophy is moot at this point. I say this because my reading of the literature at this point tells me that there is still very little interest in these quarters, not to mention considerable controversy and, dare I say, confusion on this matter of how to practice one's craft in these sectors of North American campuses too.

The Need for Sport to Be Challenged

In Part 2 of essay, I am reaffirming my belief that sport must be challenged on an ongoing basis by various categories of people in a variety of ways. The hope is that sport will continue to be conducted in its various settings now and in the future, both generally and specifically, in a manner that will encourage its proper educational and recreational uses. If this were to be the case, sport might possibly retain those aspects that can contribute value to individual and social living. To do this, however, we must first define our terms accurately so that we are fully aware of that which we are critiquing. Based on both everyday usage and dictionary definition, the term "sport" still exhibits radical ambiguity, and this adds to the present confusion. For the purpose of this paper, therefore, when the word "sport" is used it refers unless indicated otherwise to "an athletic activity requiring skill or physical prowess and often of a competitive nature, as racing, baseball, tennis, bowling, golf, wrestling, boxing, hunting, fishing, etc." *(The Random House Dictionary of the English Language,* 1987, p. 1944).

Two Basic Approaches to Criticizing and/or Philosophizing

In any effort to critique the use and abuse of sport, it is necessary to explain one's approach to such analysis. It can be argued that there are at least two basic ways to criticize and/or philosophize and thereby translate theory into practice: one would involve narrowing an issue down and examining it in great detail to refine possible ways to effect ends. The second would be to consider all possible ramifications of an issue in order to arrive at a synthesis and/or conclusion with the greatest possible application to life in the eyes of the majority. A triangular figure, either in its normal position or upside down with the narrow or pointed end on the bottom, can be used to explain how a philosopher could approach his or her task in one way or the other. In this paper I am obviously inclined strongly toward arriving at a synthesis and conclusion that will lend itself toward application of sport and developmental physical activity to life.

In this process of critiquing competitive sport, we should also maintain an effort to keep its drawbacks in check to the greatest possible extent. In recent decades we have witnessed the rise of sport throughout the land to the status of a fundamentalist religion. In this case sport is being called upon to serve as a redeemer of wayward youth, for example, but, in the process, is becoming a destroyer of certain fundamental values of individual and social life. Concurrently, onrushing science and technology have also become the tempters of many coaches and athletes and added another dimension to the personal and professional conduct of those people who are unduly anxious for recognition and financial gain. Beliefs such as these have created a vacuum of positive belief for others like me who would view "educational" competitive sport as a life-enhancer (e.g., intercollegiate sports that are not sustained through gate receipts--golf, tennis, gymnastics, soccer, and all of women's sport).

In this second part of the paper, therefore, I am simply stating what I believe to be the obvious: sport has become an extremely powerful social force in society. Secondly, if we grant that sport now has such power in our North American culture and around the world for that matter--a power indeed that appears to be growing--we should also recognize that any such social force affecting society can be dangerous if perverted (e.g., nationalism, commercialism). Thus, I believe that sport, albeit a powerful social force, has somehow become an active societal institution without an adequately defined underlying theory. Somehow, most of society seems to be proceeding generally on the previously stated assumption that "sport is a good thing for society to encourage, and more sport is even better!" (Also, and this adds to this confusion, the term "sport" still exhibits radical ambiguity based on both everyday usage and dictionary definition, thereby adding to the present problem and accompanying confusion.)

Need for a Theory of Sport

I believe further that governmental agencies (especially!) sponsoring "amateur" sport competition should be able to state in their relationship to sport that, if such-and-such is done with reasonable efficiency and effectiveness within sporting activities, then such-and-such will (in all probability) result. Accordingly, we should by now be able to argue, also, that sport is a "relatively homogeneous substance" that can serve at least reasonably well as an indispensable balm or aid to human fulfillment within an individual life (Barzun, 1974, p. 12). Further, we might argue logically that--through the process of total psycho-physical involvement--sport provides "flow experiences" (Csikszentmihalyi, 1993, p. 183).

However, Wilcox (1991), for example, in his empirical analysis, challenges "the widely held notion that sport can fulfill an important role in the development of national character." He stated that "the assumption that sport is conducive to the development of positive human values, or the 'building of character,' should be viewed more as a belief rather than as a fact." He concluded that his study did "provide some evidence to support a relationship between participation in sport and the ranking of human values" (pp. 3, 17, 18, respectively).

Assuming Wilcox's view has reasonable validity, those involved in any way in the institution of sport--if they all together may be considered a collectivity-- should contribute a quantity of redeeming social value to our North American culture, not to mention the overall world culture (i.e., a quantity of good leading to improved societal wellbeing). On the basis of this argument, the following questions are postulated initially for possible subsequent response by concerned agencies and individuals (e.g., federal governments, state and provincial officials, philosophers in the discipline and related professions):

> (1) Can, does, or should a great (i.e., leading) nation produce great sport?

> (2) With the world being threatened environmentally in a variety of ways, should we now be considering an "ecology" of sport in which the beneficial and disadvantageous aspects of a particular sporting activity are studied through the endeavors of scholars in other disciplines?

> (3) If it is indeed the case that the guardian of the "functional satisfaction" resulting from sport is (a) the sportsperson, (b) the spectator, (c) the businessperson who gains monetarily and, in some instances, (d) educational administrators and their respective governing boards, who in society should be in a position to be the most knowledgeable about the immediate objectives and long range aims of sport?

> (4) Additionally, if the answer to question No.3 above is that this person should be the trained sport and physical activity professor, is it too much of a leap to also expect that this group of persons should work to achieve consensus about what sport should accomplish and then also should have some responsibility as the guardians (or at least the assessors) of whether those aims and objectives are being approximated to a greater or lesser degree?

This initial listing of several questions that need answers brings us to the second broad section of the paper. Arguably, if there could be affirmative agreement about the answers to the final two questions immediately above, sport and physical education philosophers should be about their business of determining more accurately what the aims and objectives of such human physical activity are at point when the world gets ready to enter the 21st century of the common era (C.E.). Also, it can be argued reasonably that we should attain a consensus of how (and IF!) sport, exercise, and similar physical activity, considered collectively, is currently being used to help in the fulfillment of these aims and objectives.

Following this argument a bit further, we might postulate that sport philosophers by virtue of their background and training could also be taking the lead in analyzing and promoting ethical behavior in sport. The time is past due when sport philosophers should be looking more vigorously for at least tentative answers to the questions No.1 and No.2 raised above. (How these vital questions that need answers may be approached through an improved variety of philosophic approaches, including analytic techniques, along with substantively greater production of scholarly and professional literature directed to the achievement of these ends, is an issue that will be discussed later in Part 3.)

Conflicting Views on Philosophy and Philosophic Thought

The pendulum swings back and forth, or the merry-go-round goes round and round. Take your pick, because we are indeed once again finding sharply conflicting views on the subject of philosophy and philosophic thought. Hartshorne (1975), in arguing that philosophy concerns itself with problems more general than those functioning in the sciences, argues that:

> philosophers investigate not only facts and ideas but also
> values and ideals, and not only actualities but
> possibilities, and not only possibilities as determined the
> actual constitution of our world (i.e., as determined by
> scientists), but also possibilities transcending the actual
> world, that is to say the possibility of natural laws otherthan
> those which in fact obtain. . . . (p. 8).

Hartshorne's recommendations about the proper concerns of the discipline of philosophy were part of an excellent issue of Philosophy in Context in which a solid effort was made to define the nature and role of philosophy. (This fine journal as cited immediately above is no longer published by the Department of Philosophy, Cleveland State University, OH.) Other insightful recommendations as to our function, approaches that could be readily adapted to departmental sport philosophy, were made by R. Fox, F.E. Sparshott, E. Shmueli, G.J. Massey, L.F. Werth, L. Armour, K. Nielsen, and H. Butler. Butler (1975), for example, to select only one other recommendation in addition to that of Hartshorne above, explains that "history demonstrates that confrontation with reality is at best difficult for man" (p. 113). He asserts further:

For philosophers to offer any meaningful help, the concept of an academic philosophy must be abandoned. There are at least two compelling reasons for this. First, social practice occurs in the real world. For philosophers, this means that they must abandon the armchair to become participant observers since to do otherwise is to develop a theory without action. Since social practice is action, this is not possible. A theory of action must be grounded in action and becoming an actor involves risk. To take risks, philosophers must develop commitment.

Butler's second reason for urging "abandonment of academic philosophy" for philosophers in some of their efforts at least is that, to be of any assistance to the social world, a philosophy must be empirically grounded. Arguing that "concepts must emerge from action, and confirmation must occur in action," he offers as an example to prove his point the contrast between the theories of Dewey and the distortions that occurred within the progressive education movement when the practitioners subsequently attempted to do the theoretical grounding (p. 113).

Since these broadly encompassing statements were made, it has become ever more apparent that there is indeed a "need for a recovery of philosophy." This belief has come to our attention increasingly from a variety of sources over these past 20 years. One such statement was made as a presidential address before the American Philosophical Association by John E. Smith in 1981. Smith believes that three beliefs have prevented the discipline of philosophy from having the impact on society that it might have had. The first relates to the belief that it is possible to attain certainty; the second is the belief that to engage a philosophical issue our intellectual apparatus must be ordered appropriately; and the third belief is that philosophy can be made "scientific" by reducing it to irrefutable logic and certifiable scientific solutions (p. 8). In his effort to counteract these questionable beliefs, Smith spells out four conditions that, if met, would "contribute greatly to the recovery of philosophy as a significant force in American society."

Further evidence of the changing philosophical environment comes from a "mini–course" offered to senior citizens by Steven Ross (1990), a Hunter College philosophy professor, in the American Association of Retired Persons publication Modern Maturity (can you believe a self-respecting philosopher analyzing philosophy here?). Tracing developments within the discipline of philosophy, he states: "It came to seem ridiculous that philosophy could have nothing to say about ongoing moral controversies when American political life was forcing all of us to thinker harder about such things than we ever had before" (p. 57). He concludes his interesting analysis by stating:

Philosophy will always be special in its willingness to work out abstract answers to abstract puzzles. But today philosophers interested in saying something insightful about such questions will find themselves also taking a more active, aggressive interest in those bits of everyday life that lie just behind these questions. And this great shift in orientation is no mere change in intellectual fashion: It is rather the direct result of powerful arguments made within recent philosophy itself.

Additionally, to cite a still more recent effort to analyze the current situation as it applies to the departmental philosophy of education, Pratte (1992) believes that analytic philosophy has simply neglected to focus sufficiently on substantive questions. He explains that "the underlying assumptions of analytic philosophers have been challenged by a number of competing views, including postmodernism, poststructuralism, feminism, and neo-Marxism" (pp. x-xi). Thus, we are finding considerable divergence of interests along with an increasing pluralism of philosophical methods employed to confront the many normative considerations arising in contemporary society.

Finally, still further evidence of the changing philosophical environment, for example, comes from Borradori in The American Philosopher (1994). Here she discusses insightfully her hopes for a breaching of the "Atlantic Wall" in a period of post-analytic philosophy (pp. 3-4; see, also, Rajchman & West, 1985). While agreeing that analytic philosophy has provided "an essential means of intellectual progress," she believes that by understanding its intent a "mainly unexplored channel" has been created to narrow the philosophical gap that has developed between North America and Europe (p. 3). Also, the ultimate result of the programmatic anthology by Rajchman & West (1985) suggests consideration of the composite term "post-analytic philosophy" to describe some of the directions that American philosophy seems to be taking after the analysis era--i.e., "the emergence of a new 'public' engagedness in philosophy, a general tendency toward 'de-disciplinization' . . . ., and a renewed interest in historical perspective, completely removed from the scientific basis of the analytic genre" (p. 4). What this means, therefore, is that there has developed a move toward making American philosophy something more of a "socially engaged interdisciplinary enterprise" instead of a highly specialized occupation.

Assessment--The Aftermath of an "Elitist Approach"

In my opinion we--individually as professors and collectively as the International Association for Philosophy of Sport (formerly the PSSS)--have "paid dearly at the box office" in the past for this scholarly elitism exhibited by some of us and the minute number of our erstwhile colleagues from the mother discipline who had almost all parted from our midst. Fortunately, the tide does appear to be turning in this respect. However, I said then (in 1994), and I reiterate today that, because of the different, often conflicting approaches to "doing" philosophy, most of the members of the IAPS are not communicating as well with each other as they should be, much less communicating with their colleagues in the discipline in which they were primarily educated. By this I mean that (a) annual meetings are very poorly attended based on the small total membership of the Society, and a NASPE "sport and physical education presence" is barely noticeable even though 2800 members listed philosophy as their primary scholarly interest; (b) until recently newsletters, although well done, have been scarce; (c) only one issue of a journal was appearing each year (and its appearance was irregular, although this is typically not the editor's fault); (d) proceedings of annual meetings have very rarely been available; (e) attendance at the few sessions scheduled unofficially in the past at the annual meeting of the American Philosophical Association was almost non-existent (albeit true that a few curious philosophers did wander into the room often by mistake when such sessions were arranged); and (f) there have been no articles on either physical education or sport philosophy in either the annual proceedings of the Philosophy of Education Society or in their journal titled Educational Theory in the 25+ years I have carried a nominal membership in this society (except one by me!).

Based on all of the above and other observations, I must conclude that the Society is having absolutely no impact on (a) the public generally; (b) the people active in amateur, semiprofessional, and professional sport; (c) the overwhelming majority of professors who function in the discipline of philosophy; (d) the professors teaching in educational philosophy; (e) the large majority of professors who teach in this area generally in our professional preparation programs in physical education; and, finally, (f) the entire profession of sport and physical education within the Alliance in the USA and in CAHPER in Canada! Have I forgotten any group that the Society is not influencing?

Present Improper Modeling
of the Reality of Competitive Sport

To recapitulate: because there seems always to be an ever-changing pecking order among and within subject-matters in academic circles, so-called pure analytic philosophers gradually over the decades steadily assumed a more lofty position than those in their academic units struggling with other philosophic approaches, not to mention philosophy's possible application to specialized subject-matter fields (i.e., educational philosophy, physical education philosophy). As a result, analytic philosophers were accordingly aped by educational philosophers beginning in the mid-1950s. Then, I believe that those scholars emerging from early physical education and sport philosophy into the "true" sport philosophy of the early 1970s and thereafter have arguably become poor windows for the assessment of true reality in sport. This occurred inevitably, I believe, because those scholars attempting to function as disciplinarians alongside those laboring in the traditional academic disciplines are seemingly forced by their very specialization to avoid large, broader areas of knowledge, areas that are often much more important when the big picture is considered.

The result, I believe is that the present overall reality of competitive sport in world culture is improperly modeled through the purely disciplinary approach of a relatively small group of sport philosophers. Similarly, I believe also that most scholars in the mother discipline are doing something quite similar with their own issues, as are policy theoreticians in professional education who have merged with others in a socio–cultural area seeking to analyze the plight of the field of education as it timidly prepares to enter the 21st century. (A very close associate of ours is now functioning in a campus unit known as "cultural studies in education," and another close associate of mine is excited about the term "cultural kinesiology" to describe our field's socio-cultural aspects.)

My strong belief is that we in our field still need scholars who take a more holistic approach to doing philosophy about sport, physical activity, and expressive movement so that this aspect of professional preparation can begin to assist its *POTENTIAL* publics to appreciate what the finest type of sport and physical activity can contribute to the improvement of individuals functioning in society, as well as to the actual improvement of that society as a whole.

What has happened, I believe, is that scientists and scholars functioning in the many disciplines and sub disciplines of the modern world--and this includes those presently functioning within kinesiology and human kinetics units on North American campuses--are presenting to society fragmented images of reality daily through their research reports. The attempts at trans disciplinary, cross-disciplinary, and interdisciplinary endeavor appear futile and are failing to offer people a reasonably consensual understanding of overall reality. Here is where philosophers, and interested sport philosophers if they only choose to do so diligently, are in a position to model reality for people of all ages conjecturing about the purposes of sport and physical activity in their lives. There are indeed systemic relationships that need to be clarified. We have the real life stage, the actors, the plot, the action, and the time. As Brady (1994) suggests in connection with the overall educational curriculum, we in sport philosophy with the above categories related systemically are in a position to create the picture on the lid of the jigsaw puzzle box that models sport.

At the same time those sport philosophers who follow a more specialized approach are needed to identify the inaccuracies and inconsistencies that may be apparent in the larger picture presented by the sport philosophers seeking to help people of the present and future generations to move toward understanding of the role that sport and developmental physical activity can play in their human experience.

Religion, both organized and natural, and other wisdom traditions at least provide their adherents and potential recruits with an orienting image (however dubious that may be). We of the modern age have become imbued with the tenets of science and accompanying technology, but in the process have become so specialized in our endeavors that we don't see the big picture or even any orienting image. Or, if we do postulate a "big picture," it is useful only on Sunday or special occasions and not during our workaday week.

What Is the Aim of Sport in Culture?

By the way, what is the aim of sport and how is sport being used to help in the fulfillment of such an aim? Can we argue that sport is better than life (a truer reality)? Or do we recommend that sport be used as a means to living a better life-

-i.e. serve a transformational function? Or should sport involvement provide a human with a more natural life because of its spontaneity? Can we make the case in one or more of the following ways for sport participation as a sanctuary from life, as a "life-enhancer," or as a detergent that cleanses away life's many impurities? Whichever purpose is adopted, in the final analysis the guardian of the "functional satisfaction" resulting from the sport enterprise should be the sports participant and the spectator.

I ask further why we, as sport philosophers, should not understand what constitutes ethical behavior in sport? Moreover, should not the guardian of the ethics of sport be the sport philosopher? Everything considered, I believe that the time has arrived when sport philosophers should be providing at least tentative answers to these questions through a variety of approaches (including the prevailing analytic techniques).

Recommended Approaches Leading to a Possible Recovery in Sport and Physical Activity Philosophy

In the third part of the paper, I offer some ideas as to how we might strengthen our approaches to doing sport and physical activity philosophy in the 21st century. I point out that the "need for a recovery of philosophy" to a position of even relative eminence in society (compared to former years, that is) has come to our attention from a variety of sources for the past 20 years at least (e.g., see Zeigler, 1989b). If we consider the question "Who should do what to whom in this world?", it can be argued that politicians should save the cities, while do-gooders should help the disadvantaged. Accordingly, we might say that preachers should save souls, and that businessmen should make money for their stockholders. Leaping quickly to our realm, what should physical educators, coaches, and sport philosophers do? Arguably, physical educators should develop attitudes and skills that lead to healthy bodies through lifelong involvement in exercise and sport. Coaches, we might say, should help in the development of fine young people and adults through the development of skills that can be used in competitive sport. Finally, what should sport philosophers do? To answer "philosophize about sport" takes us right back to square one again.

So, after first looking backward to refresh ourselves as to where so-called sport philosophy has been over the past 100 years, we still need to actively and creatively seek some of the answers to questions that were being asked toward the end of the 19th century (and indeed as far back as the end of the Archaic Period in early Greek history).

One approach, in addition to what is presently being done and that actually was suggested by Zeigler (1975; see pages 124-160 and especially pp. 139-154) to improve the current situation, would be to examine the results of the extraordinary range of 20th-century social scientific inquiries available from history, psychology, sociology, and anthropology. Interestingly, this is exactly what

Wilson (1993) has recommended for the mother discipline of philosophy and which was "seconded" by MacIntyre (1993). As Wilson states, "The truth, if it exists, is in the details." This could be supplemented in currently designated kinesiology units in universities, of course, by the ever-mounting body of evidence becoming available from the efforts of our hard scientists (and those in related disciplines). Let us grant, however, that we shouldn't enthrone the sciences--both the social sciences and the natural sciences--by affirming that anything that can't be quantified should be regarded as useless.

A second counterbalancing approach, if we are indeed in or approaching "the postmodern age," would be to help humankind "create a passage beyond the failed assumptions of modernity and a radical reorientation that preserves the positive advantages of the liberal tradition and <its> technological capacities. . . ." Such a "passage" and such a "reorientation" should be "rooted in ecological sanity and meaningful human participation in the unfolding story of the Earth community and the universe" (Spretnak, 1991). Those who might be called "deconstructive postmodernists" argue basically that modernity and modern technology fled from the insights of the so-called wisdom traditions (e.g., God, Marxism, science and technology). Spretnak, who describes her position as "ecological postmodernism," critiques the deconstructive-postmodern orientation from four perspectives: ecological/cosmological, spiritual, activist-political, and feminist. Another interesting treatment titled postmodern realism is recommended by Borgmann (1992) in Crossing the postmodern divide. There can be little doubt but that there is a need for the development of individual and societal attitudes (psychologically speaking) toward the mounting ecological crisis (as recommended by Zeigler, 1978).

(**Note**: However, although I believe we should listen to them, I stress that I am not encouraging any significant involvement with the trendy, but obfuscating language of the deconstructionists and postmodernists. For example, I am not certain what the former mean when they call for a "critical pedagogy" based on a critique of our culture. After they "deconstruct," they need to "reconstruct!" Also, while I must agree that with the postmodernists claim that "broad social and political movements invariably suppress certain points of view," I must agree with Kneller (1994): "Groups cannot coalesce unless some are promoted over others" (p. 184). Yet, it should be obvious to all that micro–politics should be encouraged so that specific causes seeking reform are given adequate hearings. For an insightful discussion of this topic, see McGowan (1991) whose Postmodernism and its critics explains postmodernism's precursors (e.g., Marx, Nietzsche) and the problem of freedom in postmodern theory, yet concludes with a redeeming approach to positive freedom within the political scene.)

221

A third approach, one that builds on earlier work in the 1950s by Metheny and subsequently by Kleinman, Thomson, Stone, Kretchmar and others, is that recommended by Fahlberg and Fahlberg (1994) in which investigation is based on what is termed a "realities-based framework." Titling their article "A human science for the study of movement: An integration of multiple ways of knowing," the investigators urge the use of "multiple epistemologies" in an integrated framework. They argue that, in this age of post positivism, research questions about human movement should be viewed in relation to one integrated reality with two different levels of meaning: (1) the material world of objects moving in space that may be analyzed empirically, and (2) a human world of meaning in which the experience of the mover is determined by either psychological phenomenology and/or psychosocial hermeneutics (pp. 101-102).

A fourth obvious approach with the increased emphasis on applied ethics in the mother discipline is for sport/kinesiology philosophers to place greater emphasis on the topic of applied or practical philosophy and ethics. Kretchmar's (1994) Practical philosophy of sport represents a needed, recent contribution in this direction, as were earlier texts by McIntosh (1979), Fraleigh (1984), and Zeigler (1984). Zeigler's application of a scientific ethics to sport decisions is another effort of this type (1989a). The Center for Sport Ethics at Idaho developed by Sharon Stoll, and the Center for Applied Sport Philosophy and Ethics Research at De Montfort University Bedford, UK where Simon Eassom labors, offer hope for the future.

A fifth not-so-obvious approach would be for some one sport and physical education philosopher with a historical bent, or several people if need be, to undertake an intellectual history of the subject similar to the approach of Bronowski and Mazlish (1975) that traced the Western intellectual tradition from "Leonardo to Hegel." In this case, the lives of selected scholars and leaders who spoke or wrote cogently throughout history on competitive sport and physical education could be integrated with the intellectual, political, and social developments of the period (e.g., from Plato to Weiss).

A sixth approach, similar to that adopted by the several societies within the American Philosophical Association, might be for the International Association for the Philosophy of Sport to establish a permanent section where papers could be presented annually looking to the possible contribution that competitive sport and physical education might make toward the goal of world peace. This idea urging our profession to contribute meaningfully toward a patterned search for world peace was stressed by Zeigler (1994).

A seventh feasible approach, one that Zeigler (1964, 1977, 1989b, 2003, 2010) introduced to the field is called a "persistent problems approach." This could be most useful to sport and physical educational professionals today if it were employed wisely in professional preparation programs. The idea is to examine the various social forces (e.g., values, economics, ecology) and the many professional concerns (e.g., defining amateurism, semi–professionalism, and professionalism, the role of management, coaching ethics) as they impact upon the professional practitioner (1989b, pp. 205-358).

Looking to the Future: How 'Resuscitation' Could Be Applied to The Philosophy of Physical Activity Education (including Sport)

In defense of the scholarly output of the International Association for the Philosophy of Sport, I am prepared to argue that in the long run we will discover that its scholarly output through its journal is helpful in ways other than procuring publications, some travel money, and possible tenure of employment for the relatively few involved. However, the public, people active in all levels of sport, and the members of the profession of physical activity education (including sport) need so much more assistance with their understanding of the aims and objectives of competitive sport and developmental physical activity.

What happened during the turmoil of the 1960s and early 1970s is that many of us professing in this area "threw out the baby with the bath water." In so many instances the principles of physical education course was eliminated except in those universities where the faculty members concerned with philosophy were out of touch with the academic world of philosophy. What was substituted for the old "principles" course was typically buffeted about in the curricular struggle of the time because staff members in other sub-disciplines, having themselves as students taken "useful" courses could not understand the possible value of the newer analytic approach. Soon sport philosophy was typically relegated to elective status, and in my opinion it has never filled the bill for professional physical education students. Of course, I am not advocating a return to exactly the same sort of unsophisticated principles course today that was taught formerly. I am recommending, however, an approach that includes a required course in this area in every curriculum that introduces people to applied sport and physical education philosophy, an approach that urges students to take their first philosophy course in the philosophy department, and that then goes on in our unit to give them a working understanding of applied ethics as related to our own field.

This curricular idea can--and should--be carried out most effectively by physical educators with solid interests in philosophy and by those associated with the Philosophy Academy of NASPE within the Alliance. (I would hope that the Executive Committee of the PSSS might lend support to this recommendation, and that this be the decision of all of the members of the Society--not just the Executive.) No group other than NASPE's Philosophy Academy, with the possible exception of the National Association for Physical Education in Higher Education (NAPEHE), seems ready and willing and is reasonably capable of using its influence to restore a required, applied sport and physical education philosophy course for the benefit of the profession.

And so, in conclusion, I urge you--in fact, as a dedicated professional I implore you--to give this recommendation top priority right now. I believe the basic and applied knowledge and possible subsequent "ethical competency" that would accrue to our professional students--and eventually to all with whom they come in contact--are vital for our profession in the years immediately ahead. Our struggle as a field for true professional status is far from won yet. A sound understanding of our philosophic base--the meaning and significance of what the profession stands for--must undergird our development at all times.

Finally, all of this leads to the thought that, if we as sport and physical education philosophers are truly to make a contribution to humankind, we should be examining the ways in which sport as a social institution can contribute positively and increasingly to our culture's development. Also, we should be experimenting with new approaches to philosophizing that can truly serve humankind. In this sense we would be affirming the thesis that "sport was made for man, and not man for sport" (Steinhaus, 1952), as well as the idea that such men and women in their various sport undertakings should in no way defile the earth as a result of human thoughtlessness.

Note

1. I want to express my gratitude and appreciation to Dick Morland, Professor Emeritus, Stetson University, DeLand, Florida for his comments after carefully reading this paper in 1994. Of course, he should not be held responsible for anything said in the final version.

References

Barrett, W. (1959). *Irrational man: A study in existential philosophy*. Garden City, NY: Doubleday.

Barrows, I. C., ed. (1899) *Proceedings of the Conference on Physical Training*. Boston: Press of G. H. Ellis.

Barzun, J. (1974*). The use and abuse of art*. Princeton: Princeton Univ. Press.

Borgmann, A. (1993). *Crossing the postmodern divide*. Chicago: University of Chicago Press.

Borradori, G. (1994). *The American philosopher*. Chicago: Univ. of Chicago Press.

Brady, M. (March/April 1994). Correspondence. *Utne Reader*, 62:6-7.

Bronowski, J. & Mazlish, B. (1975) *The Western intellectual tradition*. NY: Harper & Row.

Butler, H. (1975). Lifting the veil of ignorance with a philosophy of commitment. *Philosophy in Context*, 4: 111-117.

Csikszentmihalyi, M. (1993). *The evolving self: A psychology for the third millennium*. NY: HarperCollins.

Davis, E. C. (1961). *The philosophical process in physical education*. Philadelphia: Lea & Febiger. (Includes several excellent analyses by Roger Burke.)

Davis, E. C. (1963). *Philosophies fashion physical education*. Dubuque, IA: Wm.C.Brown.

Ellfeldt, L. E., & Metheny, E. (1958). Movement and meaning: Development of a general theory." *Research Quarterly for Exercise and Sport*, 29, 264-273.

Fahlberg, L. L., & Fahlberg L. A. (1994). A human science for the study of movement: An integration of multiple ways of knowing. *Research Quarterly for Exercise and Sport.* 65, 100-109.

Fraleigh, W. P. (1984). *Right actions in sport.* Champaign, IL: Human Kinetics.

Hartshorne, C. (1975). *The nature of philosophy.* Philosophy in Context, 4: 7-16.

Henry, N. B., ed. (1942). *The Forty-First Yearbook of the National Society for the Study of Education. (Part I).* Chicago: University of Chicago Press.

Kaminsky, J. (1993*). A new history of educational philosophy.* Westport, CT: Greenwood Press.

Kaplan, A. (1961). *The new world of philosophy.* NY: Random House.

Keating, J. W. (1964). Sportsmanship as a moral category. Ethics, LXXV, 1:25-35.

Kleinman, S. (1964). The significance of human movement--a phenomenological approach. A paper presented to the National Association of Physical Education for College Women Conference, June 17.

Kretchmar, R. S. (1994). *Practical philosophy of sport.* Champaign, IL: Human Kinetics.

Macintyre, A. (August 29, 1993). The truth is in the details. *The New York Times Book Review.*

McGowan, J. (1991). *Postmodernism and its critics.* Ithaca: Cornell University Press.

McIntosh, P. (1979). *Fair play.* London: Heinemann.

Morland, R. B. (1958). *A philosophical interpretation of the educational views held by leaders in American physical education.* Ph.D. dissertation, New York University.

Nietzsche, F. *The use and abuse of history.*

Osterhoudt, R. G. (1971). *A descriptive analysis of research concerning the philosophy of physical education and sport.* Ph.D. dissertation, University of Illinois, C-U.

Paddick, R. J. (1967). *The nature and place of a field of knowledge in physical education.* M.A. thesis, University of Alberta.

Patrick, G. D. (1971). *Verifiability (meaningfulness) of selected physical education objectives.* Ph.D. dissertation, University of Illinois, C-U.

Pearson, K. (1968). "Inquiry into inquiry." An unpublished paper presented to the graduate seminar at the Univ. of Illinois, C-U.

Pearson, K. (1971). *A structural and functional analysis of the multi-concept of integration-segregation (male and/or female) in physical education classes.* Ph.D. dissertation, University of Illinois, C-U.

Pratte, R. (1992*). Philosophy of education--two traditions*. Springfield, IL: Charles C. Thomas.

Rajchman, J. & West, C. (Eds.). (1985). *Post-analytic philosophy*. NY: Columbia Univ. Press.

Random House Dictionary of the English Language, The. 1987. (2nd Ed., Unabridged). NY: Random House.

Rorty, R. (1982). *Consequences of Pragmatism* Minneapolis: Univ. of Minnesota Press.

Ross, S. (1990). Rethinking thinking, *Modern Maturity*, 33, 1:52-61.

Schrag, F. (1994). A view of our enterprise. Educational Theory, 44, 3:361-369.

Slusher, H. S. (1967). Man, sport and existence. Philadelphia: Lea & Febiger.

Smith, J. E. (September 1982). The need for a recovery of philosophy. In *Proceedings and Addresses of the American Philosophical Association*, 56, 1: 5-18.

Sparkes, A. W. (1991). *Talking philosophy: A wordbook*. London and NY: Routledge.

Spencer-Kraus, P. (1969). *The application of "linguistic phenomenology" to the philosophy of physical education and sport*. M.A. thesis, University of Illinois, Urbana.

Spretnak, C. (1991). *States of grace: The recovery of meaning in the postmodern age*. NY: Harper/SanFrancisco.

Stevenson, L. (1987). *Seven theories of human nature*. (2nd Ed.). NY: Oxford Univ. Press.

Steinhaus, A. H. (1952). Principal principles of physical education. In *Proceedings of the College Physical Education Association*. Washington, DC: AAHPER, pp. 5-11.

Stone, R. (1969). *Meanings found in the acts of surfing and skiing*. Ph.D. dissertation, University of Southern California.

Thomson, P. L. (1967). *Ontological truth in sports: A phenomenological analysis*. Ph.D. dissertation, University of Southern California.

Weiss, P. (1969). *Sport: A philosophic inquiry*. Carbondale, IL: Southern Illinois Press.

Wilcox, R. C. (1991). Sport and national character: An empirical analysis. *Journal of Comparative Physical Education and Sport*, XIII, 1: 3-27.

Wilson, J. Q. (1993). *The moral sense*. NY: The Free Press.

Zeigler, E. F. (1964). *Philosophical foundations for physical, health, and recreation education*. Englewood Cliffs, NJ: Prentice-Hall.

Zeigler, E. F. (1972). The black athlete's non-athletic problems. *Educational Theory*, 22, 4, 420-426.

Zeigler, E. F. (1974). A brief analysis of the ordinary language employed in the professional preparation of sport coaches and teachers. A paper presented to the Philosophy of Sport and Physical Activity Section, Canadian Association for Health, Physical Education and Recreation, Ottawa, May 27.

Zeigler, E .F. (1975). An analysis of the implications of reconstructionism for physical, health, and recreation education. In E. F. Zeigler, *Personalizing sport and physical education philosophy*. Champaign, IL: Stipes. (Originally presented to the presented to the AAHPERD Convention, Cincinnati, OH, May 1, 1964).

Zeigler, E. F. (1976). In sport, as in all of life, man should be comprehensible to man. *Journal of the Philosophy of Sport*, III, 121-126.

Zeigler, E. F. (1977). *Physical education and sport philosophy*. Englewood Cliffs, NJ: Prentice-Hall.

Zeigler, E. F. (1982). Philosophy of sport and developmental physical activity, in *The Sport Sciences* (Eds. J.J. Jackson and H.A. Wenger). Victoria, BC: Physical Education Series (Number 4).

Zeigler, E. F. & Rosenberg, D. (1983). Methodology and techniques employed in philosophic inquiry in sport and physical education. An unpublished paper.

Zeigler, E. F. (1984*). Ethics and morality in sport and physical education: An experiential approach*. Champaign, IL: Stipes.

Zeigler, E. F. (Late Winter 1988). How the profession "lost its principles." *The Physical Educator*, 45, 1, 14-18.

Zeigler, E. F. (1989a). Application of a scientific ethics approach to sport decisions, in P.J. Galasso, (Ed.), *Philosophy of sport and physical activity* (pp. 83-89). Toronto: Canadian Scholars' Press.

Zeigler, E. F. (1989b). *Sport and physical education philosophy: An Introduction*. Dubuque, IA: WCBrown/Benchmark.

Zeigler, E. F. (1994). *Physical education and kinesiology in North America: Professional & scholarly foundations*. Champaign, IL: Stipes.

Selection #16
Sport in the Postmodern World:
Servant or Master?

The word "adventure" is defined as either an "exciting experience" or a "bold undertaking" (*Encarta World English Dictionary*, 1999, p. 23). Our thoughts turn to the "adventure" of civilization as Earth moves into what is commonly termed "The 21st Century" (C.E.). Either definition is appropriate as we comprehend that any such pondering must be indelibly influenced by the events of September 11, 2001. Nevertheless, life goes on inexorably as an *adventure* in what we call "developing" civilization.(1)

Within the world culture of the 20th century, competitive sport gradually but steadily became an increasingly large component as one significant social institution in society's adventure. Whether its "use" will be characterized as that of "servant" or "master" is the subject of this analysis. The outcome of this "social institution's" development will be important to society in the years ahead.

The "Adventure" of Civilization

Before considering what is here conceived as sport's use as our "servant" or its abuse as our "master," let's put the question in perspective. Recall that the adventure of civilization included technological headway probably because of now-identifiable forms of early striving that embodied elements of great creativity (e.g., the invention of the wheel, the harnessing of fire). Subsequent development in technology, slowly but steadily, gradually offered humans a steadily increasing surplus of material goods over and above that needed for daily living. For example, the early harnessing of nature created the irrigation systems of Sumer and Egypt, and these accomplishments led to the establishment of the first cities.

Here material surpluses were collected, managed, and sometimes squandered. Nevertheless, early accounting methods were necessarily created and subsequently expanded in a way that introduced writing to the human scene. As we now know, the development of this form of communication in time helped humans expand their self-consciousness and to evolve gradually and steadily in all aspects of culture. The world's present, blanketing communications network has now actually exceeded humankind's ability to cope with it. For better or worse, the end result of social and material progress steadily presented a mixed agenda to humankind, an evolutionary process that has been characterized by both good and evil to the present day.

Muller (1952) concluded, "the adventure of civilization is necessarily inclusive" (p. 53). By that he meant that evil will probably always be with humankind to some degree, but it is civilization that sets the standards and accordingly works to eradicate at least the worst forms of such evil. Racial prejudice, for example, must be overcome. For better or worse, there are now

228

more than six billion people on earth, and that number appears to be growing faster than a national debt! These earth creatures are black-, yellow-, brown-, red-, or white-skinned, but fundamentally we now know from genetic research that there is an "overwhelming oneness" in all humankind that we dare not forget in our overall planning (Huxley, 1957).

As various world evils are overcome, or at least held in check, scientific and accompanying technological development will be called upon increasingly to meet the demands of the exploding population. Gainful work and a reasonable amount of leisure will be required for further development. Unfortunately, the necessary leisure required for the many aspects of a broad, societal culture to develop fully, as well as for an individual to grow and develop similarly within it, has come slowly. The average person is far from a full realization of such benefits. Why "the good life" for all has been so slow in arriving is not an easy question to answer. Of course, we might argue that times do change slowly, and that the possibility of increased leisure has really come quite rapidly--once humans began to achieve some control of their environment.

"Universal Civilization or the Clash of Civilizations?

Naipaul (1990) theorized that we are developing a "universal civilization" characterized by (1) the sharing of certain basic values, (2) what their societies have in common (e.g., cities and literacy, (3) certain of the attributes of Western civilization (e.g., market economies and political democracy), and (4) consumption patterns (e.g., fads) of Western civilization. Samuel Huntington (1998), the eminent political scientist, doesn't see this happening yet, however, although he does see some merit in these arguments. He grants that Western civilization is different than any other civilization that has ever existed because of its marked impact on the entire world since 1500. However, he doesn't know whether the West will be able to reverse the signs of decay already present and thus renew itself.

Sadly, there have been innumerable wars throughout history with very little if any let-up to the present. Nothing is so devastating to a country's economy as war. Now, whether one likes it or not, the world is gradually sliding into what Huntington has designated as "the clash of civilizations." It appears that the American government in power has seized upon his analysis as a justification to move still further in the War on Terrorism by the installation of what has euphemistically been called a "modernized regime" in Iraq. It is argued that this "accomplishment" would help toward the gradual achievement of worldwide democratic values along with global capitalism and so-called free markets.

The Misreading of Huntington's Thought. This misreading of Huntington's thought, however, needs to be corrected. As it stands, he asserts, "Western belief in the universality of Western culture suffers three problems. . . .It is false; it is immoral; and it is dangerous" (p. 310). He believes strongly that these religion-based cultures, such as the Islamic and the Chinese, should be permitted to find their own way in the 21st century. In fact, they will probably do so anyhow, no matter what the West does. Then individually (hopefully not together!), they will probably each become superpowers themselves. The "unknown quality" of their future goals will undoubtedly fuel the desires of those anxious for the United States to maintain overwhelming military superiority along with continually expanding technological capability.

While this is going on, however, the United States needs to be more aware of its own internal difficulties. It has never solved its "inner-city problem," along with increases in antisocial behavior generally (i.e., crime, drugs, and violence). Certainly the decay of the traditional family (i.e., husband, wife, two children) could have long-term implications as well. Huntington refers further to a "general weakening of the work ethic and rise of a cult of personal indulgence (p. 304). Still further, there is a definite decline in learning and intellectual activity as indicated by lower levels of academic achievement creating a need for course grade "aggrandizement" (i.e., the gentleman's "C" is "history"). Finally, there has been a marked lessening of "social capital" (the amount of "volunteering" including personal trust in others to meet individual needs).

Schlesinger's Analysis of America. These conflicting postulations by Huntington and Naipaul are stated here merely to warn that the present "missionary culture" of the United States is, in many ways, not really a true culture anyhow. So states Arthur Schlesinger, Jr. (1998), the distinguished historian. He points out that in recent years the U.S.A. has gradually acquired an ever-increasing multi-ethnicity. In *The Disuniting of America,* he decries the present schisms occurring in the United States. He is most concerned that the melting pot concept formerly so prominent in the States is becoming a "Tower of Babel" concept--"just like Canada!" he says. He understands, however, that "Canadians have never developed a strong sense of what it is to be a Canadian" by virtue of their dual heritage (p. 17).

Huntington explains further that an attempt to export democratic and capitalistic values vigorously to the world's other cultures may be exactly the wrong approach. He believes that they may well be looking mainly for stability in their own traditions and identity. Japan, for example, has shown the world that it is possible to become "rich and modern" without giving up their illiberal "core identity." Struggle as all cultures do for renewal when internal decay sets in, no civilization has proven that it is invincible indefinitely. This is exactly why Muller characterized history as somehow being imbued with a "tragic sense."

The "Tragic Sense" of Life

This "tragic sense' that history has displayed consistently was described by Herbert Muller (1952), in his magnificent treatise titled *The Uses of the Past* . Muller disagrees with the philosopher Hobbes (1588-1679), however, who stated in his De homine that very early humans existed in an individual state of nature in which life was anarchic and basically "solitary, poor, nasty, brutish, and short."

Muller argued in rebuttal that life "might have been poor and short, but that it was never solitary or simply brutish" (p. 6).

Accordingly, Muller's approach to history was in the spirit of the great tragic poets, a spirit of reverence and/or irony. It is based on the assumption that the tragic sense of life is not only the profoundest, but also the most pertinent for an understanding of both past and present (p. viii). Muller believed that the drama of human history has been characterized up to now by high tragedy in the Aristotelian sense. As he stated, "all the mighty civilizations have fallen because of tragic flaws; as we are enthralled by any golden age we must always add that it did not last, it did not do" (p. viii). This brings to mind that conceivably the 20th century of the modern era may turn out to have been the "Golden Age" of the United States. As unrealistic as this may sound because today the United States is the most powerful nation in the history of life on Earth, there could be misgivings developing about the blind optimism concerning history's malleability and compatibility in keeping with American ideals.

"The Future as History"

More than a generation ago, Heilbroner (1960) arrived at this position similarly. He explained in his "future as history" concept that America's belief in a personal "deity of history" may be short lived in the 21st century. As he stated this, he emphasized the need to search for a greatly improved "common denominator of values" (p. 170) in the face of technological, political, and economic forces that are "bringing about a closing of our historic future." As the world turns today in 2002, one may laugh at this prediction. Yet, looking at the situation from a starkly different perspective even earlier, Toynbee (1947) came to a quite similar conclusion in his monumental *A Study of History* from still another standpoint. He theorized that humankind must return to the one true God from whom it has gradually but steadily fallen away. You can challenge him on this opinion, as the author (an agnostic) most assuredly does. Yet, no matter--the way things are going at present--we on the Earth had best try to use our heads as intelligently and wisely as possible. As we get on with striving to make the world as effective, efficient, and humane as possible, we need to make life as replete with good, as opposed to evil, as we possibly can. With this plea for an abundance of righteousness, the reader may no longer be wondering where this analysis is heading. Let us turn now to whether the "use" and "possible abuse" of sport have provided humankind with a "helpful servant" or a "demanding master."

The Use and Abuse of Sport

At this point, having placed the "adventure" of civilization in some perspective, this analysis now shifts its focus to competitive sport and related physical activity. Here is a societal institution that became an ever-more powerful social force in the 20th century. Thus, I am attempting to analyze philosophically and sociologically what I call the "use" and "possible abuse" of sport. Basically, the argument is that society is governed by strong social institutions (i.e., "forces").

Among those social institutions are (1) the values (including created norms based on these values), (2) the type of political state in vogue, (3) the prevailing economic system, (4) the religious beliefs present, etc. To these longstanding institutions, I have added the influence of such others as education, science and technological advancement, concern for peace, *and now sport itself.* (Zeigler, 2003, 74). Of these, the values, and the accompanying norms developed, form the strongest institution of all.

Crossing the Postmodern Divide. Whether we recognize it or not, the burgeoning sport enterprise will also be forced to cross what has been termed the postmodern divide. An epoch in civilization approaches closure when many of the fundamental convictions of its advocates are challenged by a substantive minority of the populace. It can be argued that indeed the world is moving into a new epoch as the proponents of postmodernism have been affirming over recent decades. Within such a milieu there are strong indications that highly commercialized sport is going to have great difficulty crossing this chasm, this so-called, postmodern divide.

A diverse group of postmodern scholars argues that many in democracies, under–girded by the various rights being propounded (e.g., individual freedom, privacy), have come to believe that now they too require--and deserve!--a supportive "liberal consensus" within their respective societies. Conservative, essentialist elements prevail at present and are functioning strongly in many Western political systems. With their more authoritative orientation in mind, conservatives believe the deeper foundation justifying this claim of a need for a more liberal consensus has never been fully rationalized. However, it can be argued that postmodernists now form a substantive minority supporting a more humanistic, pragmatic, liberal consensus in which highly competitive sport is viewed as an increasingly negative influence on society (Borgman, 1993, p. 78). If this statement has merit--there are strong indications that the present sport enterprise--as known today--will have difficulty crossing this post-modern divide that has been postulated.

Characterizations of Competitive Sport

Having stated that "sport" has become a strong social institution, it is true also that there has been some ambiguity about what such a simple word as sport means. The word "sport" is used in many different ways as a noun. The number of definitions is now 14 in the most recent *Encarta World English Dictionary* (1999, p. 1730). In essence, what is being described here is an athletic activity requiring skill or physical prowess. It is typically of a competitive nature as in racing, wrestling, baseball, tennis, or cricket. For the people involved, sport is often serious, and participants may even advance to a stage where competitive sport becomes a semi-professional or a professional career choice. For a multitude of others, however, sport is seen more as a diversion, as recreational in nature, and as a pleasant pastime.

A Social Institution Without a Theory. Viewed collectively, my argument here is that at present the "totality" of sport appears to have become a strong social institution--*but one that is without a well-defined theory.* This assertion may have been recognized by others too. Yet, at this point the general public, including most politicians, seems to believe that "the more competitive sport we have, the merrier!" However, those who seek to promote sport ought right now to be able to answer such questions as (1) what purposes competitive sport has served in the past, (2) what functions it is fulfilling now, (3) where it seems to be heading, and (4) how it should be employed to serve all humankind.

How Sport Serves Society . In response to these questions, without careful delineation or any priority at this point, I can state that sport as presently operative can be subsumed in a non-inclusive list as possibly serving in the following ways:

1. As an organized religion (for those with or without another similar competing affiliation)
2. As an exercise medium (often a sporadic one)
3. As a life-enhancer or "arouser" (puts excitement in life)
4. As a trade or profession (depending upon one's involvement with it)
5. As an avocation, perhaps as a "leisure-filler" (at either a passive, vicarious, or active level)
6. As a training ground for war (used throughout history for this purpose)
7. As a "socializing activity" (an activity where one can meet and enjoy friends)
8. As an educational means (i.e., the development of positive character traits, however described)

In retrospect, I finds it most interesting that I didn't list sport "as a developer of positive character traits" until last! Now I wonder why. . . .

This listing could undoubtedly be larger. It could have included such terms as (1) sport "the destroyer," (2) sport "the redeemer," (3) sport "the social institution being tempted by science and technology," (4) sport "the social phenomenon by which heroes and villains are created," or, finally, (5) sport "the social institution that has survived within an era characterized by a vacuum of belief for many." However, I must stop. believing this listing is sufficient to make the necessary point here.

The hope is that you, the reader, will agree that those people involved in the sport enterprise truly need to understand what competitive sport has become in society. Frankly, I don't believe that a great many of its promoters know they are confronted with a stark dilemma. My argument here is that sport too--as is true for all other social institutions--is inevitably being confronted by the postmodern divide. In crossing this frontier, many troubling and difficult decisions, often ethical in nature, will have to be made as those related to commercialized sport in one of several ways. For example, what sort of professional preparation should prospective sport managers and coaches have, those men and women who will guide sport into becoming a responsible social institution? The fundamental question facing the profession is: "What kind of sport does it want to promote to help shape what sort of world in the 21st century?"

Is Sport Fulfilling Its Presumed Educational and Recreational Roles Adequately?

What implications does all of this have for sport as it enters the 21st century? As I view it, there are strong indications that sport's presumed educational and recreational roles in the "adventure" of civilization are not being fulfilled adequately. Frankly, the way commercialized, over-emphasized sport has been operated, it can be added to the list of symptoms of American internal decay enumerated above (e.g., drugs, violence, decline of intellectual interest, dishonesty, greed). If true, this inadequacy inevitably throws a burden on sport management as a profession to do something about it. Sport, along with all of humankind, is facing the postmodern divide.

Reviewing this claim in some detail, Depauw (Quest, 1997) argues that society should demonstrate more concern for those who have traditionally been marginalized in society by the sport establishment (i.e., those excluded because of sex or "physicality"). She speaks of "The (In)Visibility of DisAbility" in our culture. Depauw's position is backed substantively by what Blinde and McCallister (1999) call "The Intersection of Gender and Disability Dynamics."

A second point of contention about sport's contribution relates to the actual "sport experience." The way much sport has been conducted, the public has every right to ask, "Does sport build character or 'characters'?" Kavussannu & Roberts (2001) recently showed that, even though "sport participation is widely regarded as an important opportunity for character development," it is also true that sport "occurs in a context that values ego orientation (e.g. winning IS the most important thing)."

Sport's Contribution Today. What is competitive sport's contribution today? Delving into this matter seriously might produce a surprise--or perhaps not. It may well be that sport is contributing significantly in the development of what are regarded as social values--that is, the values of teamwork, loyalty, self-sacrifice, and perseverance consonant with prevailing corporate capitalism in democracy and in other political systems as well. Conversely, however, it may also be that there is now a great deal of evidence that sport is developing an ideal that opposes the fundamental moral virtues of honesty, fairness, and responsibility in the innumerable competitive experiences provided (Lumpkin, Stoll, and Beller, 1999).

234

Significant to this discussion are the results of investigations carried out by Hahm, Stoll, Beller, Rudd, and others in the late 1980s and 1990s. The Hahm-Beller Choice Inventory (HBVCI) has now been administered to athletes at different levels in a variety of venues. It demonstrates conclusively that athletes will not support what is considered "the moral ideal" in competition. An athlete with moral character should demonstrate the moral character traits of honesty, fair play, respect, and responsibility whether an official is present to enforce the rules or not. This finding was substantiated by Priest, Krause, and Beach (1999). They reported that the four-year changes occurring in college athlete's ethical value choices were consistent with other investigations. The findings showed decreases in "sportsmanship orientation" and an increase in "professional" attitudes associated with sport.

On the other hand, even though dictionaries define social character similarly, sport practitioners, including participants, coaches, parents, and officials, have come to believe that character is defined properly by such values as self-sacrifice, teamwork, loyalty, and perseverance (Rudd. 1999). The common expression in competitive sport is: "He/she showed character"--meaning "He/she 'hung in there' to the bitter end!" [or whatever]. Rudd confirmed also that coaches explained character as "work ethic and commitment." This coincides with what sport sociologists have found. Sage (1988, p. 634) explained: "Mottoes and slogans such as 'sports builds character' must be seen in the light of their ideological issues" In other words, competitive sport is structured by the nature of the society in which it occurs. This would appear to mean that over-commercialization, drug-taking, cheating, bribe-taking by officials, violence, etc. at all levels of sport are simply reflections of the culture in which we live.

Thus, we are left with sport's presumed relationship with moral character development that has been misinterpreted. And so, despite its early 20th-century claims to be "the last best hope on earth" for immigrants, American culture--where this "redefinition" of the term character has occurred--appears to be facing what Berman (2000) calls "spiritual death" (p. 52). He makes this claim because of "its crumbling school systems and widespread functional illiteracy, violent crime and gross economic inequality, and apathy and cynicism."

At this point, one can't help but recall that the ancient Olympic Games became so excessive with ills that the event was abolished. The Games were begun again only by the spark provided in the late 19th century by de Coubertin's "noble amateur ideal." The way things are going today, it is not unthinkable that the steadily increasing excesses of the present Olympic Games Movement could well bring about their demise again. However, they could well be only symptomatic of a larger problem confronting world culture.

This discussion about whether sport's presumed educational and recreational roles have justification in fact could go on indefinitely. So many negative incidents have occurred that one hardly knows where to turn to avoid further negative examples. On the one hand we read the almost unbelievably high standards set in the Code of Conduct developed by the Coaches Council of the National Association for Sport and Physical Education (NASPE) (2001). Conversely, however, we learn that today athletes' concern for the *presence* of moral values in sport declines over the course of a university career (Priest, Krause, and Beach, 1999).

Sedentary Living Has Caught Up With America. With this as a backdrop, we learn further that Americans are concurrently, for example, increasingly facing the cost and consequences of sedentary living (Booth & Chakravarthy, 2002). Additionally, Malina (2001) tells us there is a need to track people's physical activity across their lifespan. North America hasn't yet been able to devise and accept a uniform definition of wellness for all people. The one thought that emerges from these various assessments is as follows: Many people give every evidence of wanting their "sport spectaculars" for the few--much more than they want all people of all ages and all conditions to have meaningful sport, exercise, and physical recreation involvements throughout their lives.

In Canada, conversely, Tibbetts (2002), for example, described a most recent Environics survey that explained that "65% of Canadians would like more government money spent on local arenas, playgrounds, and swimming pools, as well as on sports for women, the poor, the disabled, and aboriginals."

Official Sport's Response to the Prevailing Situation

How does what is often called the "sport officialdom" respond to this situation? Answers to this question are just about everywhere as we think, for example, of the various types of scandals tied to both the summer and winter versions of the Olympic Games. For example, the *Vancouver Province* (2000) reported that the former "drug czar" of the U.S. Olympic Team, Dr. Wade Exum, charged that half of the team used performance-enhancing drugs to prepare for the 1996 Games. After making this statement, the response was rapid: he was forced to resign! He then sued the United States Olympic Committee for racial discrimination and harassment.

Viewed in a different perspective, as reported by Wallis (2002), Dr. Vince Zuaro, a longtime rules interpreter for Olympic wrestling, said recently: "Sports are so political. If you think what happened with Enron is political, [try] Olympic officiating. . . .Every time there's judging involved, there's going to be a payoff." Further, writing about the credibility of the International Olympic Committee, Feschuk (2002) stated in an article titled "Night of the Olympic Dead": "The IOC has for so long been inflicting upon itself such severe ethical trauma that its survival can only be explained by the fact that it has passed over into the undead. Its lifeless members shuffle across the globe in a zombie-like stupor, one hand extended to receive gratuities, the other held up in exaggerated outrage to deny any accusations of corruption."

At the same time, Dr. Ayotte, director of the only International Olympic Committee-accredited testing laboratory in Canada, explained that young athletes believe they must take drugs to compete successfully. "People have no faith in hard work and food now," she says, to achieve success in sport (Long, 2001).

Dick Pound's "Reward" for Distinguished Service. Closing out reference to the Olympic Games Movement, recall the case of Dick Pound, the Canadian lawyer from Montreal, who had faithfully and loyally striven most successfully to bolster the Games' finances in recent decades. He had also taken on the assignment of monitoring the situation with drugs and doping, as well as the bribery scandal associated with the Games held in Salt Lake City. In the election to succeed retiring President Samaranch, Pound unbelievably finished in third place immediately behind a man caught in a bribery scandal just a short time earlier (and since removed from office).

Finally, in the realm of international sport, Norwegian professor Dr. Hans B. Skaset (2002), a Norwegian professor, in response to a query, emailed me about a prediction he made at a conference on drugs in sport in November, 2002. He stated as keynote speaker that:

> Top international sport will cut itself free from its historical values and norms. After working with a clear moral basis for many years, sport by 2008-2010 will continue to be accepted as a leading genre within popular culture--but not, as it was formerly, a model for health, fairness, and honorable conduct. . . .

Switching venues, you don't see hockey promoters doing anything to really curb the neanderthal antics of professional hockey players. Considering professional sport generally, note the view of sport sociologist, Steven Ortiz, who has found in his study that "there clearly seems to be a 'fast-food sex' mentality among professional athletes" (Cryderman, 2001).

In addition, in the realm of higher education, Canadian universities are gradually moving toward the athletic-scholarship approach that certain universities in the East and Midwest sections of Canada have been following for years illegally (Naylor, 2002)! In September, 2001, a Halifax, Nova Scotia university team, the St. Mary Huskies, beat Mount Allison, a Sackville, New Brunswick university football team in the same conference, by a score of 105-0. In this article, one of a series sponsored by *The Globe and Mail* (Toronto), various aspects of this lopsided development were considered. Interestingly, funding for recruited athletes is just "penny-ante" compared to the support provided for the scholarship programs of various upper-division university conferences in the United States .

How to Reclaim Sport (Weiner). In writing about how society's obsession with sport has "ruined the game," Weiner (2000), a sport *critic* with the *Minneapolis Star-*

Tribune, asked the question: "How far back must we go to remember that sports matter?" Recalling the time when "sports had meaning," and "sports were accessible," he recommends that society can only "reclaim sports from the corporate entertainment behemoth" if it does the following:

1. "Deprofessionalize" college and high school sports,
2. Allow some form of public ownership of professional sports teams,
3. Make sports affordable again, and
4. Be conscious of the message sport is sending.

To summarize, the "sport industry" have quite simply conducted themselves in keeping with the prevailing political environment and ethos of the general public. They have presumably not understood and accordingly not accepted the contention that there is an urgent need for sport to serve as a beneficent social institution with an underlying theory looking to humankind's betterment (a necessary "IF 'this,' THEN 'that' will result" type of approach).

Of course, it can be argued that society does indeed believe that competitive sport is doing what it is intended to do--i.e., provide *both* non-moral and moral values to those involved. (The non-moral values could be listed as recognition, money, and a certain type of power, whereas the moral values could be of a nature designed to help the team achieve victory--dedication, loyalty, self-sacrifice.) If this assessment is accurate, the following question must be asked: Does the prevailing ethos in sport competition need to be altered so that this activity truly helps boys and girls, and men and women too, to learn honesty fair play, justice, responsibility, and beneficence (i.e., doing good)?

Seemingly the only conclusion to be drawn today is that the sport industry is "charging ahead" driven by the prevailing capitalistic, "global village" image of the future. Increasingly in competitive sport, such theory is embraced ever more strongly, an approach in which winning is overemphasized with resulting higher profits to the promoters through increased gate receipts. This same sport industry is aided and abetted by a society in which the majority do not recognize sufficiently the need for sport to serve as a social institution that results in a substantive amount of individual and social good.. On the one hand there are scholars who argue that democratic states, under girded by the various human rights legislated (e.g., equal opportunity), urgently need a supportive "liberal consensus" to maintain a social system that is fair to all. Yet, conservative, essentialist elements functioning in the same social system evidently do not see this need for a more humanistic, pragmatic consensus about the steadily mounting evidence showing a need for ALL people to be active physically throughout their lives.

This is the substantive aspect of the basis for the argument that commercialized sport will have great difficulty "crossing the post-modern divide." Zeigler (1996) pointed out that almost every approach to "the good life" stresses a need for an individual's relationship to developmental physical activity such as sport and fitness. Question: Should not governments and professional associations worldwide be assessing the social institution of sport to determine whether the way sport is presented to students is resulting in their becoming imbued with a desire to promote the concept of "sport for all" to foster overall human betterment?

Functioning With an Indeterminate, Muddled Theory. Once again, before considering future societal scenarios that world culture is facing, the argument should be made again that today sport is functioning vigorously with an indeterminate, muddled theory. The general implication is that sport competition builds both "moral" ***and*** "social" character traits consonant with democracy and capitalism. Crossing the post-modern divide means basically also that sport management educators, for example, should see through the false front and chicanery of the developing economic and technological facade of the global hegemony. They should see to it that their students understand this development. Face it: Sport is simply ***being used*** as a powerful institution in this "Brave New World" of the 21st century.

What Kind of A World Do You Want for Your Descendants?

The ultimate question here is whether society is fully cognizant of, and truly approves of, the situation as it has developed. Are we simply "going along with the crowd" while taking the path of least resistance? Can we do anything to improve the situation by perhaps implementing reforms that could help to make the situation more wholesome? More precisely, the question is whether the world can, and indeed should, re-orient itself to play a significant role in helping sport and related physical activity become a social institution exerting a positive influence in the ongoing "adventure" of civilization.

To do this, countries should determine what sort of a world they and their citizens should be living in. If a person as a concerned citizen considers himself or herself to be an environmentalist, for example, the future looks bleak at present. If he/she is business oriented, however, the belief is that continued economic and technological growth could well be the answer to all upcoming problems. Finally, a person who is something of a "New Ager" can only hope for some sort of mass spiritual transformation will take place.

Homer-Dixon (2001), in his *The Ingenuity Gap*, believes that humans are changing their relationship with the world and are "careening into the future." He explains his belief that an "ingenuity gap" has been created, and he questions whether humans will be able to solve the environmental, technological, and social problems that have somehow developed. The searching question to all who are involved with sport management is in a similar vein. Will you have the necessary ingenuity to close the gap that has been created by the "commercialized sport juggernaut?" Will you live up to the highest purposes of any profession--that is, to serve humankind best through the means at your disposal?

Finally, it is probably the case that the sport management "establishment" is at the moment conforming blindly to the power structure as they use the medium of education and recreation--i.e., sport--for their selfish purposes. The author, as one aging person who encountered corruption and sleaze in the intercollegiate athletic structure of several major universities in the United States, retreated to a Canadian university where the term "scholar-athlete" still implied roughly what it says. However, problems are now developing even in Canadian inter-university sport as well.

Two Approaches to Consider. What can this analysis possibly mean to members sport management worldwide? Actually there are several choices. One choice is to do nothing, meaning that organized sport continues in the same vein as at present. This would require no great effort. In the process, "business as usual" will be supported one way or the other--by "hook or by crook". What people are doing unfortunately is devoting themselves to the type of sport that in the final analysis means least to our society and ignoring that which could mean the most! Society should be seeking the answers to such questions as (1) what is sport's prevailing drift?; (2) what are the advantages and disadvantages of sport involvement for life?; and (3) what is sport's residual impact on society?

I was personally involved in sport competitively throughout high school and college. Then I coached university football, wrestling, and/or swimming over a period of 15 years. Finally I served as overall administrator of a university faculty in which inter-university athletics was housed. Yet, despite this involvement encouraging my son and daughter to become involved, I have personally been conducting an informal boycott of the NFL, NBA, and NFL, and of all *overly commercialized* university sport for a number of years. Frankly, to me it has become disgusting, because it is basically almost amoral. It certainly is not characterized by honesty and sportsmanship, not to mention the "good foul" and other "deviational maneuvers" to "foil the enemy"! It also involves too much passive "spectatoritis". Frankly, as presently conducted, I believe it is actually subversive to the higher purposes of democracy.

Further, I am convinced that the commercialized Olympic Movement with its drugs, officiating, free-loading officials, and bribery problems--not to mention its millionaire basketball, hockey, and tennis performers etc.--will eventually suffer the same fate as the ancient Games did in 336 C.E. unless radical change takes place soon. The late Baron de Coubertin and Avery Brundage must indeed be "whirling in their graves" at a rate to soon exceed the sound barrier!

Concluding Statement

Am I being unduly pessimistic, having reached the "old-curmudgeon" stage? Perhaps this is true. However, those worldwide who are truly concerned about the future of "value-laden," competitive sport, wherever you may be, are strongly urged to get involved now with the reforms that seem so necessary. In the immediate future, please seek the answer to two fundamental questions. The response to the first question might well cause action to be taken in the future to answer question #2. These questions are: (1) in what ways can we accurately assess the present status of sport to learn if it is--or is not--fulfilling its role as a presumably beneficent social institution? and (2)--depending on whether the answer to #1 is negative, of course--will you then have the motivation and professional zeal to do your utmost to help sport achieve what could well be its rightful place in society?

References

Berman, M. (2001) *The twilight of American culture*, NY: W.W. Norton.

Blinde, E. M. & McCallister, S. G. (1999). Women, disability, and sport and physical fitness activity: The intersection of gender and disability dynamics. *Research Quarterly for Sport and Exercise*, 70, 3, 303-312.

Booth, F. W., & Chakravarthy, M. V. (2002). Cost and consequences of sedentary living: New battleground for an old enemy. *Research Digest (PCPFS)*, 3, 16, 1-8.

Borgman, A. (1993) *Crossing the postmodern divide*. Chicago: The Univ. of Chicago Press.

Cryderman, K. (2001). Sport's culture of adultery. *The Vancouver Sun* (Canada), August 21, C5.

Depauw, K. P. (1997). The (in)visibility of disability: Cultural contexts and "sporting bodies," *Quest*, 49, 416-430

Encarta World English Dictionary, The. (1999). NY: St. Martin's Press.

Feschuk, S. (2002). Night of the Olympic dead. *National Post (Canada)*, Feb. 16, B10.

Hahm, C. H., Beller, J. M., & Stoll, S. K. (1989). *The Hahm-Beller Values Choice Inventory*. Moscow, Idaho: Center for Ethics, The University of Idaho.

Homer-Dixon, T. (2001). *The ingenuity gap*. Toronto: Vintage Canada.

Huntington, S. P. (1998). *The Clash of Civilizations (and the Remaking of World Order*. NY: Touchstone.

Huxley, J. (1957). *New wine for new bottles*. NY: Harper & Row.

Kavussanu, M. & Roberts, G. C. (2001). Moral functioning in sport: An achievement goal perspective. *Journal of Sport and Exercise Psychology*, 23, 37-54

Long, W. (2001. Athletes losing faith in hard work. *The Vancouver Sun* (Canada), Jan. 31. E5.

Lumpkin, A., Stoll, S. K., & Beller, J. M. (1999). *Sport ethics: Applications for fair play* (2nd Ed.). St. Louis: McGraw-Hill.

Malina, R. M. (2001). Tracking of physical activity across the lifespan. *Research Digest (PCPFS)*, 3-14, 1-8.

Muller, H. J. (1952) *The uses of the past*. NY: Mentor.

Naipaul, V. S. (Oct 30, 1990). "Our Universal Civilization." The 1990 Winston Lecture, The Manhattan Institute, *New York Review of*

Books, p. 20.

National Association for Sport and Physical Education. (2001). The coaches code of conduct. *Strategies,* Nov.-Dec., 11.

Naylor, D. (2002), In pursuit of level playing fields. *The Globe and Mail* (Canada), March 9, S1.

Priest, R .F., Krause, J. V., & Beach, J. (1999). Four-year changes in college athletes' ethical value choices in sports situations. *Research Quarterly for Exercise and Sport*, 70, 1, 170-178.

Province, The (Vancouver, Canada) (2000). Drug allegations rock sports world. July 3, A2.

Rudd, A., Stoll, S. K., & Beller, J. M. (1999). Measuring moral and social character among a group of Division 1A college athletes, non-athletes, and ROTC military students. *Research Quarterly for Exercise and Sport,* 70 (Suppl. 1), 127.

Sage, G. H. (1988, October). "Sports participation as a builder of character?" *The World and I,* Vol. 3, 629-641.

Schlesinger, A. M. (1998). (Rev. & Enl.).*The disuniting of America.* NY: W.W. Norton.

Skaset, H. B., Email correspondence. May 14, 2002.

Tibbetts, J. (2002). Spend more on popular sports, Canadians say, *National Post* (Canada), A8, April 15.

Toynbee, A. J. (1947). *A study of history.* NY: Oxford University Press.

Wallis, D. (2002). Annals of Olympics filled with dubious decisions. *National Post (*Canada), Feb. 16, B2.

Weiner, J. (Jan.-Feb. 2000). Why our obsession has ruined the game; and how we can save it. *Utne Reader,* 97, 48-50.

Zeigler, E. F. (2003). *Socio-Cultural Foundations of Physical Education and Educational Sport.* Aachen, Germany: Meyer and Meyer Sport.

Zeigler, E. F. (1996). Historical perspective on "quality of life": Genes. memes, and physical activity. *Quest ,* 48, 246-263.

Selection #17
Delineating the "Common Denominators" of Physical Activity Education for the 21ˢᵗ Century

The basic premise of this analysis is reflected in its title. First, I believe that–in a sense–American physical (activity) education lost its way in the course of the 20ᵗʰ century. Second, I believe this happened because the developing value orientation of America was largely responsible for this deviation from its important objectives. Third, for the field to find its way back in the 21st century, I recommend that physical activity educators can carry out their mission best by emphasizing in a balanced fashion. those "essences" that emerged as its "common denominators" in the century recently completed.

To begin to explain what happened during this period, there was an urgent need historically for American children and young people to be more active physically in the last half of the 19th century as America experienced vast industrialization. As a result, when this need was recognized generally, a "battle of foreign systems" of exercise ensued with the result that all sorts of physical activity program were recommended for consideration.

These years from 1880 to 1890 in which this happened, undoubtedly formed one of the most important decades in the history of physical education in the United States. The colleges and universities, the YMCAs, the *Turners*, and proponents of the various foreign systems of gymnastics–all made contributions during this brief period. However, instead of one of these competing systems winning out, something unique gradually emerged. That "something" became known as "American physical education."

The Association that promoted this "American physical education" was called the Association for the Advancement of Physical Education (now AAHPERD) that was founded in 1885. (The word "American" was added in 1886.) This professional organization was the first of its kind in the field and undoubtedly stimulated teacher education markedly at the turn of the century and thereafter. An important early project was the plan for developing a series of experiences in physical activity--physical education--the objectives of which would be in accord with the existing pattern of general education. The struggle to bring about widespread adoption of such a program followed. Early legislation implementing physical education was enacted in five states before the turn of the 20th century.

The late 19th century also saw the development also of sporadic efforts in organized recreation and camping for children living in underdeveloped areas in large cities. The first playground was begun in Boston in 1885. New York and Chicago followed suit shortly thereafter, no doubt to a certain degree as a result of the ill effects of the Industrial Revolution. This was actually the meager beginning of the present tremendous recreation movement in America. Camping, that activity begun by both private individuals and organizational camping, started before the turn of the century as well. Both have flourished similarly since that time and has been an important supplement to the entire movement.

Although criticism of the educational system as a whole was present between 1870 and 1890, it really assumed large–scale proportions in the last decade of the 19th century. All sorts of innovations and reforms were being recommended from a variety of quarters. The social movement in education undoubtedly had a relationship to a rise in what may be termed "political progressivism." Even in the universities, the formalism present in psychology, philosophy, and the social sciences was coming under severe attack. Out in the public schools, a different sort of conflict was raging. Citizens were demanding that the promise of American life should be reflected through change and a broadening of the school's purposes.

However, although the seeds of this educational revolution were sown in the 19th century, the story of its accomplishment belongs to the 20th century.

The 20th Century

The tempo of life in the United States seemed to increase in the 20th century. The times were indeed changing as evidenced, for example, by one war after another. In retrospect there were so many wars--World War I, World War II, the Korean War, the Vietnam War, the seemingly ever-present "cold war" the seemingly began after the global conflict of the 1940s. Inescapably they have had a powerful influence of society along with the earlier worldwide depression of the 1930s. Looking back on 20th century history is frightening; so much has happened, and it has happened so quickly. *(The phenomenon of change is as ubiquitous today at the beginning of the 21st century as are the historic nemeses of death and taxes.)*

In the public realm, social legislation and political reform made truly significant changes in the lives of people despite the leavening, ever-present struggle between conservative and liberal forces. Industry and business assumed gigantic proportions, as did the regulatory controls of the federal government. The greatest experiment in political democracy in the history of the world was grinding ahead with deliberate speed, but with occasional stopping-off sessions while "its breath was caught." The idealism behind such a plan–a vision that amounted to "democratic socialism"–was at times challenged from one or more quarters. Also, wars, financial booms–and depressions or perhaps recessions–weren't the types of developments that made planning and execution simple matters. All of these developments mentioned above had their influence on the subject at hand–education (and, of course, what I am here delineating as physical **activity** education).

In the early 20th century, United States citizens began give serious thought to their educational aims or values. The earliest aim in U.S. educational history had been religious in nature, an approach that was eventually supplanted by a political aim consistent with emerging nationalism. However, then an overwhelming utilitarian, economic aim seemed to overshadow the political aim. The tremendous increase in high school enrollment forced a reconsideration of the aims of education at all levels of the system. An educational program to be mastered by "the many" supplanted training for "the elite." It was at this time also that the beginnings of a scientific approach to educational problems forced educators to rationalize the development based on theory and (2) to devise a scholarly rationale other than one forced on the school simply because of a sheer increase in numbers.

Next, an effort on the part of many people followed to consider aims and objectives from a sociological orientation. For the first time, education was conceived in terms of complete living as a citizen of an evolving democracy. The influence of John Dewey and others encouraged the viewing of the curriculum as child-centered rather than subject-centered—a rather startling attempt to alter the long-standing basic orientation that involved the rote mastery of an amalgam of educational source material. What was called the Progressive Education Movement placed great emphasis on individualistic aims. This was subsequently countered by a demand for a theory stressing a social–welfare orientation rather than one so heavily pointed to individual development.

The relationship between school health education and physical education grew extensively during the first quarter of the 20th century. This included their liaison with the entire system of education. Health education in all its aspects was viewed seriously, especially after the evidence surfaced from the draft statistics of World War I. Many states passed legislation requiring varying amounts of time in the curriculum devoted to the teaching of physical education. National interest in sports and games grew at a phenomenal rate in an era when economic prosperity prevailed. The basis for school and community recreation was being well laid.

Simultaneously with physical education's achievement of a type of maturity brought about legislation designed to promote "physical fitness" and "healthy bodies," the struggle between the inflexibility of the various foreign systems of gymnastics and the individual freedom of the so-called "natural movement" was being waged with increasing vigor. Actually, the rising interest in sports and games soon made the conflict unequal, especially when the concept of "athletics for all" really began to take hold in the second and third decades of the century.

Conflicting Educational Philosophies

Even today at the beginning of the 21st century, however, the significance of play and its possibilities in the educative process have not really been comprehended. Viewed historically, until well up in the 1800s in the United States, the entire educational system was opposed to the idea of what would be included in a fine program of physical activity education today. It was the organized German-American Turners primarily, along with certain others, who came to this continent from their native Germany and advocated that mental and physical education should proceed hand in hand in the public schools. The Turners' opposition to military training as a substitute for physical education contributed beneficially to the extremely differentiated pattern of physical education in the post-Civil War era. Their influence offset the stress on military drill in the land-grant colleges created by Congress passing the Morrill Act in the United States in 1862. The beginning of American competitive sport as we know it also dates to this period. However, college and university faculties took the position consistently that games and sport were not a part of the basic educational program. In the realm of "physical training," however, the colleges and universities, the YMCAs, the Turners, and the proponents of the various foreign systems of gymnastics all made contributions during the last quarter of the 19th century.

In the early 20th century Americans began to do some earnest thinking about their educational aims and values. Whereas the earliest aim in U.S. educational history had been religious in nature, this was eventually supplanted by a political aim consistent with emerging nationalism. However, an overwhelming utilitarian, economic aim then seemed to overshadow the political aim. It was at this time. Also, that the beginnings of a scientific approach to educational problems forced educators to seek understanding of the development based on a rationale other than the sheer increase in student enrollment.

Then there followed an effort to consider aims and objectives from a sociological orientation. For the first time, education was conceived in terms of complete living as a citizen in an evolving democracy. The influence of John Dewey and others encouraged the viewing of the curriculum as child-centered rather than subject-centered. Great emphasis was placed on individualistic aims with a subsequent counter demand for a theory stressing more of a social welfare orientation.

The relationship between health and physical education and the entire system of education had strengthened during the first quarter of the 20th century. Many states passed legislation requiring physical education in the curriculum, especially after the damning evidence of the draft statistics in World War I. Simultaneous with physical education's achievement of a type of maturity through such legislation, the struggle between the inflexibility of the various foreign systems of gymnastics and the individualistic freedom of the so-called "natural movement" was being waged with increasing vigor. Actually the rising interest in sports and games soon made the conflict unequal, especially when the concept of athletics for all really began to take hold in the second and third decades of the century.

The natural movement was strengthened further by much of the evidence gathered by many natural and social scientists. A certain amount of the spirit of Dewey's philosophy took hold within the educational environment. This new philosophy and the accompanying methodology and techniques appeared to be more effective in the light of the changing ideals of an evolving democracy. Despite this pragmatic influence, however, the influence of idealism remained strong also, with its emphasis on the development of individual personality and the possible inculcation of moral and spiritual values through the transfer of training theory applied to sports and games.

Embryonic Emergence of the Allied "Professions"

School health education developed greatly during the period also. The scope of school hygiene increased, and a required medical examination for all became more important. Leaders were urged to conceive of school health education as including three major divisions: health services, health instruction, and healthful school living. Educator and citizen alike gradually accepted the value of expansion in this area. For example, many physical educators began to show a concern for a broadening of the field's aims and objectives, the evidence of which could be seen by the increasing amount of time spent by many on coaching duties. Conversely, the expansion of health instruction through the medium of many public and private agencies tended to draw those more directly interested in the goals of health education away from physical education.

Progress in the recreation field was significant as well. The values inherent in well-conducted playground activities for children and youths were increasingly recognized; the Playground Association of America was organized in 1906. At this time there was still an extremely close relationship between physical education and recreation, a link that remained strong because of the keen interest in the aims of recreation by a number of outstanding physical educators. Many municipal recreation centers were constructed; it was at this time that the use of some of the schools–relatively few, actually–for "after-hour" recreation began. People began to recognize that recreational activities served an important purpose in a society undergoing basic changes. Some recreation programs developed under local boards of education; others were formed by the joint sponsorship of school boards and municipal governments. A large number of communities placed recreation under the direct control of the municipal government and either rented school facilities when possible, or gradually developed recreational facilities of their own.

Professional Associations Form an Alliance

The American Association for Health, Physical Education, and Recreation became the American Alliance for Health, Physical Education, Recreation, and Dance in 1968. As such it has undoubtedly accomplished a great deal in a strong united effort to coordinate the various allied professions largely within the framework of public and private education. Despite membership losses during the 1970s, its success story continues today with those functions that properly belong within the educational sphere. The Alliance is also gradually increasing its influence on those seeking those services and opportunities that we can provide at the various other age levels as well.

Additionally, for better or worse, there are many other health agencies and groups, recreational associations and enterprises, physical education associations and "splinter" disciplinary groups, and athletics associations and organizations moving in a variety of directions. One example of these is the North American Society for Sport Management that began in the mid-1980s and has grown significantly since. Each of these associations or societies is presumably functioning with the system of values and norms prevailing in the country (or culture, etc.) and the resultant pluralistic educational philosophies extant within such a milieu.

We have seen teacher education generally, under which physical education has been bracketed, and professional preparation for recreational leadership also, strengthened through self-evaluation and accreditation. The dance movement has been a significant development within the educational field, and those concerned are still determining the place for this movement within the educational program at all levels. A great deal of progress has been made in physical education, sport, and (more recently) kinesiology research since 1960.

Achieving Some Historical Perspective

It is now possible to achieve some historical perspective about the second and third quarters of the 20th century as they have affected physical education and sport, as well as the allied professions of health education, recreation, and dance education. The Depression of the 1930s, World War II, the Korean War, the Vietnam War, the subsequent cold war with the many frictions among countries, and now the "War on Terrorism" have been strong social forces directly influencing sport, physical education, health education, recreation, and dance in any form and in any country. Conversely, to what extent these various fields and their professional concerns have in turn influenced the many cultures, societies, and social systems remains yet to be accurately determined.

It would be simplistic to say (1) that physical educators want more and better physical education and intramural-recreational sport programs, (2) that athletics-oriented coaches and administrators want more and better athletic competition for the "physically gifted," (3) that health and safety educators want more and better health and safety education, (4) that recreation personnel want more and better recreation, and that (5) dance educators want more and better dance instruction. Yet, this would probably be a correct assessment of their wishes and probably represents to a large degree what has occurred.

"Common Denominators" in Program Development

Each one of the future allied professions or fields (listed immediately above) developed to a point where its advocates "saw clearly" its own program objectives. Hence, each decided to seek separate status and broke free from a direct relationship with physical education. Nevertheless, each of these "allied professions" has had a greater or lesser influence on the stated objectives of physical education during the 20th century. The resultant, presumably consensual objectives of physical education presented below give an indication of this influence as to what toward the middle of the century was designated as physical education at all educational levels.

In addition, even today at the beginning of the 21st century, with only slight modification–these "common denominators" of human motor performance (i.e., of physical activity) within what is here being called "developmental physical activity" of humans in exercise, sport, and expressive movement are still intact. Listed below, we find considerable agreement on them in countries all over the civilized world:

"Common Denominators"
of
Developmental Physical Activity
in
Exercise, Sport, and Expressive Movement

1. That regular physical activity education be required for all children and young people (who are presumably still in school) up to and including 16 years of age.

2. That human movement fundamentals through various expressive activities are basic in the elementary, middle, and high school curricula.

3. That physical vigor and endurance are important for people of all ages. Progressive standards should be developed from prevailing norms.

4. That boys and girls (and young men and women) should have an experience in competitive sport at some stage of their development. The important goal here is the development of an athlete of character, one who is honest, fair, responsible, respectful, and compassionate (Stoll and Beller, 1998)

5. That remediable defects should be corrected through exercise therapy at all school levels. Where required, adapted sport and physical recreation experiences should be stressed.

6. That a young person should develop certain positive attitudes toward his or her own health in particular and toward community hygiene in general. Basic health knowledge should be an integral part of the school curriculum.

(N.B.: Note that this "common denominator"
should be a specific objective of the field of physical
activity education only as it relates to developmental
physical activity.)

7. That exercise, sport, and expressive movement can make a most important contribution throughout life toward the worthy use of leisure.

8. That character and/or personality development is vitally important to the development of the young person, and therefore it is especially important that men and women with high professional standards and ethics guide all human movement experience in sport, exercise, and expressive movement at the various educational levels.

(See Zeigler, 2003, pp. 185-186, for an elaboration
of these proposed common denominators.)

A Call for Professional Reunification

Physical activity educators in the United States recognize that there are indeed allied professions represented to a greater or lesser extent in the American Alliance (AAHPERD). It is no longer a question of bringing these other fields or professions back into the physical activity education fold; they are gone forever. However, in their interest as well as that of physical activity education and educational sport, these "allied fields" must be kept closely allied to the greatest extent possible.

What is really crucial at the moment is that physical activity educators seek to bring about a recognizable state of *REUNIFICATION* within what is here being called the physical (activity) education and (educational) sport. If the present splintering process taking place is not reversed, both in the United States and in Canada, prospects for the future may be bleak indeed.

The discipline of developmental physical activity-however it is eventually defined and named (!)—relates directly to exercise, sport, and related expressive movement. Those who are qualified and officially recognized and officially certified in the theory and practice of such human movement should be designated as professionals. This applies to performers, teachers/coaches, teachers of teachers/coaches, scholars and researchers, practitioners in alternative careers, or other professional practitioners not yet envisioned.

Selection #18
The 21st Century: What Do We Do Now That We're Here?

> Look not mournfully to the past--it comes not back again;
> wisely improve the present--it is thine; go forth to meet
> the shadowy future without fear, and with a manly heart.
> --Longfellow

The words of Longfellow above, it seems to me, are among the best I have seen for general guidance We have made our mistakes in the past; we have a fairly good idea of where we are at the present; and we must move into the future strongly and boldly, but with great care and concern.

I plan to spell out here what I consider the necessary steps for us to take as we "sculpt the future" of physical activity education and educational sport. First, however, what I propose to say here will be offered in a somewhat different perspective or slant. It will be somewhat more general socially, and also more normative philosophically. I am very matter of fact and very specific as to how our field has been "modified." This occurred to a certain extent because of the impact of various social forces (e.g., economics), but also because of our many sins of omission and commission.

If I were not worried about the future generally, and about the future of our own field specifically, I don't believe that I would have undertaken this task. I want to make it clear that I don't for one minute buy the thought expressed by Sir Arthur Wing Pinero in his *The Second Mrs. Tanqueray* to the effect that "the future is only the past again, entered through another gate." I am much more inclined to the sentiment expressed by Henrik Ibsen in a letter to Georg Brandes in which he stated, "I hold that man is in the right who is most closely in league with the future." Indeed, but there's the rub, I suppose: Just how does one "get in league with the future"? The answer to this question is probably--"With some difficulty." Nevertheless, I think we would all agree that the achievement of such understanding is our task alone; no one else is going to do it *for* us.

Forecasting the Future

"Getting in league with the future" may come true, I presume, by making a sincere, solid effort to understand what "futurology" is all about. I turned first for some guidance to *Visions of the Future* (Melnick, 1984), a publication of the well-known Hudson Institute. Initially, we are told that there are three ways of "looking at the future": (1) the *possible* future, (2) the *probable* future, and (3) the *preferable* future (p. 4). The next step is to decide which of the three ways to consider first to apply these findings in our lives. Initially, then, it is the *possible* future of the profession of what I call physical activity education and educational sport that I consider first.

.

As you might imagine, the *possible* future includes everything that *could* happen. Thus, perceptions of the future can be formed by us either individually and collectively. The *probable* future refers to occurrences that are likely to happen, and here the range of alternatives should be considered. Finally, the *preferable* future relates to an approach whereby people first make choices that indicate how they would like things to happen. Underlying any thought, there are certain basic assumptions or premises:

(1) that the future hasn't been predetermined by some
    force or power,
2) that the future cannot be accurately predicted
    because we don't understand the process of
    change fully, and
(3) that the future will undoubtedly be influenced by
    choices that people make, but won't necessarily
    turn out the way they want it to be (Amara, 1981).

As we all appreciate, people have been predicting the future for thousands of years, undoubtedly with a limited degree of success. Considerable headway has been made, of course, since the time when animal entrails were examined to provide insight about the future (i.e., one of the techniques of so-called divination). Nowadays, for example, methods of prediction include forecasting by the use of trends and statistics. One most recent approach (Megatrends, 1982) along this line has been of great interest to me because I have been using a variation of this technique for more than 40 years, one that originated with John S. Brubacher (1947). It is termed a "a persistent problems approach". I have used it to help analyze my own field (see Zeigler, 1964, 1968, 1977a, 1977b, 1984, 1988, 1989, 1990, 1992, 1994a, 1994b, 2003, 2005).

John Naisbitt and The Naisbitt Group (<u>Megatrends</u> 1982 and subsequent publications) believe that "the most reliable way to anticipate the future is by understanding the present" (p. 2). Thus, they monitor occurrences all over the world through a technique of descriptive method known as *content analysis*. They actually monitor the amount of space given to various topics in newspapers, an approach they deem valid because "the news-reporting process is forced choice in a closed system" (p. 4).

Melnick and associates (1984) discussed a further aspect of futurology—the question of "levels of certainty." They explain that the late, great scholar, Herman Kahn, often used the term "Scotch Verdict" when he was concerned about the level of certainty available prior to making a decision. He borrowed this idea from the Scottish system of justice in which a person charged with the commission of a crime can be found "guilty," "not guilty," or "not been proven guilty." This "not been proven guilty" (or "Scotch") verdict implies there is enough evidence to demonstrate that the person charged is guilty, but that insufficient evidence has been presented to end *all reasonable doubt* about the matter. Thus, a continuum has been developed at one end of which we can state we are 100% sure that such-and-such is *not* true. Accordingly, at the other end of the continuum we can state we are 100% sure that such-and-such is the case (pp. 6-7). Obviously, in between these two extremes are gradations of the level of certainty. From here this idea has been carried over to the realm of future forecasting.

Next we are exhorted to consider the "Great Transition" that humankind has been experiencing, how there has been a pre-industrial stage, an industrial stage and, finally, a post-industrial stage that seems to have arrived in North America first. Each of the stages has its characteristics that we recognize. For example, in the pre-industrial era there was slow population growth, people lived simply with very little money, and the forces of nature made life very difficult. When the industrial stage or so-called modernization entered the picture, population growth was rapid, wealth increased enormously, and people became increasingly less vulnerable to the destructive forces of nature. The assumption here is that comprehension of the transition that is occurring now can give us some insight as to what the future might hold. We cannot be "100% sure", but at least we might be able to achieve a "Scotch Verdict" (p. 47). If North America is that part of the world that is the most advanced economically and technologically, and as a result will complete the Great Transition by becoming a post-industrial culture, then we must be aware of what this will mean to our society. Melnick believes that we have probably already entered a "super-industrial period" of the Industrial Stage in which "projects will be very large scale, services will be readily available, efficient and sophisticated, people will have vastly increased leisure time, and many new technologies will be created" (pp. 35-37).

It is important that we understand what is happening as we move further forward into what presumably is the final or third stage of the Great Transition. First, it should be made clear that the level of certainty here about predictions is at Kahn's "Scotch Verdict" point on the continuum. The world has never faced this situation before; so, we do not know exactly how to date the beginning of such a stage. Nevertheless, it seems to be taking place right now (i.e., with the super-industrial period starting after World War II). As predicted, those developments mentioned above (e.g., services readily available) appear to be continuing. It is postulated that population growth is slower than it was 20 years ago; yet it is true that people are living longer. Next, it is estimated that a greater interdependence among nations and the steady development of new technologies will contribute to a steadily improving economic climate for underdeveloped nations. Finally, the forecast is that advances in science and accompanying technology will bring almost innumerable technologies to the fore that will affect life styles immeasurably all over the world.

This discussion could continue almost indefinitely, but the important points to be made here are emerging rapidly. First, we need a different way of looking at the subject of natural resources. In this interdependent world, this "global village" if you will, natural resources are more than just the sum of raw materials. They include also the application of technology, the organizational bureaucracy to cope with the materials, and the resultant usefulness of the resource that creates supply and demand (p. 74). The point seems to be that the total resource picture (as explained here) is reasonably optimistic *if correct decisions are made* about raw materials, energy, food production, and use of the environment. These are admittedly rather large **"IFS"** (pp. 73-97).

Finally, in this "forecasting the future" section, the need to understand global problems of two types is stressed. One group is called "mostly understandable problems," *and they are solvable.* Here reference is made to:

(1) population growth,
(2) natural resource issues,
(3) acceptable environmental health, (
4) shift in society's economic base to service occupations, and
(5) effect of advanced technology.

However, it is the second group classified as "mostly uncertain problems," that could bring on disaster! First, the Great Transition is affecting the entire world, and the eventual outcome of this new type of cultural change is uncertain. Thus, we must be ready for these developments attitudinally. Second, in this period of changing values and attitudes, people in the various countries and cultures have much to learn and they will have to make great adjustments as well. Third, there is the danger that society will, possibly unwittingly-, stumble into some irreversible environmental catastrophe (e.g., upper-atmosphere ozone depletion). Fourth, the whole problem of weapons, wars, and terrorism, and whether the world will be able to stave off all-out nuclear warfare. Fifth, and finally, whether bad luck and bad management will somehow block the entire world from undergoing the Great Transition successfully, obviously a great argument for the development of management art and science (pp. 124-129).

What Should We Avoid in the 21st Century?

Before recommending what we, in the field of physical activity education and educational sport under girded by the scholarly contributions of kinesiology or exercise science, *should do* as we move along in the 21st century, we should undoubtedly give brief consideration to the question of *what to avoid* along this path. First, there is evidence to suggest that we should maintain flexibility in our philosophical approach. This will be difficult for some who have worked out definite, explicit philosophic stances. For those who are struggling along with *an implicit sense of life* (as defined by Rand, 1960), however, having philosophic flexibility may be even more difficult because they don't fully understand "where they are coming from"! We all know people for whom Alvin Toffler's concepts of "future shock" and "third wave world" have become a reality. Life has indeed become stressful for these individuals.

Second, I believe that we as individuals should avoid what may be called either "naive optimism" or "despairing pessimism" in the years ahead. What we should assume, I believe, is a philosophical stance that is named "positive meliorism", a position that assumes that we should strive consciously to bring about a steady improvement in the quality of our lives. This "what-to-avoid" item is related to the recommendation above concerning flexibility in philosophical approach, of course. We cannot forget, however, how easy it is to fall into the seemingly "attractive traps" of either blind pessimism or blind optimism.

Third, I believe the professional in physical activity education and educational sport should continue to strive for "just the right amount" of "freedom" in his or her life generally and in one's professional affairs as well. Freedom for the individual is a fundamental characteristic of a democratic state, but it should never be forgotten that such freedom as may prevail in all countries today had to be won "inch by inch." It is evidently in the nature of the human animal that there are always people in our midst who "know what is best for us," and who seem anxious to take our hard-won freedoms away. This seems to be true whether crises exist or not. Of course, the concept of 'individual freedom' can not be stretched to include anarchy. On the other hand, the freedom to *teach* what we will responsibly in physical activity education and educational sport, or conversely the freedom to *learn* what one will in such a process, should be guarded almost fanatically.

A fourth pitfall in this matter of avoidance along the way is the possibility of the development of undue influence of certain *negative* aspects inherent in the various social forces capable of influencing our culture and everything within it (including, of course, physical activity education and educational sport). Consider the phenomenon of nationalism and how an overemphasis in this direction can soon destroy a desirable world posture or even bring about unconscionable isolationism. Another example of a "negative" social force that is not understood generally is the clash between capitalistic economic theory and the environmental crisis that has developed. "Bigger" is not necessarily "better" in the final analysis.

Fifth, moving back to the realm of education, we must be careful that our field doesn't contribute to what has consistently been identified as a fundamental anti-intellectualism in the United States. On the other hand, "intelligence or intellectualism for its own sake" is far being the answer to our problems. As long ago as 1961, Brubacher asked for the "golden mean" between the cultivation of the intellect and the cultivation of a high degree of intelligence because it is need as "an instrument of survival" in the Deweyan sense (pp. 7-9).

Sixth, and finally, despite the cry for a "return to essentials" in the final quarter of the 20th century–and I am not for a moment suggesting that Johnny or Mary shouldn't know how to read and calculate mathematically–we should avoid imposing a narrow academic approach on students in a misguided effort to promote the pursuit of excellence. I am continually both amazed and discouraged by decisions concerning admission to professional programs in undergraduate physical activity education programs made *solely* on numerical grades, in essence a narrowly defined academic proficiency. Do not throw out academic proficiency testing, of course, but by all means broaden the evaluation made of candidates by assessing other dimensions of excellence they may have—i.e., the actual life competencies they have achieved! Here, in addition to ability in human motor performance, I include such aspects as "sensitivity and commitment to social responsibility, ability to adapt to new situations, characteristics of temperament and work habit under varying conditions of demand," and other such characteristics, traits, and competencies as recommended as long ago as 1970 by the Commission on Tests of the College Entrance Examination Board (*The New York Times*, Nov. 2, 1970)

What *Should* We Do in the 21st Century?

What should we do--perhaps what *must* we do--to ensure that the profession will move more decisively and rapidly in the direction of what might be called <u>true</u> professional status? Granting that the various social forces will undoubtedly influence us, what can we do collectively in the years immediately ahead? These positive steps should be actions that will effect a workable consolidation of purposeful accomplishments on the part of those men and women who have a concern for the future of developmental physical activity as a valuable component of the entire life of a human. The following represent a number of categories joined with action principles that are related to the listing of "modifications" that have occurred in the past 30 years. We should seek a North American consensus on the steps spelled out below. Then we, as dedicated professionals, should take as rapid and strong action as we can muster through our professional associations in the United States and Canada. These recommended steps are as follows:

1. A Sharper Image. In the past the field of physical education has tried to be "all things to all people," and now does not know exactly what it does stand for. Now we should now sharpen our image and improve the quality of our efforts by focusing primarily on developmental physical activity—specifically, human motor performance in sport, exercise, and related expressive movement. As we sharpen our image, we should make a strong effort to include those who are working in the private agency and commercial sectors. This implies further that we will extend our efforts to promote the finest type of developmental physical activity for people of all ages in "normal, accelerated, or special" populations.

2. Our Field's Name. All sorts of name changes have been implemented to explain either what people think we are doing or should be doing, or to camouflage the presumed "unsavory" connotation of the term "physical education" that evidently conjures up the notion of a "dumb jock" working with the lesser part of a tri-partite human body. Nevertheless, we should continue to focus primarily on developmental physical activity as defined immediately above while moving toward an acceptable working term for

our profession. In so doing, we should keep in mind the profession's bifurcated nature in that it has both theoretical and practical (*or disciplinary and professional*) aspects. At the moment we are still called physical education and sport professionally and physical and health education in a significant number of elementary and secondary schools in Canada where the professional association just changed its name to Physical and Health Education Canada. A desirable disciplinary name might be developmental physical activity, and we could delineate this by the addition of "in sport, exercise, and expressive movement." *Within education, we could be termed physical activity educators.*

3. A Tenable Body of Knowledge. Various social forces and professional concerns have placed us in a position where we don't know where or what our body of knowledge is, we will strongly support the idea of disciplinary definition and the continuing development of a body of knowledge based on such a consensual definition. From this should come a merging of tenable scientific theory in keeping with societal values and computer technology so that we will gradually, steadily, and increasingly provide our members with the knowledge that they need to perform as top-flight professionals. As professional practitioners we simply must possess the requisite knowledge, competencies, and skills necessary to provide developmental physical activity services of a high quality to the public.

4. Our Own Associations. There is insufficient support of our own associations for a variety of reasons. Thus, we need to develop voluntary and mandatory mechanisms that relate membership in professional organizations both directly and indirectly to stature within the field. We simply must commit ourselves to work tirelessly and continually to promote the welfare of professional practitioners who are serving the public in areas that we represent. Incidentally, it may be necessary to exert any available pressures to encourage people to give first priority to our own groups (as opposed to those of related disciplines and/or allied professions). The logic behind this dictum is that our own survival comes first for us!

5. Professional Licensing. Teachers/coaches in the schools, colleges, and universities are protected indefinitely by the shelter of the all-embracing teaching profession. However, we should now move rapidly and strongly to seek official recognition of our endeavors in public, semi-public, and private agency work and in commercial organizations relating to developmental physical activity through professional licensing at the state or provincial level. Further, we should encourage individuals to apply for voluntary registration as qualified practitioners at the federal level in both the United States and Canada.

6. Harmony Within The Field. An unacceptable series of gaps and misunderstandings has developed among (1) those in our field concerned

primarily with the bio-scientific aspects of human motor performance, (2) those concerned with the social-science and humanities aspects, (3) those concerned with the general education of all students, and (4) those concerned with the professional preparation of physical educators/coaches, all at the college or university level. Hence, we should strive for a greater balance and improved understanding among these essential entities within the profession.

7. Harmony Among The Allied Professions. The field of physical education spawned a number of allied professions down through the years of the 20th century. Now we should seek to comprehend what they claim that they do professionally, and where there may be a possible overlap with what we claim that we do. Where disagreements prevail, they should be ironed out to the greatest extent possible at the national level within the Alliance (AAHPERD) and within Physical and Health Education Canada (the former CAHPERD).

8. The Relationship With Intercollegiate Athletics. For several reasons an ever-larger wedge has been driven between units of physical education and interscholastic and intercollegiate athletics in educational institutions where gate receipts are a strong and basic factor. Such a rift serves no good purpose and is counter to the best interests of both groups. Thus, we will work for greater understanding and harmony with those people who are primarily interested in the promotion of highly organized, often commercialized athletics. At the same time it is imperative that we do all in our power to maintain athletics in a sound educational perspective within our schools, colleges, and universities.

9. The Relationship with Intramurals and Recreational Sports. Intramurals and recreational sports is in a transitional state at present in that it has proved that it is "here to stay" at the college and university level. Nevertheless, intramurals hasn't really taken hold yet, generally speaking, at the high school level, despite the fact that it has a great deal to offer the large majority of students in what may truly be called recreational (educational?) sport.

Both philosophically and practically, intramurals and recreational sports ought to remain within the sphere of the physical education field. It is impractical and inadvisable to attempt to subsume all non-curricular activities on campus under one department or division. Thus, departments and divisions of physical (activity?) education and athletics ought to work for consensus on the idea that intramurals and recreational sports are co-curricular in nature and deserve regular funding as laboratory experience in the same manner that general education course experiences in physical education receive their funding for instructional purposes.

10. Guaranteeing Equal Opportunity. "Life, liberty, and the pursuit of happiness" are guaranteed to all in North American society. As members of a field within the education profession—and a potential profession in the public sector—we should move positively and strongly to see to it that equal opportunity is indeed provided to the greatest possible extent to women, to minority groups, and to special populations as they seek to improve the quality of their lives through the finest type of experience in the many activities of our field.

11. The Physical (Activity) Education Identity. In addition to the development of the allied professions (e.g., school health education) in the second quarter of the twentieth century, we witnessed the advent of a disciplinary thrust in the 1960s that was followed by a splintering of many of the field's "knowledge components" to form many different sub disciplinary societies. These developments have undoubtedly weakened the overall field of physical education in both educational institutions and in the larger society. Thus, it is now more important than ever that we hold high the physical education identity as we continue to promote vigorously the professional and scholarly foundations of our field.

12. Applying the Competency Approach. The failures and inconsistencies of the established educational process have become increasingly apparent. Thus, we will as a field within education explore the educational possibilities of a competency approach as it might apply to general education, to professional preparation, and to all aspects of our professional endeavor in public, semi-public, private, and commercial agency endeavors. This means that initially we will indicate clearly what state or quality we are asking students to achieve in the various theoretical and practical experiences outlined in the curriculum. Then we will see to it that they achieve sufficient knowledge and skill to fulfill the curricular requirements before they advance to the next stage of their development.

13. Managing the Enterprise. All people employed in the unique field of sport and physical education are managers--but to varying degrees. The "one course in administration in the undergraduate curriculum" approach with no laboratory or internship experience of earlier times is simply not sufficient for the future. There is an urgent need to apply a competency approach in the preparation (as well as in the continuing education) of those who will serve as managers either within educational circles or elsewhere in the society.

14. Ethics and Morality in Physical Activity Education and Educational Sport. In the course of the development of the best professions, the various, embryonic professional groups have gradually become conscious of the need for a set of professional ethics—that is, a set of professional obligations that are established as norms for practitioners in good standing to follow. Our field within the education profession needs a well-defined

creed, as well as a detailed code of ethics as we move ahead in our development. Such a move is important because, generally speaking, ethical confusion prevails in North American society. Such a sound code of ethics should be combined with steady improvement in the three essentials of a fine profession would relatively soon place us in a much firmer position to claim that we are indeed what we claim to be. These three "essentials" are (1) an extensive period of training, (2) a significant intellectual component that must be mastered before the profession is practiced, and (3) a recognition by society that the trained person can provide a basic, important service to its citizens (Zeigler, 1984, 1992, 2002, 2007).

15. Reunifying the Field's Integral Elements. There now appears to be reasonable agreement that what is now called physical (activity) education and (educational) sport is concerned primarily with developmental physical activity as manifested in human motor performance in sport, exercise, and related expressive movement. Thus, we will now work for the reunification of those elements of our profession that should be uniquely ours within our disciplinary definition.

16. Cross-Cultural Comparison and International   Understanding. We have done reasonably well in the area of international relations within the Western world due to the solid efforts of many dedicated people over a considerable period of time. However, we now need to redouble our efforts to make cross-cultural comparisons of physical education and educational sport while reaching out for international understanding and cooperation in both the so-called Western and Eastern blocs. Much greater understanding on the part of all of the concepts of 'communication,' 'diversity,' and 'cooperation' is required for the creation of a better life for all in a peaceful world. Our field can contribute significantly toward this long–range objective.

17. Permanency and Change. The "principal principles" espoused for physical education and sport by the late Dr. Arthur Steinhaus of George Williams College still apply most aptly to our professional endeavors. These are the overload principle, the principle of reversibility, the principle of integration and integrity, and the principle of the priority of man and woman). We should now emphasize that which is timeless in our work, while at the same time accepting the inevitability of certain societal change. (See, also, "Physical education's 13 principal principles" by E.F. Zeigler, 1994).

18. Improving the Quality of Life. Our field is unique within education and in society. Since fine living and professional success involve so much more than the important verbal and mathematical skills, we will emphasize strongly that education is a lifelong enterprise. Further, we will

stress that *the quality of life can be improved significantly through the achievement of a higher degree of kinetic awareness and through heightened experiences in sport, exercise, and related expressive movement.*

19. Reasserting Our "Will to Win". The developments of the past 40 years have undoubtedly created an uneasiness and concern about the future of the field within education. Doubts have been raised by some as to the field's "will to win" through the achievement of the highest status within the education profession. *We pledge ourselves to make still greater efforts to become vibrant and stirring through absolute dedication and commitment in our professional endeavors within education.* Ours is a high calling as we seek to improve the quality of life for all through the finest type developmental physical activity in sport, exercise, and related expressive movement.

The Professional Task Ahead

What, then, is the educational task ahead? First, we should truly understand why we have chosen this field within the education profession as we rededicate ourselves anew to the study and dissemination of knowledge, competencies, and skills in human motor performance in sport, exercise, and related expressive movement. Concurrently, of course, we need to determine exactly what it is that we are professing.

Second, as either professional practitioners within the educational system or as instructors involved in the professional preparation of practitioners, we should search for young people of high quality in all the attributes needed for success in the field. Then we should follow through to help them develop lifelong commitments so that our field can achieve its democratically agreed-upon goals. We should also prepare young people to serve in the many alternative careers in sport, exercise, dance, and recreational play that are becoming increasingly available in our society.

Third, we must place *quality* as the first priority of our endeavors. Our personal involvement and specialization should include a high level of competency and skill under girded by solid knowledge about the profession. It can be argued that our task is as important as any in society. Thus, the present is no time for indecision, half-hearted commitment, imprecise knowledge, and general unwillingness to stand up and be counted in debate with colleagues within our field and in allied professions and related disciplines, not to mention the public.

Fourth, the obligation is ours. If we hope to reach our potential, we must sharpen our focus and improve the quality of our effort as professional educators. Only in this way will we be able to guide the modification process that the field is currently undergoing toward the achievement of our highest goals within the education profession. This is the time, right now, to employ sport, exercise, dance, and play to make our reality more healthful, more pleasant, more vital, and more life enriching. By "living fully in one's body," behavioral science men and women will be adapting and shaping this phase of reality to their own ends.

Finally, such improvement will not come easily; it can only come through the efforts of professional people making quality decisions, through the motivation of people to change their sedentary lifestyles, and through our professional assistance in guiding people as they strive to fulfill such motivation in their movement patterns. When our black brothers and sisters speak about the concept of 'soul,' they mean placing a special quality into some aspect of life (e.g., soul music). Our missions in the years ahead is to place this special quality in all of our endeavor.

References and Bibliography

Amara, R. (1981). The futures field. *The Futurist*, February.

Brubacher, J. S. (1947). *A history of the problems of education*. New York: McGraw-Hill.

Brubacher, J. S. (1961). Higher education and the pursuit of excellence. *Marshall University Bulletin*, 3:3.

Melnick, R. (1984). *Visions of the future*. Croton-on-Hudson, NY: Hudson Institute.

Naisbitt, J. (1982). *Megatrends*. New York: Warner

New York Times, The. (1970). Report by Commission on Tests of the College Entrance Examination Board, Nov. 2

Rand, A. (1960). *The romantic manifesto*. New York: World Publishing.

Zeigler, E. F. (1951). *A History of Professional Preparation for Physical Education in the United States* . Eugene, OR: University of Oregon Microform Publications, 1951).

Zeigler, E. F. (1968). *Problems in the History and Philosophy of Physical Education and Sport* Englewood Cliffs, NJ: Prentice-Hall.

Zeigler, E. F. (Ed. & Au.).(1975). *History of Sport and Physical Education in the United States and Canada. Champaign, IL:* Stipes, 1975).

Zeigler, E. F. (1979). *Issues in North American Physical Education and Sport*. Washington, DC: AAHPERD, 1979.

Zeigler, E. F. (1986). *Assessing Sport and Physical Education: Diagnosis and Projection* Champaign, IL: Stipes.

Zeigler, E. F. (1991). *Sport and Physical Education: Past, Present, Future*. Champaign, IL: Stipes, 1991).

Zeigler, E. F. (1994). Physical Education's 13 Principal Principles. *Journal of Physical Education, Recreation, and Dance*, 69:7, 4-5.

Zeigler, E. F. (2003). *Socio-Cultural Foundations of Physical Education and Educational Sport*. Aachen: Germany: Meyer & Meyer.

Zeigler, E. F. (2005). *History and Status of American Physical Education and Educational Sport*. Victoria, Canada: Trafford.

Zeigler, E. F. (2007). *Applied Ethics for Sport and Physical Activity Professionals*. Victoria, Canada: Trafford

Epilogue
The "World of the Future"

Postmodernism as One of Four World Views

Walter Truett Anderson (1996) identified postmodernism as one of four prevailing world views. These four worldviews that he postulated are:

(1) the postmodern-ironist, which sees truth as socially constructed,

(2) the scientific-rational in which truth is 'found' through methodical, disciplined inquiry,

(3) the social-traditional in which truth is found in the heritage of American and Western civilization and

(4) the neo-romantic in which truth is found either through attaining harmony with nature and/or spiritual exploration of the inner self.

Each of these defines truth differently: "what truth is - where and how you look for it, how you test or prove it."

"Futures of the Self"

In the following year (1997), Anderson, then president of the American Division of the World Academy of Art and Science, went one step further as he sketched four different scenarios as postulations for the future of earthlings in this ongoing adventure of civilization. In this essay "Futures of the Self," taken from The future of the self: Inventing the postmodern person (Tarcher–Putnam, 1997), Anderson argued convincingly that current trends were adding up to an identity crisis for humankind. The creation of the present "modern self," he explained, began with Plato, Aristotle, and with the rights of humans in Roman legal codes.

The developing conception of self ran into trouble in the Middle Ages, but fortunately was resurrected in the Renaissance Period described by many historians as actually the second half of The Middle Ages.

Since then the human "self" has been advancing like a "house a fire" as the Western world has gone through an almost unbelievable transformation. Scientists like Galileo and Copernicus influenced philosophers such as Descartes and Locke to foresee a world in which the self was invested with human rights.

"One World; Many Universes"

Anderson's "One World, Many Universes" version seems the most likely to occur . This is a scenario characterized by high economic growth, steadily increasing technological progress, and globalization combined with high psychological development. Such psychological maturity, he predicts, will be possible for a certain segment of the world's population because "active life spans will be gradually lengthened through various advances in health maintenance and medicine" (pp. 251-253)

Nevertheless, a problem has developed with this dream of individual achievement of inalienable rights and privileges, one that looms large as the world moves along in the 21st century. The modern self envisioned by Descartes, a rational, integrated self that Anderson likens to Captain James Kirk at the command post of (the original Starship Enterprise, appears to be having an identity crisis. The image of this bold leader (he or she!) taking us fearlessly into the great unknown has begun to fade as alternate scenarios for the future of life on Earth are envisioned.

In a world where globalization and economic "progress" seemingly must be rejected, or at least scaled back drastically, because of catastrophic environmental concerns or "demands," the bold-future image could well "be replaced by a post-modern self; de–centered, multidimensional, and changeable" (p. 50).

Of the four different types of civilizations postulated *by* Anderson, his "One World, Many Universes" version is the most likely to occur. This is a scenario characterized by (1) high economic growth, (2) steadily increasing technological progress, and (3) globalization combined with high psychological development. Such psychological maturity, he predicts, will be possible for a certain segment of the world's population because "active life spans will be gradually lengthened through various advances in health maintenance and medicine" (pp. 251-253).

Nevertheless, a problem has developed with this dream of individual achievement of inalienable rights and privileges, one that looms large at the beginning of the 21st century. The *modern self* envisioned by Descartes, a rational, integrated self that Anderson likens to Captain Kirk at the command post of the original Starship Enterprise, appears to be having an identity crisis. The image of this bold leader (he or she!) taking us fearlessly into the great unknown has begun to fade as alternate scenarios for the future of life on Earth are envisioned. In a world where globalization and economic "progress" seemingly *must be rejected* because of accompanying catastrophic environmental concerns or "demands," the bold-future image could well "be replaced by a postmodern self: de–centered, multidimensional, and changeable" (p. 50).

Captain Kirk (or Barack Obama!) as he "boldly went where no man had gone before" presumably to rid the world of terrorists and evil leaders, also faces a second crucial change. As he, and subsequent elected officials, seek to shape the world of the 21st century based on Anderson's analysis, there is another force--*the systemic-change force mentioned above*--that is shaping the future. This all-powerful force gives every reason for humankind to comprehend that it may well exceed the Earth's ability to cope.

As gratifying as such factors (i.e., terms used by Anderson) as "globalization along with economic growth" and "psychological development" may seem to the folks in a coming "One-World, Many Universes" scenario, there is a flip side to this prognosis. Anderson identifies this image as "The Dysfunctional Family" scenario. All of these benefits of so-called progress are highly expensive and available now only to relatively few of the six billion *plus* people on earth. Anderson foresees this as "a world of modern people happily doing their thing; of modern people still obsessed with progress, economic gain, and organizational bigness; *and of postmodern people being trampled and getting angry*" [italics added by this author] (p. 51). As people get angrier, who dare deny that the extent of present-day terrorism in North America and elsewhere will seem like child's play.

"The Future as History"

Concluding in a broader vein, more than a generation ago, Heilbroner (1960) showed foresight as he explained his "future as history" concept. This was a theory that America's belief in a personal "deity of history" may be short-lived in the 21st century. He emphasized the need to search for a greatly improved "common denominator of values" (p. 170) in the face of technological, political, and economic forces that are "bringing about a closing of our historic future." As the world turns today, some may scoff at this prediction.

Yet, looking at the situation from a starkly different perspective even earlier, Toynbee (1947) came to a quite similar conclusion in his monumental *A Study of History, but* from another standpoint. He theorized that humankind must return to the one true God from whom it has gradually but steadily fallen away. You can challenge him on this opinion, as the author (an agnostic) most assuredly does. Yet, no matter--the way things are going at present--we on the Earth had best try to use our heads as intelligently and wisely as possible. As we get on with striving to make the world as effective, efficient, and humane as possible, we need to make life for all humans on Earth as replete with good, as opposed to evil, as we possibly can.

Concluding Statement

However, those worldwide who are truly concerned about the future of "value-laden," competitive sport, wherever you may be, are strongly urged to get involved now with the reforms that seem so necessary (e.g., the institution, generally, and public ownership of professional sport). In the immediate future, please seek the answer to two fundamental questions.

The response to the first question might well cause action to be taken in the future to answer question #2. These questions are:

(1) in what ways can we assess the present status of sport and
related physical activity accurately to learn if it is--**or is not**--
fulfilling its role as a presumably beneficent social institution?
and

(2) depending on whether the answer to #1 is positive or negative,
will you then have the motivation and professional zeal to do
your utmost to help sport and related physical activity (and
related health education) achieve what should be its rightful
place in society?

The author's stance is that the message for the human organism is the same no
matter which scenario he or she resides:

> ***Sport and related physical activity, broadly interpreted
> and experienced under wise educational or recreational
> conditions, can serve humankind as a worthwhile social
> institution contributing vitally to the well being, ongoing
> health, and longevity of humankind.***

References

Anderson, W. T. (1996). *The Fontana Postmodernism
Reader.* London: Fontana Press.

Anderson, W. T. (1997). *The future of the self: Inventing the
postmodern person.* NY: Tarcher/Putnam.

Heilbroner, R. L. (1960). *The future as history.* New York: Harper &
Row.